Waiting for the

Waiting for the Barbarians

A Tribute to Edward W. Said

EDITED BY MÜGE GÜRSOY SÖKMEN AND BAŞAK ERTÜR

VERSO

London • New York

This edition published by Verso 2008

Published in Turkey as *Barbarları Beklerken: Edward Said'i Anıyoruz*
© Metis Yayınları Ltd, 2008
© in the contributions to the individual authors 2008
© in this English collection Verso 2008
All rights reserved

The moral rights of the authors and translators have been asserted

1 3 5 7 9 10 8 6 4 2

Verso
UK: 6 Meard Street, London W1F 0EG
USA: 20 Jay Street, 10th Floor, Brooklyn, NY 11201-8346
www.versobooks.com

Verso is the imprint of New Left Books

ISBN: 978-1-84467-245-5 (hb)
ISBN: 978-1-84467-246-2 (pb)

British Library Cataloguing in Publication Data
A catalogue record for this book is available from the British Library

Library of Congress Cataloging-in-Publication Data
A catalog record for this book is available from the Library of Congress

Typeset in Bembo by Hewer Text UK Ltd, Edinburgh
Printed in the USA by Maple Vail

Contents

Acknowledgements

This book is a collection of papers presented at a two-day conference organized by Metis Publications and the Department of Sociology at Boğaziçi University, in Istanbul in May 2007. The conference was part of a series of events, including a photography exhibition by Jean Mohr, a piano concert by Saleem Abboud-Ashkar, and a literary reading event with Elias Khoury and Murathan Mungan, all organized in an effort to pay tribute to, revisit and engage with the richly variegated erudition and seminal scholarship of Edward Said.

First of all we would like to acknowledge our companions and partners in this venture, with the hope that this expression of gratitude will not be mistaken as a claim of primary ownership on our part. The prime mover behind the initiative was Rasha Salti, who wished to bring about a space that would facilitate a conversation among Said's colleagues, students, friends, and readers from across the globe; a space that may rekindle our hope in the face of lived experience full of such violent conflict and subject to the political imperative that rules our present. At an early stage in the organizing process, Mariam C. Said kindly gave us her endorsement, and never hesitated to lend a hand in times of need. We have been honored by her trust and are grateful for her efforts. The Department of Sociology at Boğaziçi University graciously agreed to co-organize and host the event, and we owe our smooth partnership to the vital labor of Faruk Birtek, Nükhet Sirman, Zafer Yenal, Aslı Zengin, and Oyman Başaran. We would also like to acknowledge our colleagues at Metis Publications – Semih Sökmen, Emine Bora, Bülent Doğan, and Sabahattin Göksu – for their goodwill, patience and unconditional support.

We are grateful to Emel Kurma and Didem Ermiş at Helsinki Citizens' Assembly for their excellent advice. Fırat Genç and Özlem Dalkıran produced logistical magic in the midst of much confusion; we would not have succeeded without them. Translators Nur Deriş Ottoman and Sungur Savran were as outstanding as ever, making a profound dialogue possible during the two-day marathon. We were very much honored by Jale Parla's contributions as a moderator. Thanks also to our volunteers at the university who gave of their time and energy with zest and imagination: Elif Aydıntuğ, Sevi Bayraktar, Cemre Baytok, Melek Cevahiroğlu, Nur Sümeyye Ensari, Zeynep Güzel, Hazal Halavut, Seda Karsıloğlu, Aytaç Köktürk, Fırat Kurt, Ömer Özcan, and Hazal Övarış. We were fortunate to have the auspicious assistance of Alisa Lebow who not only contributed to the organization of the tribute but also helped with the editing of this book. Sibel Gökçen and Çiğdem Arşıray's efforts and ideas were indispensable.

The exhibition "Israelis and Palestinians, Side by Side or Face to Face: Fifty Years of Photography by Jean Mohr" was part of the tribute event thanks to the willingness and solidarity of Jean Mohr, the support of the Swiss Consulate-General in Istanbul, and the efforts of İz Öztat, Levent Duran, Ahmet Çakaloz, and Jean-François Berger. We would like to thank the authors Elias Khoury and Murathan Mungan for being willing to take part in the literary reading event, as well as Najla Said for her impeccable delivery of Cavafy's "Waiting for the Barbarians." Saleem Abboud-Ashkar provided a wonderful finale to the tribute with a solo piano concert.

Of course, many thanks go to our gracious and tolerant conference participants whose papers you will read in this volume. Tanya Reinhart had kindly accepted our invitation to participate in the tribute events along with her partner Aaron Shabtai. The devastating news of her death came shortly after enthusiastic and delightful email exchanges with her. She will be missed deeply. Ranajit Guha had to cancel his participation due to unforeseen circumstances but was very kind in sending a note of solidarity to the conference. Two participants at the conference whose papers we could not include in this volume were Masao Miyoshi and Akeel Bilgrami; we would like to thank them for braving the long journey to Istanbul and for their lively and insightful presentations.

Last but not least, we owe a debt of gratitude to our sponsors, without whom all of this would have remained a sweet dream: The Plum Foundation of Denmark, with special thanks to Christian Harlang and Birgitte Rahbek; the Istanbul, Beirut, Washington, and Ramallah offices of the Heinrich Böll Foundation, with special thanks to Ulrike Dufner, Aylin Örnek and Layla Al-Zubaidi. We would also like to thank our fiscal sponsor, the New York Foundation for the Arts, and our individual sponsors Jean Stein and Gürhan Ertür.

Müge Gürsoy Sökmen and Başak Ertür

Preface: Edward and Istanbul

Mariam C. Said

The organizers have asked me to welcome you all and I am delighted that so many of Edward's colleagues, friends, students, and others are participating in this forum of ideas.

Istanbul has been forever the bridge that connects East and West, Asia and Europe, Christianity and Islam, and a place where one can look backwards and forward at the same time, literally and figuratively. At this time in history, I feel no other place would resonate as well with Edward's rich legacy than this beautiful city on the Bosphorus. This is indeed a great tribute to one of the greatest public intellectuals of the twentieth century, whose legacy extends into several fields and has resulted in new disciplines.

As I speak I can see Edward's hands and hear his voice saying to me, "do you know that Auerbach wrote *Mimesis* as an exile in Istanbul during World War II? He wrote it from memory. Can you imagine, from memory?" Edward would say this often, and every time he mentioned it, it was as if he was making this discovery for the first time. He seemed always amazed by how Auerbach managed to produce his masterpiece here in this city.

Auerbach was one of many literary giants Edward admired. Edward's Introduction to the 2003 edition of Auerbach's *Mimesis: The Representation of Reality in Western Literature*[1] appeared a few months before he passed away. Edward writes that "only a small number of books seem perennially present and, by comparison with the vast majority of their counterparts, to have an amazing staying power. Certainly this is true of Erich Auerbach's magisterial *Mimesis*." The same could be said of Edward's many books, especially his magisterial *Orientalism*, mostly written in exile in various places between the Atlantic and Pacific Oceans.

The first and last time Edward visited Istanbul was in 1995 when we spent a lovely week here. In retrospect it was here that he began to take in the seriousness of his illness. His treatments early that summer did not go well and we were worried, but Edward was determined not to lose one second of whatever time was left. We must press on, he always said when things seemed desperate.

His projects were many and varied. He stood on the shoulders of past giants and his vision went beyond theirs. He was a master at finding alternate ways of seeing. He explained the Question of Palestine to the West from a totally new perspective, went on to link the Palestinian struggle to the other liberation movements of the world, and until his last breath followed daily and in detail the current events as they unfolded. He never tired of writing and analyzing the situation in Palestine/Israel. His monumental output attests to that. In the end he saw only one solution, the idea of a bi-national state. He was by no means the first to advocate this, nor was he the only one, but what he did was to articulate brilliantly, I must say, why the end result has to be a bi-national state. He left the details of implementation for the Palestinians and Israelis to determine their future together. This vision is very much the conversation of today.

In March 2003 we flew to Cairo and Beirut where Edward was scheduled to lecture. The political mood was very tense; it was literally days before the invasion of Iraq, and I kept thinking what he could possibly say during this awful time. Finally I asked him what he would lecture on. Ever the optimist Edward answered with one word – humanism – and added that this is the only hope. Edward ends his Introduction to *Mimesis* with these words:

> But the triumph of *Mimesis*, as well as its inevitable tragic flaw, is that the human mind studying literary representations of the historical world can only do so as all authors do – from the limited perspective of their own time and their own work. No more scientific a method or less subjective a vision with learning, dedication, and moral purpose. It is this combination, this mingling of styles out of which *Mimesis* emerges. And to my way of thinking, its humanistic example remains an unforgettable one, fifty years after its appearance in English.[2]

Edward left us with several "humanistic examples." The last book he finished was *Humanism and Democratic Criticism*.

In January 2003 he gave a lecture at SOAS – "Memory, Inequality, and Power: Palestine and the Universality of Human Rights" – where he devoted the last part of the lecture in telling the story of the Weimar project, which is the story of the West Eastern Divan workshop and orchestra. Marina Warner, in her talk at a panel discussion at Columbia University last fall on Edward's book *On Late Style*, described the West Eastern Divan project as Edward's "late style." This humanistic, educational, and musical endeavor – a project Edward established with his friend the conductor and pianist Daniel Barenboim, where equality, co-operation, and co-existence prevail – is a way of challenging the status quo, defying the occupation, and offering a ray of hope to the young generation living in confusion and turmoil. This is how Edward summed up his description of the project:

> In our work and planning and discussions our main principle is that separation between people is not a solution for any of the problems that divide peoples. And certainly ignorance of the other provides no help whatever. Cooperation and co-existence of the kind that music lived as we have lived, performed, shared and loved it together might be. I for one am full of optimism despite the darkening sky and the seemingly hopeless situation for the time being that encloses us all.[3]

These words were uttered in January 2003. Four years later the sky is completely dark and the situation that encloses us as I speak is more than hopeless, but the West Eastern Divan project is ongoing. It is opening up the minds of the young musicians, and offering them a realm of possibilities which allows them to take intellectual risks. The orchestra is first rate and has become world-renowned. In the summer of 2006 the workshop took place despite the war. Today in Palestine/Israel many similar projects that involve the other in theatre, art, and music exist against all odds, in defiance of the occupation and as a protest against the concrete wall that is being built as a separation barrier.

I wanted to tell you briefly about my involvement in part of Edward's legacy. However, I am here eager to listen and learn more about Edward's academic contributions as a scholar and intellectual, and to hear the various interpretations and discussions based on his legacy.

Notes

1 Erich Auerbach, *The Representation of Reality in Wester Literature*, translated by Willard R. Trask, with a new Introduction by Edward W. Said, Princeton: Princeton University Press, 2003, p. xxxxii.
2 Ibid.
3 Edward Said, "Memory, Inequality, and Power: Palestine and the Universality of Human Rights", unpublished lecture delivered at SOAS in January 2003, p. 25.

Keynote Address:
The Intellectual and the Double Exile

Elias Khoury

What happened in 1967 to the young American man teaching at Columbia University in New York City? This is the question of the second beginning to which Edward Said did not attend in his autobiographical book *Out of Place*. In this book Said, like Taha Hussein in *Al Ayyam*, wrote his childhood. Said's autobiography begins with the question of ambiguity and contradiction. Edward, the English name, and Said, the Arabic surname. Hussein's autobiography also began with an ambiguity, that of darkness and light. In both cases the two writers built from the ambiguities of childhood the beginnings of their simultaneous consciousness.

The young American man of Arab origins, walking alone in the streets of New York, in the midst of euphoric happiness at Israel's quick victory and the Arab defeat, all of a sudden discovered his estrangement in the place where he lived. He saw darkness surrounding the world of human values he believed in, and decided to become a Palestinian. He went to Lebanon and studied Arabic culture and language with Anis Frayha. And in Beirut the idea of his major book *Orientalism* arose; he returned to the United States with two names, the way he was born, and the way he had lived his childhood in Jerusalem and Cairo.

The concept of Nakba that was formulated by Constance Zureik in 1948 – in his small book *The Meaning of the Nakba*, which tried to articulate a possible national reply to the Palestinian catastrophe – would take on a new dimension with Said's work, and would be understood as being at the heart of Orientalist discourse.

The young man was born twice: the first time in Jerusalem in 1935; the second time in 1967 between New York and Beirut. And between these two births, he studied in the colonial schools of Cairo, spent summers in

Dhour El Shweir in Lebanon, played piano, read English literature, saw the marvels of Tahiya Karioka's body shivering in her belly dance suit under the eyes of her admirers, completed his undergraduate studies at Princeton, then graduated from Harvard where he discovered Conrad and was searching for the beginnings.

Without being aware of what he was doing, Said incarnated in his works the two Arab al-Nahdas. He was an American like the group of the "Rabita Kalamiya," an Egyptian like the intellectuals of Lebanon, Syria, and Palestine who found refuge in Cairo at the beginning of the twentieth century, and a Beiruti like the vast numbers of Arab intellectuals who lived in Beirut during the 1960s and 1970s. A Palestinian, Egyptian, Lebanese, and American who wrote in English and read Arabic and other languages; a French intellectual, a Palestinian militant and a New York academic who spoke Arabic with Lebanese and Egyptian and Palestinian accents, and, when he couldn't find his words, would switch back to English.

In his life and works Edward Said constructed his own model of an American and Arab intellectual. He was not haunted by nostalgia like many other immigrants. He returned to his Palestinian and Arab identity in order to be a witness who cannot but identify with the victims. He didn't write in English in order to find a linguistic home for himself, but rather in the Conradian tradition that shakes and discovers. He didn't return to Palestine in search for his roots, but rather to discover the future, in an attempt to put Palestine on the map of human pain.

He was a project of a beginning, and as he wrote in his book *Beginnings*, the beginning cannot be discovered or found, but must be made. This was his secret and his way, that of a man who makes the beginnings with consciousness, challenging concepts in order to create a new secular and worldly vision.

It is easy to situate Said in the process of the development of humanities and literary criticism in the Western cultural field. Although he remained an outsider, we can still trace a lineage that links him to Lukács, Vico, Auerbach, Gramsci, Foucault, and Fanon. This lineage gave him a horizon he would use in his deep critique of the mechanisms of power and knowledge, especially in his two great works: *Orientalism* and *Culture and Imperialism*, and in his masterpiece *The Representations of the Intellectual*.

The real difficulty is to identify his Arabic lineage. A difficulty due not only to the rarity of his works in this field, but also the scarcity of Arabic references in his works. It is true that he wrote about modern Arabic literature and played a major intellectual and political role in the Arab cultural scene, especially with *Orientalism* and his texts on Palestine; nevertheless it remains very difficult to discern his status in a cultural structure that he entered from outside. I would suggest a reading of his works through two approaches.

1. *Modernism*. This can be effectively achieved by comparing his approach with the emergence of Arabic modernism in the works of Taha Hussein. This pairing refers not, as one might initially suspect, to the impact of their two autobiographies, but rather to the different approaches towards modernism that categorically separated the two writers. Hussein went a long way in his relationship with European culture, starting from a position of admiration and appropriation, and using rational and modern methods in reading the Arabic cultural heritage. Although he sometimes took this approach to a level of excess, as in his book *Pre-Islamic Poetry*, he was still able to create a radical change in the cultural structure through questioning the sacred and the forbidden. On another level, as a way of escaping the predestination of Egyptian-Arabic identity, Hussein adopted Mediterraneanism as a cultural approach without a critical position against colonialism.

Edward Said succeeds Taha Hussein by contradicting his views. Said was part of the radical tendencies of the West. His theoretical production was at the center of a postcolonial approach, which questioned the relationship between culture and power through a vision that prioritizes the idea of national liberation in the context of a radical criticism of the dominant Arabic culture.

The huge difference between their approaches can be understood in relation to the history of the Arab Awakening, to use George Antonius' term, where Taha Hussein represents the incarnation of al-Nahda's ideology. Here the awakening is perceived as a combination of two pasts, the Arab Golden cultural age and modern Western culture, thus neglecting the present and its contradictions. On the other hand, Said represents a new awareness that transcends the idea of authenticity and the endorsement of a closed, finite identity, because he saw ideas as fields of contradictions.

2. *The Nakba and the Idea of Palestine*. In his book *The Question of Palestine*, unfortunately not yet translated into Arabic, Said continues Constantine Zureik's approach and creates a total rupture with it at the same time. Zureik, the nationalist, modernist, and secular thinker, saw the Arabic face of the Palestinian Nakba, coined the term, and understood it in the light of a modernist revolutionary thought that came to influence the Arab elite and paved the way for the military coups that dominated Arab political life. Said reread the Nakba from a new perspective, putting it at the heart of world history. *The Question of Palestine* is a concrete political application of his book *Orientalism*, where the Nakba is seen in its human global dimension,

presenting a profound analysis of the mechanisms of struggle in its different levels.

Said situated the idea of Palestine at the center of modern history, as the struggle between the present and interpretation, and as part of understanding the colonial project in Palestine and the Arab world. This attempt to read Said in the modern Arab cultural field will not be complete without reading the influence of Said on modern Arabic thought and literature, and his approach to the idea of the intellectual. One can speak about a lot of misreading, especially with regard to *Orientalism*, but one can nonetheless see the traces of his influence on the works of historians, political analyses and literature. To explore this properly would need a conference of its own.

As far as his concept of the intellectual goes, I suppose that in his small book Said proposed a new approach which offers a guideline for the Arab intellectual in these times of decomposition of the national movement. Here I will speak from my personal experience in Beirut, where through the text and model of Said one can open a window towards the optimism of the will.

When I went to New York in January 2001 to begin my academic career at New York University, my feeling was that I was going to the city of Edward Said. He introduced the city to me, and showed me what he would later describe – in the introduction to his book *Reflections on Exile* – as the turning point that isolated the city from its Bohemian leftist intellectual tradition. I was coming from the long Lebanese Palestinian experience of Beirut. The distance enabled me to see my Beirut experience with new eyes. I looked behind me to see the shadow of my city, and realize that what happened between the resistance against the Israeli invasion in 1982 and the beginning of the new century was so big – the war and the Syrian domination that replaced it. The political and ideological language had to go through different levels of transformation, to the extent that language itself was on the verge of losing its relationship with meaning.

Between 1992 and 1998, I was the director of the Theatre of Beirut, and the editor of *Mulhak* (the weekly literary supplement of *An-Nahar*), a post which I still hold. With some friends we had the dream of reinventing the meaning of Beirut. Among the things we did was organize a tribute to Edward Said held in 1997, and a commemoration of the 50 years of the Palestinian Nakba in 1998. We felt that we were in a kind of race with time, and that through deep intellectual work with a penetrating, critical, approach we could reinvent our relation with the place. But we had not realized that the defeat of the national movement both in Lebanon and Palestine was irreversible, and that the Arab East was going through a long journey in the darkness of tyranny, occupation, and a very vague Islamic project.

New York was a window that enabled me to see how profound our crisis as Arab intellectuals was. And with the madness of September 11, I began to realize the deep solitude of the Third World intellectual in the new world disorder. The struggle for the idea of Palestine was threatened on one side by a new generation of fighters who were ready to exercise the Orientalist discourse by adapting all its premises, and on the other side by a new conservative establishment that was waiting for this moment in order to hide the colonial project behind the language of the war of civilizations and the end of history. It is a huge cultural battle that aims to destroy the humanist approach in culture and replace it with a new racist colonial discourse.

I once asked Edward Said if there was still a place for everybody. I was referring to his quotation from Aimé Césaire in his book *Reflections on Exile*.[1] At that time Said was writing his last work on humanism. He was aware that life had become so short, but nonetheless chose not to isolate himself with pain or be haunted by death. Even though one witnessed the great struggle he waged against cancer, his last battle was not against his death as one may suppose, but was rather for a humanist approach, as if he could see the dangers that can destroy the role of intellectuals in the Arab world. In *The Question of Palestine*, Said put forward his major approach to the Palestinian tragedy, only to discover later, with the Oslo agreement and the emergence of the Palestinian authority, that the struggle for national liberation could not achieve its goals under a bureaucracy that became the victim of its illusions.

I don't remember his answer to my question, or even if he answered at all. I wanted to discuss with him my feeling of the isolation of the Arab intellectual in the new world emerging under one superpower, but time was short as always, and the question remained with me.

In *Representations of the Intellectual*, Said tried to draw a personal portrait through combining Gramsci's organic intellectual, "who is actively involved in society," with Benda's cleric "whose activity is essentially not the pursuit of practical aims." This combination represents the first features of the intellectual of the twenty-first century; the model that was based on the statement of Zola's "j'accuse" and reached its peak with Sartre's universal intellectual who would gradually disappear under Foucault's specific intellectual, before becoming totally dissolved in the global market of ideas. For Said, the intellectual is

> an individual endowed with a faculty of representing, embodying, articulating a message, a view, an attitude, philosophy or opinion to,

as well as for, a public. And this role has an edge to it, and cannot be played without a sense of being someone whose place it is publicly to raise embarrassing questions, to confront orthodoxy and dogma (rather than to produce them), to be someone who cannot easily be co-opted by governments or corporations, and whose *raison d'être* is to represent all those people and issues that are routinely forgotten or swept under the rug.[2]

The synthesis of Gramsci and Benda, a Marxist philosopher and an idealist thinker whose models ranged from Socrates to Jesus of Nazareth, was an attempt to face in an oblique way the crisis of the intellectual in our postmodern world, and in particular the crisis of the Third World intellectual who feels total isolation both in his/her country and in the world. The double exile of the Third World intellectual is not only an outcome of the status of the intellectual in the Western world and his/her continuous isolation, but has its specific reasons:

1. The weakness of the idea of international solidarity. The price of the fall of the totalitarian Soviet regime, and the rise of a new conservatism in the Western world, replaced the idea of internationalism with the idea of globalization. The Third World intellectual feels that his/her cause in defending freedom and democracy in his/her country is becoming a tool to be manipulated by the empire. Either that or the cause is totally neglected. The price paid for this isolation is becoming extremely high, because it parts the intellectual from his/her language, i.e., the ability to circulate a complex truth in a world dominated by a flat language of war between good and evil. The examples of this difficulty are numerous, from Iraq to Palestine. The simplistic language of the "war against terror" tries to destroy the mere idea of justice, and pushes language to the edge of becoming meaningless.

2. This breakdown of meaning, which creates the feeling of isolation, is part of a political and social decomposition in the Arab Mashriq itself. It is an outcome of the impotence of the Arab regime in face of the long Israeli occupation of the West Bank, Gaza, and the Golan Heights, coupled with the Arab regime's terrible oppressive nature, the latter being a product of the military or the oligarchy. The political decomposition is not an outcome of the rise of fundamentalism, it is rather the reverse: fundamentalism itself is an outcome of this decomposition, and an instrument that was used first in the Cold War before it became a party to the so-called war of civilizations. The inability of the Arab regime to make peace or declare war created a kind of

political and moral stagnation that is leading it towards self-destruction. In the face of this decomposition, the need to formulate a new language is inevitable, but it encounters a kind of calcification of the old leftist and nationalist discourses that were based upon an approach that called for a coup, as put forth by Aflaq, and the Stalinist concept of "the writer and intellectual as an engineer of the human soul."

3. The crisis of the political regime reflects a deep crisis in the project of social change that was appropriated and destroyed by the military. "The treason of the clerks," to borrow Benda's title, took on tragic dimensions in the destruction of Beirut, the exile of the Iraqi intellectuals, the dilemma of the Egyptian intellectuals having to choose between assassination and collaboration with the state apparatus, and the marginality of the Palestinian critic (and here lies the special importance of Said, remaining a critical voice until the end).

The old Arab intellectual, forged under the twin influences of Sartre and Marxist ideology, has disappeared. The models of Ghassan Kanafani, who was assassinated by Israel in 1972, and of Hussein Mroueh and Mahdi Amel, both assassinated in the 1980s by the fundamentalists and the Syrian intelligence, have disappeared to be replaced by the assassinations of Algeria during the civil war and the assassinations of Beirut during the Lebanese Intifada of independence.

The clarities of the national struggle have been replaced by the ambiguities of our times of disintegration, and the organic intellectual has found himself in an indeterminate situation. The relationship with the popular movement has become enigmatic, and a new era represented by technicians of culture and formulated through NGOs will try to fill the gap without any real success, because it is actually part of a global approach towards specific problems that can only find their solution in politics.

Edward Said's model of the intellectual offers a possible answer to the crisis of the Arab intellectual, where the word is facing the sword, and the battle is both local and global. In the local dimension he is engaged in a battle that has three levels:

1. The innovation and production of a critical position.

2. Facing occupation through resistance and building institutions of civil society.

3. Leading the cultural opposition to dictatorship, and working to recreate the liberation movement outside both the dead nationalistic ideology and

the fundamentalist discourse that is, in one of its aspects, an echo of the Orientalist discourse.

Success at these levels cannot be achieved without being part of the world. Edward Said taught us that being present in the world involves being critical and becoming partners by destroying barriers to create a multiple identity.

Raef Zureik wrote that we were unfair to Said when we didn't believe his illness and his coexistence with death. Today we will be even more unfair to him if we believe in his death and create from his work a closed text. He used to speak about anger as an antidote to cancer. His anger against injustice must become ours, and his pen that challenged the sword must become our weapon in the battle for human values.

Notes

1 "And no race possesses the monopoly of beauty, of intelligence, of force, and there is a place for all at the rendezvous of victory."
2 Edward Said, *Representations of the Intellectual*, New York: Pantheon, 1994, p. 11.

PART I

The Power of Literature

The Making of a Counter-Tradition

Timothy Brennan

In the wake of Edward Said's death, a number of eulogies sought to capture his free-flowing imagination and openness to many, even incompatible, points of view. All of this was fitting at the time given the inclination of close friends to rescue him from the accusations of partisanship that were already beginning to emerge with renewed strength among his adversaries. But as I knew him, Said was much more settled in his convictions, much less ambivalent than some of these memorials suggested.

If there is no mystery why well-wishers retreated to a place of ambiguity, holding it up as a supreme value (what better way to defend the life of a man often vilified as an iconoclast?), still there was good reason to doubt the portrait's accuracy. The deification of ambiguity was for Said one of the central doctrines of academic cultural theory during the years of his greatest influence, and one of the primary reasons he was so impatient with many of the forms it had taken. This is not to say that he did not deploy ambiguity on occasions for rhetorical cover, only that this was a tactical move that cannot obscure the persistent affiliations that marked his outlook. What I would like to do here is give that outlook a name.

After these initial attempts by allies to protect his name, the goal of any engagement with Said's work can no longer be content with extolling the author or the man alone. The point now would be to address his leads, returning to those aspects of his intellectual project that are inspiring or that need to be revised or deepened. To allude to his favorite poem by Cavafy, one he frequently cited, we can no longer be waiting for the barbarians (they seem already to have crashed the gates!), or even less, lighting a candle at his vigil. The project would necessarily have to be about a *tradition* – what is by definition always larger than one person and what gathers its power only over many generations by way of the coherence of its orientation, which is not to say the uniformity of its ideas.

It is a specific tradition I have in mind, and it is based on a *literary* authority – which I will try to describe since I do not want to be misunderstood as saying that it is based on a *textual* authority, which is a very different thing. A textual authority relies on the specialized interpretive techniques of the professional cleric, monk, rabbi, or theologian with proprietary claims to the meaning of Text (the model, basically, of one type of modern literary critic – say, for example, Jacques Derrida). "Literary," by contrast (for Said at least) meant intentionally useless, curious, imaginatively driven, idealistic, drawn to ideas for their own sake, polymorphous in one's intellectual wanderings and experiments: all that is disparaged by a technocratic commercialism gullibly awed by science like that of the United States (although this seems to be the general profile of neoliberalism itself at present, and so true of a number of other countries as well).

This bid for the polymorphous, in other words, must not be misunderstood. Said was not applauding *difference* – which in academic theory usually refers to the elusiveness of reality structured by language or to the multiple identities that make up society. Instead, he was trying to express the need for a departure from the *way* one approaches knowledge, and what one understands it to be. The general culture is dulled by its faith in science, which has come to mean little more than an unreflective confidence in the 'facts' of experimental evidence and the self-evident utility of technology. The most elementary philosophical insights – for example, questioning the cultural framing of the questions asked, or the degree to which the researcher affects the outcome of any inquiry in advance – are not even posed, much less satisfactorily dealt with by the scientific community or its uncritical public.

He was saying that the humanities pose no serious challenge to these proclivities by counter-posing to them a form of textualism that closes itself off from all debate in the carapace of an essentially aesthetic retreat. He evoked open-endedness, yes, but not in the name of indeterminacy. Rather, he meant a type of alert intellectual hunger devoted to humanist principles that had fallen into disrepute. When I speak of his tradition, I am not saying Said created it. On the contrary, he recognized that one can not create such a thing. There were no gurus in his pantheon, and no acolytes. It is true that his intellectual heroes – the ones he frequently chose as topics for his essays – were always exceptional, brave, and stubborn individuals, burning with a different vision. But they were never living myths – never enamored of power or iconic. So although he did not invent his tradition, he nevertheless translated it into a particular idiom. This translation was his most general achievement.

This tradition – if I can begin now to characterize it – is based, first of all, on historical agency: a view, we must remember, that was under furious attack on the academic left throughout his career. It is based as well on the idea of the university as a refuge from the commercial and political world; on the view of humanistic learning as the weapon of non-instrumental thinking; on a skepticism towards philosophy and philosophical thinking; and on the concept of what he called the "gentile intellect" – which is to say a non-Biblical mode of thinking, rejecting on principle any claim to being a special, chosen, or elect group or race on the basis of one's inheritances.[1] In order to understand this tradition, we need first to make some distinctions regarding its literary character.

All of what Said was, everything that gave him the authority to speak in so many areas (including Palestinian politics), had to do with the fact of his being a professor of literature. This is a methodological point. As he saw it, the mode of intellectual engagement uniquely available in the generalist knowledge of the humanities allowed for the non-prescriptive outlook that enabled his political and critical insights. They would not have been possible otherwise. My view also is that his points of departure, his political imagination, the constellation of thinkers that affected his outlooks and tastes all grew out of a specifically literary training and sensibility. But here we meet an impasse if our goal is to understand the tradition from which he gathered strength. For we have to be honest and note that literary authority is often derived from ostentatious leisure, as Thorstein Veblen once famously pointed out.

In Ivy League colleges, the literary scholar still evokes an earlier time (and this redolence of the past is sharply felt and shared even today). The wide reading of the humanist in that earlier time was as much a mark of detachment as curiosity, for it was primarily his wealth that freed him from work and was the pre-condition for his learning. By choosing this career, he was announcing that he did not have to prepare for a trade.[2] This sort of humanist is not about intellectual adventure at all, and has little in common with that rigorous, theoretical training of the sort Said describes in *Orientalism* when he marvels at the skills of the great philologists of the last century. This enterprise is rather about the smell of money, and the cultural finish that allows one to feel at home in the pages of the *New York Times Magazine*. To a degree, then, the Saidian example is non-transferable, since it has so much to do with his ethnic and class location, not only with his talents and choices. And for complicated reasons, his Palestinian ethnicity gave him a particular authority when combined with his other privileges. Had he written everything he did, it would not have been so widely read or so influential had he not been a Palestinian living in New York. His genius was to have done something special on the enviable grounds that he occupied, within that closed, far from generalizable, environment.

On the other hand, Columbia's ivy walls deflected some of the heat that came his way for defending Palestine. The university was to this degree a refuge, and he was very open about conceding this aspect of its attractions for him. Escaping the vituperative exchanges in newspapers and television talk shows was a way to refresh his thinking, and to participate in a different type of engagement that was about intellectual exploration and speculative knowledge rather than programmatic clashes. But even if we are not likely to see debates in the humanities as being politically consequential, we have to acknowledge that they were so for Said. He took them very seriously. He saw a direct connection between debates in the humanities and the production of intellectuals capable of making a difference in the public sphere. In a sense, you could say that he diagnosed trends in the humanities very closely for just this reason, and he believed (as I do) that theoretical trends in the humanities after the 1970s were at least partly responsible for taking an entire generation out of politics.

But to say "refuge" gives a false sense of the way Said thought of the university, and wrongly implies that he thought the media and the political marketplace more vital arenas, and the university a simple pastime or vacation from serious public persuasion. This was not his position at all. He was just as likely to think of the media as a viciously empty-headed place populated by celebrated inanities like Larry King or Paula Zahn. Said was skeptical, as I have said, about difficult philosophical writing, and claimed even not to know how to think abstractly (saying, for instance, that he had never read Theodor Adorno's *Negative Dialectics*, the major philosophical work by the thinker he frequently cited in his work on music). But he perfectly understood that all critical projects have a philosophical foundation. One cannot challenge the dominant or pose any kind of political alternative without a clarity of concept that is nothing if not *philosophical*. And it is only in the university – in fact, it is only in the humanities of the university – that such orientation can be achieved. Many have addressed themselves, and quite rightly, to Said's practical impact on Middle East perspectives and Palestinian options. But these practical interventions grew out of a tradition whose philosophical foundation he alluded to throughout his career in piecemeal fashion, but that he never actually named for tactical reasons.

Said's habit was to return to earlier traditions to mine their lessons for current, reconfigured use, and indeed, the historical sense for him meant precisely to reject the modernist fantasy that we live in a period of ruptures rather than misrecognized continuities. This is by far the most emphatic point made in his first important book, *Beginnings*, published in 1975: that literary modernism – including that modernism known as postmodernism –

thought of itself as setting bravely out from the year zero of the now, whereas we are all really naively adapting and reassembling older patterns, and are part of a conversation we often take to be a monologue.

We think of Said as not being a joiner, and no doubt, although he has often been attacked personally for his outspoken and often angrily expressed views, one particular line of attack on him was avoided by refusing (for most of his career at least) to be a member of a political organization. In this way he could not be tarnished by a collective brush. This organizational agnosticism, in fact, is one of the more questionable legacies he left us in my opinion. At any rate, it is against that background that I am trying to emphasize that he in fact did join an intellectual lineage. He came to a point during his apprenticeship years as a young professor in the late 1960s and early 1970s when he discovered that he was already within a movement larger than himself. From *Beginnings* on, he set about militating for a counter-tradition that he sought to keep alive and to bring others to. His rhetorical dilemma (one he solved, I think) was how to polemicize against a then-dominant Cartesian and Spinozist intellectual tradition in such a way that did not appear polemical, and in such a way that he would even be misunderstood as being so.

Said often presented himself as someone defined by roaming among various exemplary and notably odd individuals in his essays (one thinks of his fascination with André Gide and Glenn Gould, for instance). He went out of his way to portray this gesture as the exuberance of the literary intellectual for all manner of human variety and quirkiness. Alongside this dalliance with non-conformists and intellectual misfits, he was busy articulating a passion for a tradition that many of us think of today as purely Vichian – that is, based on the early eighteenth-century humanist, Giambattista Vico – although Vico did not launch this tradition either. We understand better what Said was trying to point us towards when we pay more attention to the antinomian sides of his character revealed in this counter-tradition, since it would not have been possible for an individual or a mere iconoclast, however talented or privileged, to have done what he did without wading into an intellectual steam that came out of the past and moved towards the future.

Conveniently placed outside the contemporary critic's range of reference, Vico was useful for Said's veiled polemical purposes because he carried with him no offensive connotations, and was therefore a perfect figure for Said's strategy of indirection. For Vico dedicated his career to obliterating the unsavory attractions of Descartes and Spinoza. Descartes was, to him (as to Said), the perfect twin embodiment of French philosophical idealism and scientific arrogance. In other words, what Said means to say is that he identifies with Vico's struggle against the lonely ego of mathematical rationalism that leads, after so many twists and turns, to the Cartesianism rampant in literary and cultural theory of the late 1970s and 1980s. This Cartesianism takes a slightly different form today in the lionizing of Spinoza, who has recently attracted a number of critical communities, including Italian ex-communists and even mainstream scholars of the seventeenth century like Jonathan Israel, as the truly subversive, truly subterranean fountainhead of the radical Enlightenment.

This Spinozist twist on the problem was one that Said never diagnosed – it came to prominence too late – nor did he fully recognize the importance of the even more formidable and depressing turn in theory over the last decade to interwar reactionaries like Martin Heidegger, who have come to assume the role of holy sages freeing intellectual inquiry from the stigma of being intellectual, and enacting instead a poetic experience of truth based on a strategy of dissimulation. But the larger point is that Saidian criticism owes the same debt to Vico that poststructuralist theory does to Spinoza, and Vico's new science – the science of history – was antipathetic to a notion of originality as rupture. Confronting claims to novelty, Vico observed, according to Said, that "only by reproducing can we know what was produced and what the meaning is of verbal production for a human being: this is the quintessential Vichian maxim"; or similarly, that language is *re-writing* – "history conditioned by repetition, as encipherment and dissemi-nation – the instability, and the richness of a text as practice and as idea."[3] He perfectly anticipated Said's method in that his approach was based on complementarity: the lateral as opposed to the linear and sequential, the concept of beginning as a repetition of worthy precursors, the conceiving of language itself as "the rewriting [which is to say, the writing again] of history," and the unfolding of a thesis, not in prophetic explosions, but by way of "a gradually developing exemplary discourse."[4]

It is already in the mid-1970s, keep in mind – that is, before *Orientalism* – that Said lays out his case for humanist philology as a model for public and political intervention by literary intellectuals on the grounds that literary intellectuals, by virtue of their capacious understandings and verbal flair, are best positioned to attain "mass density and referential power" – provided they forego a politics that satisfies itself with the insurrectionary poses of "radical" readings of texts. This latter is what we see today, for example, in the pretentious Deleuzian politics of rupture in thinkers such as Antonio Negri and Paolo Virno, whose Spinozist "linear thinking" is everywhere evident in the structure of their books which march forward like scholastic theology manuals, displaying categories and subpoints deductively laid out.

Said recoiled from this sort of thinking, and instead found the political edge of the critic not in a strategy of reading but in the palpable curiosity of humanists, their command of speech and unpredictable range of reference, which are themselves potent acts of authorial self-fashioning. These give literary critics decisive advantages over the arid specialists of military, market, and media (who use a model of specialization, as I noted before, that textualist approaches to literature unfortunately emulate). Second, it is in the book *Beginnings* that Said first announces his intention of making Vico his point of departure, the person through whom he will reorient comparative literature and change the (to him) fatal directions of criticism and public commentary at the dawn of the Age of Reagan. And Said establishes himself there also as a thinker fully conversant with contemporary theory and a creative re-interpreter of it, one who sought to place it – that is, historicize it – by means of comparisons that deprived it of its aura and brought it crashing back to earth.

I want to be clear that when I say a Vichian tradition I am not simply alluding to what Said said in his three essays on Vico (one of which takes the form of the concluding chapter of *Beginnings*). And I am not simply saying that Said's way of reading literature, or his practice as a literary critic, was influenced by Vico's humane and populist approach to the Homeric epics, or by the latter's focus on the early European vernaculars, or on the clever critique of religion couched in Vico's "providential history" of self-making found in *The New Science*. In fact, I am saying that there were significant gaps in Said's own account of Vico's meaning to him, and that various dimen-sions of the Italian humanist – particularly the one I am emphasizing now regarding tradition – that Said was silent about, although I would say not ignorant of.

When I say Vichian tradition, I mean, first of all, a minoritarian intellectual position that preceded Vico himself in the form of the medieval scholarly legacies, already implicitly secular, that Martin Bernal observes Vico was heir to – one that championed the legendary Egyptian founder of writing, Hermes Trismegistos (aka "Thoth," the etymological root of Greek *theos* or God) as the founder of non-Biblical or "gentile" philosophy and culture.[5] I am referring also to the nineteenth- and twentieth-century philologists, the mappers of the world spirit, whom Said meticulously examines (and I think it is important to remember, extols) in *Orientalism* – a book that, as I read it, was for Said an apprenticeship that allowed him to understand how mere literary critics (the stodgy and often arcane nineteenth-century linguists, etymologists, and editors) managed to become public personalities with a voice in policy-making.

With the word "Vichian," I am referring also to the Georg Lukács of the essay "Reification and the Consciousness of the Proletariat," a decisive text in Said's formation, where Lukács speaks of the "prophetic words" of Vico, the man who averred that if we are able to "regard the whole of reality as history (that is, as *our* history, since there is no other), we shall have raised ourselves . . . to the position from which reality can be understood as our 'action.' "[6] I am alluding as well to the Vico that Hannah Arendt called (contemptuously) an "ideologist of the classless society" and that E.P. Thompson, in his remarkable polemic, *The Poverty of Theory*, claimed was "able . . . to hold in simultaneous suspension, without manifest contradiction, a Hegelian, a Marxist, and a structuralist . . . heuristic" – an obviously useful skill if I am right about the delicate rhetorical task Said faced in the 1980s and 1990s.[7] I am thinking too of the Vico alluded to in Mbwil a M. Ngal's novel about a Zairean/Congolese intellectual, whose name is "Viko," whose ambition is to write the great African novel infusing the imported European form of the novel with the "riches of traditional African orality."[8]

I am thinking, perhaps most of all, of the Vichian inspirations of V.N. Vološinov's linguistics, and the shattering riposte it offers to the abstract objectivism still dominant in our Saussurean cage, on the one hand, and the equally extremist "subjectivism" of Humboldt and his followers – the sort of infantile invocations of the invented languages of modernism (so prevalent among the lyric poets of countless American small magazines) that Said attacks so mercilessly throughout *Beginnings* as well as in numerous off-the-record comments at conferences.[9] And I am alluding to the Vico that Raymond Williams, following Vološinov, applauds under the name "Vico" in his *Marxism and Literature* in 1977.[10] In short, when I refer to the Vichian tradition, I am referring to what Proudhon referred to in *The Philosophy of Poverty* in his chapter on God, where he remarks that "the whole effort, even of those who following Bossuet, Vico, Herder, Hegel, have applied themselves to the philosophy of history, has been hitherto to establish a presence of a providential destiny presiding over all the movements of man."[11]

The name "Vico" is Said's way of alluding to something much greater, something that had to conceal itself in the prevailing critical winds of right-moving prejudice, scientism, and political intolerance, in which a left-Hegelian posture was as heterodox and as dangerously blasphemous as was secularity in the Middle Ages. But we should not for that reason fail to recognize what he meant by this combination of ideas. Let us begin with the notion of "providence," which any reader of *The New Science* cannot fail to notice or puzzle over. How can a tract like *The New Science* – which nods to religious convention, but that no attentive reader can interpret as anything but counter-religious – be simultaneously about so apparently religious a concept as "providence"? Vico is saying, among other things, that humans, however separated they are by culture, by geography, by historical experience, or mode of production – as they in fact have been throughout much of their pre-history – all happened, remarkably, to arrive at similar civil institutions in isolation from one another, and without any one group having exported the key or model as a gift of their unique genius. Each people found its way to *society*, to laws, to cultural achievement, to economic self-sufficiency; or, as he puts it in *The New Science*, "ploughed lands were the first altars of the gentiles."[12] How could this have happened, Vico asks, if there were not some secular logic to humans themselves as social creatures, some innate capacity to express their humanity in forms recognizable to, and valued by, all?

This logic he, somewhat impishly and with a great deal of intentional paradox, calls "providence" – flirting, in this way, with the prevailing religious rhetoric he was in fact mocking – although it is exactly the idea taken up by others more famously later. For example, it is the exact idea found in Hegel's *Phenomenology of Mind* in his account of the Mind's coming to self-consciousness, the Mind's coming to recognize its common destiny with others; or it is found in Aimé Césaire's famous lines on there being room for everyone at the "rendezvous of victory" – an important element in all national independence struggles for equal sovereignty, which are often based on an equal claim to having contributed, in unrecognized ways, to a world culture now monopolized by an appropriating imperial power.[13] And these Vichian seeds have blossomed in many other fields as well.

This whole line of argument was counter-posed to Vico's opening gambit in *The New Science*, which freely conceded to orthodoxy that one people had precedence over all others – that, according to Biblical verities, the Jews as the people chosen by God were first, were exceptional, and existed as it were outside of history. The brilliance of Vico's study in part is that this apparent place of honor is actually a justification for ignoring Biblical verities, precisely on the ground that they are "outside of history." All the action of his book – all that demands our interest, and draws us in – lies in what is purportedly only "left over" after establishing the exalted character of the chosen. Let the chosen have God, he seems to say; for the rest of us, we have men and women, who are much more interesting and, in the end, more consequential. *This* is the basis upon which his providential history is built: the complete and radical non-priority of any people.

Philosophically speaking, the tradition that Said was militating against was Cartesian, although Descartes has lately been supplanted by a thinker very similar to him from the seventeenth century, one whose underground influence in self-consciously "radical" theory has been even more profound – that is, Spinoza. We hear a great deal these days about the influence of Erich Auerbach on Said, and that was of course very real; but actually, his critique of the Cartesian and Spinozist traditions comes even more directly out of Lukács (who himself derives his orientation from Vico's explicit attacks on Descartes and Spinoza in *The New Science*). Both Descartes and Spinoza represent a tempting, but ultimately false, response to transcendent thinking, thinking based on the fantasy-life of religious desire, or on an attempt to forget or play down the material world we all occupy. In opposing that particular hegemony of his time, Spinoza's philosophy, therefore, can be seen as the most extreme materialism imaginable, as the blasphemous declaration that God is nothing more nor less than the material universe. But within this immensely important and salutary claim, the whole philosophical mind of Spinoza is rigidly fixed to a mathematical model, proceeding by a method of deductive reasoning in pursuit of the unity of substance. His vision of the one who thinks and acts is highly formal, intent to purge real men and women of that irrationalism, altruism, and perversity that interferes with salvational rationalism. As Lukács puts it (in a style of argument Said copied), all givens – that is, inherited ideas considered conventionally true – are dismissed by Spinoza as non-existent, "causing [them] to vanish behind the monumental architecture of the rational forms."[14] Or, as Vico himself puts it, "Spinoza speaks of the commonwealth as if it were a society of traders" – that is, as though a set of crystalline, sharply defined, vigorously logical rules shorn of their messiness could act as a guide for human action.[15] For Spinoza, whatever is clearly and distinctly perceived is true. Doubt has no room in his philosophy except as a vacillation of the mind; the entire purpose of his project is to prove the substantiality of the "I" that knows.

One can see the attractions of such a philosophy for literary critics, given the subjective nature of their claims, who wish to benefit from such heady foundations in a purely logical truth that was associated, historically, with movements of radical opposition to authority in the seventeenth century. In the conservative years of the 1980s, Spinoza became the favorite displacement of Hegel, who in contrast to Spinoza was a philosopher of revolution, of social responsibility, of seeing philosophy itself as finding its fulfillment only in politics and the law. Spinoza became the new anti-Hegel for those in flight from agency and in pursuit of a new politics of truth based on an austere, transgressive philosophy too pure for tainted historical beings – which is the role he plays today in a variety of ostensible radicalisms. Vico, by contrast, was Said's Hegel, and without fealty to either the one or the other alone, he became the name under which Said wished to organize a counter-tradition that reached into a liberationist past of real movements and peoples without sacrificing intellectual passion, and took no outcome as inevitable, except insofar as those outcomes were shaped by the tradition that alone could allow us to perceive them.

Notes

1 Said speaks of Vico's "frighteningly godless" vision, a "human vision" of "an excruciatingly gentile mind" – in other words, a mind "which has been denied the fully integrated revelation accorded the Hebrews [creating instead] a neutral, amoral, and beautiful *mundus* of the mind that is – as he [Vico] is always ready to remind us – only an imagistic economy for the real thing" ("Vico: Humanist and Autodidact," *The Centennial Review*, 11:3, 1967: pp. 341, 351). See also his reference to Vico's "vivid account . . . of human 'gentile' existence," in "Vico on the Discipline of Bodies and Texts," *Reflections on Exile*, Cambridge: Harvard University Press, 2000, p. 84; and *Beginnings: Intention and Method*, Baltimore: Johns Hopkins University Press, 1975, pp. 349–50.

2 Thorstein Veblen, *Theory of the Leisure Class*, New York: Houghton Mifflin, 1973, pp. 215–16.

3 Said, *Beginnings*, p. 357.

4 Ibid., p. 337.

5 Martin Bernal, *Black Athena: The Afroasiatic Roots of Classical Civilization*, New Brunswick: Rutgers University Press, 1987, pp. 23–4, 170; see also Giambattista Vico, *The New Science of Giambattista Vico*, trans. Thomas Goddard Bergin and Max Harold Fisch, Ithaca and London: Cornell University Press, 1984, pp. 38–9.

6 Georg Lukács, "Reification and the Consciousness of the Proletariat," *History and Class Consciousness: Studies in Marxist Dialectics*, Boston: MIT, 1971, p. 145.

7 Hannah Arendt, "Labor, Work, Action," *The Portable Hannah Arendt*, Peter Baehr, ed., New York: Penguin, 2000, p. 169; E.P. Thompson, *The Poverty of Theory and Other Essays*, New York and London: Monthly Review Press, 1978, p. 115.

8 Mbwil a M. Ngal, *Giambatista Viko; ou, Le Viol du discourse africain* (1975), cited in David Damrosch, *What is World Literature?*, Princeton and Oxford: Princeton University Press, 2003, pp. 113–17.

9 V.N. Vološinov, *Marxism and the Philosophy of Language*, translated by Ladislav Matejka and I.R. Titanik, Cambridge, MA: Harvard University Press, 1986.

10 Raymond Williams, *Marxism and Literature*, Oxford and New York: Oxford University Press, 1977.

11 Jean-Pierre Joseph Proudhon, *System of Economical Contradictions: or, The Philosophy of Poverty* (1847), trans. Benjamin R. Tucker (1888), cited in Rod Hay's "Archive for the History of Economic Thought," at http://www.marxists.org/reference/subject/economics/proudhon/philosophy/index.htm. From "Introduction: The hypothesis of God," 2.

12 Vico, *The New Science*, p. 10.

13 G.W.F. Hegel, *The Phenomenology of Mind*, translated with an introduction and notes by J.B. Baillie, New York: Harper Torchbooks, 1967, pp. 228–40, 507–610; Aimé Césaire, *Notebook of a Return to the Native Land*, translated and edited by Clayton Eshelman and Annette Smith, Middletown, CT: Wesleyan University Press, 2001.

14 Lukács, "Reification and the Consciousness of the Proletariat", p. 117.

15 Jonathan Israel, *The Radical Enlightenment: Philosophy and the Making of Modernity 1650–1750*, Oxford: Oxford University Press, 2002, p. 666.

2

The Political Edge of Fiction

Jacqueline Rose

The tribute to Edward Said, that was the original occasion for this essay, took place close to the 40th anniversary of the Occupation, at a time when the situation in the territories, notably Gaza, was dramatically deteriorating, as it continues to do so by the day. The renewed sense of loss in relation to Said, who would have had so much to say, was therefore, and still is, acute. At the end of 2005, I attended the Limmud Festival in England, a Jewish Cultural Festival that annually attracts more than 2,000 Jewish participants worldwide. In one session campaigning *Ha'aretz* journalist, Gideon Levy, in a paper devoted to challenging the concept of Israel as a democracy, pointed out the significance of 2005 as the year in which the time of the Occupation exceeded the time between the war of 1967 and the Declaration of Israel which founded the nation-state. From this point on, he insisted, no one could any longer pretend that the Occupation was an anomaly, a regrettable and passing phase, in Israel's history. It has become the normality of the nation.

As a Jew, I feel a particular accountability for this reality. Not, I should stress, because I consider all Jews to be somehow responsible for, or identifiable with, Israeli government policy – an anti-Semitic belief as I see it, or one at least that can inflame anti-Semitic sentiment – but because Israeli governments repeatedly state that they act on behalf of all the world's Jews. I speak from outside the nation, but it is an outside whose potential otherness the Israeli government is unwilling to countenance. Thus Olmert, at the height of the second Lebanese war of 2006, stated on video link to America: "I believe this war is fought by all Jews."[1] When, a decade before that war, Israel launched Operation "Grapes of Wrath" on Beirut in 1996, I was sitting in New York with Edward and Mariam Said. He asked me why I wasn't writing to the British Press protesting policies carried out in my name. It was not something, not the kind of thing, I would have done then, but it is the kind of thing I would do now. I think that, before, I did not want to hear myself being so wrongly evoked, I wanted to refuse the assumed link. Today it seems to me unavoidable.

Our topic is "Edward Said, the Literary Critic." My preamble is not just intended to alert us to the dreadful background of this tribute. My aim is to open up the question of speech, as something that can be contested, as well as misappropriated and misread. As well as to alert us to the extent to which the unity of the spoken voice cannot be assumed without, clearly in this case, immediate political consequences. It is to suggest, therefore, the complex and disturbing ways in which politics and language are enmeshed. "Who speaks for the Jews?" raises the difficult question of what constitutes the identity of a group. Challenging Olmert's right to speak and fight wars on my behalf, I am deliberately opening up a fissure in the identity and definition of the modern Jew. I am suggesting – and for many in relation to Israel this would be the scandal – that the identity of the Jew is more than one. There is a gap between Israel and the Diaspora, there is a gap between the identity of the Jew who is content to be represented by Israeli policy and the Jew who abhors it, many of whom are inside Israel today. To open up the gap is to allow language its fullest possibilities.

For Edward Said this was, as I understand it, one of the chief tasks of criticism, as well as being modern literary writing's peculiar, and politically enabling, creativity. If Joseph Conrad was never the simple apologist for empire that someone like Chinua Achebe believed him to be, it was, in the case of *Heart of Darkness* for example, because of the dislocations in the narrator's language, which drew constant attention to the discrepancy between the "orthodox view" and his own. This is from Said's *Culture and Imperialism* of 1993: "[If] Conrad can show that all human activity depends on controlling a radically unstable reality to which words approximate only by will or convention, the same is true of empire, of venerating the idea and so forth."[2] What we might call the contingency of language in its ability to name the world, and thereby seem to control it, is wrested by Conrad into the service of an essentially exposing, destabilizing, vision. That vision reveals the limits and fragility of empire, and thereby – although Conrad might not have been aware that this is what he was doing – measures its time on earth:

> But come to an end [empire] would, if only because – like all human effort, like speech itself – it would have its moment, then it would have to pass. Since Conrad *dates* imperialism, shows its contingency, records its illusions and its tremendous violence and waste (as in *Nostromo*), he permits his later readers to imagine something other than an Africa carved

up into dozens of European colonies, even if, for his own part, he had little notion of what that Africa might be.[3]

"Imagine something other." That also could have served as the title of this essay. I want to suggest that one place we can look for such imaginings is inside Israeli writing, even though this is not a place, for political reasons, where Said himself, as far as I am aware, chose to go.

First a detour, although hopefully it will turn out not to have been one. In his essay on "Arabic Prose and Prose Fiction After 1948," Said describes the particular task of the Arab writer post-1948 as the need to create the the Arabs as a nation: "the disaster had revealed to the Arabs that their history had not yet made of them a nation."[4] This places Arab writing in a type of fissured temporality: "at the intersection of past and future stands the disaster, which on the one hand reveals the deviation from *what has yet to happen* (a unified, collective Arab identity) and on the other reveals the possibility of *what may happen* (Arab extinction as a cultural or national unit)."[5]

The Arab writer after 1948, I read Said as saying, was torn between two imperatives, or rather had to make on himself an impossible demand: to wrench from its possible extinction an identity that wasn't yet there. In this context, creating a present bore the weight of an urgent political obligation. Hence the importance of the "scene" in this literature, the site of what he terms a "restorative history." "The emphasis on the scene," he writes, "is intensified, is made more urgent: a scene formally translates the critical issues at stake in the Arab world."[6] He then proceeds to a reading of Ghassan Kanafani's 1962 novella *Men in the Sun* (*Rijal fil shams*), whose horrendous unfolding in the present, given in every tiny detail of concrete, breathing – and finally extinguished – life, bears witness to the threat of catastrophe, and the need to wrest from potential extinction the record of a people in danger of being eclipsed before it has even been born. Kanafani must "make the present"; unlike Stendhal or Dickens, this is not "an imaginative luxury", but "a literal, existential necessity."[7] Rereading this powerful, persuasive essay for today, one passage, which sums up the argument, struck me in particular: "To be in a scene is to displace extinction, to substitute life for the void. Thus the very act of telling, narrating, uttering, guarantees actuality; here the Islamic tradition of *isnad* (support, witness) is vitalised and put to a definite aesthetic purpose."[8]

It was the word "witness" that struck me. It is the title of the most famous short story by Shulamith Hareven, the Israeli writer and peace activist, whose critique of Israeli nationalism, both in her journalism and fiction, will now become my focus. It is also central to the writing of S. Yizhar, who will be another topic of this essay.

First, however, some crucial distinctions. If for the Arab writer, the threat is to a people not yet brought into being, a people in danger therefore of being erased at the very point of their emergence into history *as* a people, the issue for the Israeli writer is very different. For the Israeli, according to one predominant version of Jewish history, *the threat has already happened*. And yet the people as a people – this is the fundamental affirmation of Jewish statehood – *exist*. Israel *is* a nation (indeed that is the modern meaning of the word). Furthermore, as the Declaration of Independence of 1948 spells out explicitly, the State of Israel is viewed by its founders as the "redemption" of the historic catastrophes that have befallen the Jewish people, as well as their "return" to an existence as a people, one that existed in the past, was destroyed and is now being restored. This is therefore a very different imagined temporality. But, perhaps without always knowing it, this temporality also carries a fissure or contradiction inside itself. The Declaration of Independence is a performative that conjures into existence a nation-state based on an erasure of a people from their own history. It harbors therefore a sense of disaster inside its most radical self-affirmation. It would be wrong, I believe, to see this as ideology only, although the ideological uses and political manipulations to which it has been put by Israel in the service of state violence is now well-known. "We are a people." "We have been destroyed." This is of course just one turn from Herzl's statement: "We are one people, our enemies have made us so." It is, we might say, its radical intensifier. But it is very different from Said's analysis of the predicament of the Arab writer: "Not yet a people, we are in danger of extinction before we have even become one." If the urgent political task of the Arab writer is to create the present of his own people on the page, for the Israeli, the problem is very different. There is a narrative already there waiting. Indeed it is encoded into her being as a citizen of the modern world. A narrative that folds catastrophe into identity, an identity which then closes on the Palestinians and on itself.

The question is therefore what the Israeli writer does with that narrative. If we go back to the start of this essay, then at its most obvious, the Israeli writer finds her- or himself more in the position of, say, Conrad. Although any simple equation of Zionism and colonialism seems to me flawed – even if rooted in European empire, the Zionists were stateless, had no metropolitan state – nonetheless, in relation to the Palestinians, she or he is the representative of the nation with the power (the Palestinians precisely having no nation). The question then becomes how far the writer colludes with that power – and, I would want to add, with its catastrophic core – or allows us to question it. Faced with a rhetoric of statehood which can be seen as one of the most efficient and coercive of the twentieth century, on what terms, at the risk of challenging the heart of the nation, does the writer create an alternative space? If for Said it was a political imperative to write the Arab people into being, note that it was no less an imperative – a passion I would say – for him to trace the moments inside literary writing where the dominant discourse of empire had the good faith to deconstruct itself. At one level, the point of this essay is then simple. To call up, in his spirit as I like to see it, those Israeli writers who I think are performing an equivalent task in relation to Israeli nationhood. When I started working on Zionist discourse, I was not yet aware of just how powerfully critical some of the dissenting voices of this literature could be.

Little known outside Israel, Shulamith Hareven is one of the country's most famous writers. Born in Poland in 1930, she escaped the Nazis with her family and moved to British-ruled Mandatory Palestine, where, as a member of the *Hagana*, she participated in the creation of the state (she served as a medic at the front during the 1948 war). She was also a founder of *Galutz*, the Israeli military radio station, and worked with Jewish immigrants from Arab countries as an officer in the Israel Defense Force. But if her story embodies that of the new nation, her own voice is rarely in tune with the refrain of the state. She went on to be a journalist and writer – the first woman to be made a member of the Academy of Hebrew Language – a peace activist, founder of *Peace Now* in 1978, and one of the most outspoken critics of the Israeli government (in 1995, the French magazine *L'Express* nominated her as one of the hundred women who "move the world").

Throughout her writings, Hareven issued the strongest critique to the dominant rhetoric of her nation. Her strongest reproach is the price the individual has paid for such a powerful, and powerfully enforced, collective dream. "We will bring them here," Golda Meir announced, "and turn them into human beings."[9] For the state to flourish, identification with the new ethos was to be absolute. Or in the words of the teacher in her 1980 short story, "The Witness," as he exhorts the young boy, Shlomek, who has fled war-torn Poland for Palestine: "You know the expression: "Be part of the group or die?" "[10] "My role as an educator," he comments later, "was to build a new generation, proud and magnanimous and cruel" – he is citing Jabotinsky, founder of right-wing Revisionist Zionism and of its ultra-nationalist youth movement, *Betar*.[11]

"The Witness" is perhaps Hareven's most famous story. It is written in the first person voice of the young Israeli whose task it is to absorb Shlomek into the new nation. The tale is not presented as autobiography, although it is the only non-autobiographical piece Hareven chose to include in her autobiographical compilation, *Yamim Rabim*, or *Many Days*, of 2002, the last of her writings published during her life (she died in 2003). But just how closely, and critically, it brushes against her own history can be measured by the fact that the teacher, also born in Poland (a fact he prefers not to recall), came, like Hareven, to Israel at the age of eleven, and by its ironic, almost scathing representation of the young boys in the class who are being proudly groomed for recruitment by the *Hagana*, of which Hareven herself had been a member. When one such, Boaz, is on the verge of being defeated in a brawl with Shlomek, the teacher intervenes on his side: "I was sure that in the coming year when the officers of the *Hagana* arrived to look their age group over, Boaz would be chosen as commander material . . . I could not allow his leadership to be undermined."[12] With a crucially destabilizing shift of perspective, Hareven is re-telling her own story.

But if this story has become celebrated, it is for the way it documents the silencing by the *Yishuv* of what was happening to the Jews of Europe, a silencing which would only come to be fully documented as history in the 1990s in the writings of the brilliant cultural historian, Idith Zertal.[13] Through the voice of a narrator whose utter shallowness is displayed on every page, Hareven's story allows us to enter this experience from the side of the victim (although as we will see, the status of "victim" is the last one Hareven feels should be claimed by Israel). No less important, it goes back in time to that moment, decisive as she believes for the new nation, when the full extent of the horrors was not yet known. Shlomek is a survivor from the beginning, not the end of the war, who has witnessed the massacre of his whole family by the Nazis (hence the title of the story) – his father was hanged on Passover, his mother and two brothers killed in the forest when they ventured out in search of bread. No one at the school believes him. They treat him as a fantasist and liar. In the eyes of the burgeoning nation, he is no more or less than a displaced person needing to be assimilated into his new place: "Soon you'll look like everyone else and talk like everyone else, and no one will be able to tell that you weren't born here."[14] Shlomek is therefore both witness and messenger. He talks. In this alone Hareven rewrites, in something like an act of grace, the silence of her generation, gives them back their voice.

The climax of the story comes when a leader of the *Yishuv* arrives from the Jewish Agency "in a burst of glory" to address the school.[15] After a speech detailing the gravity of the war but with "prophecies of consolation," Shlomek rises to his feet, to the consternation of the gathering, and delivers his deathly message: "Comrade Benio, I have a question to ask you. There is evidence that the Germans intend exterminating all the Jews of Europe living under their rule. Have the national institutions any knowledge of this, and if so, what do they propose to do about it?"[16] It is the question of the wise fool. It is the truth (more than once the narrator has told Shlomek that the absolute truth was not the most important thing). Comrade Benio believes the claims to be exaggerated: "But, I tell you comrades, that even if this grave news, or even part of it, proves to be true . . . even then we will not be able to do anything."[17] "Our first duty, our sacred duty, is to the remnants of our people gathered here: we have no greater duty than our duty to the great pioneering venture of building Eretz Israel."[18] Shlomek flees the school that night – "without a coat, in his sandals and short trousers" – "slipping past" the Arab villages to the High Commissioner to whom he delivers his eye-witness report to events that the whole world, including the *Yishuv*, will finally be forced to recognize. "Why couldn't he have waited," the teacher declaims, "why did he run away in the night as if his conscience wasn't clean?"[19] What he doesn't ask is what difference it would have made, given that the new nation has, as Comrade Benio attests, so fully exonerated itself from any responsibility for the Jews of Europe.

Note that the Arab village appears here as an aside: "How he had succeeded in slipping past the Arab villages," comments the narrator, "I don't know."[20] Even in this expansive, self-critical examination of the nation-in-waiting, the Palestinian cannot be seen – although this is connoted as the blindness of the blindest of narrators. But if this story is important in this context it is because it draws on the history of the genocide of the Jews, insists on its imminent reality, but then proceeds to undo its most recurrent political effect. The Holocaust is not presented here as a justification for the State of Israel, since the nation in its founding moments was in such radical disassociation from it. Manipulation of the Holocaust for political purposes is therefore just that, precisely because it is so remote from the event which it evokes. In her obituary for Gideon Hausner, Attorney General at the time of the Eichmann trial, Hareven contrasts his humility in the face of the *Shoah* with the politicians "who take the name of the Holocaust in vain . . . the arrogant hacks who were not there but who have no qualms about manipulating the Holocaust, using it as a political ploy or as an excuse to turn others into victims." (Her description of the "*Shoah*oligists" and "*Shoah* Business" who "milk it for all its worth" makes Norman Finkelstein seem tame in comparison.[21]) It is because she has so vividly charted the resistance to suffering in the founding of the state that Hareven's critique of the political use of the Holocaust in Israel today acquires such moral authority.

For Hareven, suffering is not the same thing as victimhood. If, as she suggests, the nation has always been ashamed of the first, it has embraced the second as a new, fortified identity that licenses its own violence against the

Palestinians ("an excuse to turn others into victims"). "If my only identity is that of the victim, the world's deterministic and doomed victim, I may (or so it seems) commit any atrocity."[22] Why, she asks with reference to Hausner, has "the principle of statehood embodied in trial, as opposed to the ghetto mindset behind revenge . . . never been taught in our schools?"[23] Every schoolchild knows "the desperate acts of our history by rote. In how many Israeli schools are court rulings taught?"[24] Hareven is appealing to the rule of law against the rule of rhetoric; she is asking for language to be used differently. Coagulated to the past in the name of a catastrophically dreaded and anticipated future, it needs instead to submit to the painstaking scrutiny of a present fully accountable to itself.[25]

"It is as if all of Zionism," she writes in her 1986 essay "Identity: Victim," "is dependent on our not knowing and not wanting to know."[26] All that can be seen is "the eternal victim, alone in the world, who sits upright on his throne with his eyes closed, smothering all other peoples (especially the Arabs), and is always, always right, right with the cold, blind righteousness of the victim above whose head flutters the banner, 'Vengeance is mine!' "[27] In fact in the 34 years between the Declaration of Independence and the first Lebanese War, there were only five weeks of all-out war involving the bulk of the IDF; and, according to an IDF spokesman, in the years preceding the war, terrorism had in fact been in decline (37 casualties in three years, and in the year prior to the war, one). In the process, as Hareven sees it, Israel not only licenses aggression towards the Palestinians, it is also wreaking destruction upon itself: "The upshot, then, of presenting things as though Israel faced a threat to its existence, the danger of a holocaust, is that by our own talk and with our own hands we generate situations in which dozens or hundreds of times as many of our people fall as are killed in all the acts of terrorism combined, and without an iota of justification."[28] Israelis are left no chance of identity "except to be either murderers, the murdered, or both."[29] What, she laments, has any of this to do with Judaism?[30] The tradition of Judaism to which Hareven appeals is one of justice. For this reason alone, I would caution against the identification of Edward Said's thought with any concept of a "gentile culture." If only Israelis could, Hareven pleads, see themselves as the inheritors of a people with a four-thousand-year history of responsibility, conscience, and appeals for social order and justice, then: "even if, often in history, I have been the victim of others, I will never oppress those weaker than myself and never abuse my power to exile them."[31]

I don't think it is going too far to say that Hareven has taken the official rhetoric of statehood and torn it apart at the seams. There is the profoundest link between her deconstruction of the place of catastrophe in the national imagination, and the force of her critique of Israel's treatment towards the Palestinians. Contrary to the official discourse, the new nation could not acknowledge the pain or reality of the Holocaust. Paradoxically it was that very refusal which allowed it to transmute catastrophe into identity – an identity of victim-hood that then becomes a sanction for state violence against another people. This in itself should make it clear that acknowledging the Holocaust and criticizing Israel are not alternatives, not antagonistic to each other. In fact, in this alternative logic as I read it, to accord the Holocaust its rightful place as memory rather than identity, would allow – force perhaps is too strong a word – Israel to recognize what it is doing.

S. Yizhar was the pen-name of Yishar Smilansky born in 1916. He is most famous in the West for his short story "The Prisoner," written during the 1948 war, and published at the time in *Molad*, a monthly journal sponsored by Mapai, the ruling party. Yizhar was himself a member of the Knesset, like Hareven, perhaps even more so, at the seat of power. Like Hareven, his critique has the authority of belonging. "The Prisoner" tells the story of an Arab, eventually named as Hasan Ahmed, a shepherd taken captive by Israeli troops during the 1948 war, and subjected to brute interrogation before being transferred in the back of a jeep, in the final scene, to a camp "which specialized in interrogating prisoners and meted out to each just what he deserved."[32] "The Prisoner" shows startling prescience in relation to modern scenes of torture that have become so familiar to us today, notably Abu Ghraib: while the prisoner is being mocked and taunted by the Israeli soldiers on the mountainside where he is captured: "One man was taking pictures of the whole scene."[33]

But what is really remarkable about this story is the voice in which it is told. It opens lyrically in the third person:

> Shepherds and their flocks were scattered on the rocky hillsides among the woods of low terebinth and the stretches of wild rose, and even among the swirling contours of valleys foaming with light, with those golden-green sparks of rustling summer grain under which the clodded earth, smelling of ancient soil, ripe and good, crumples to grey flour at a foot's touch.[34]

But the lyricism is anguished: "We sat down on the rocks . . . A whirlpool of gleaming mountain fields, olive hills, and a sky ablaze with intense silence blinded us for moments and so beguiled our hearts that one longed for a word of redeeming joy."[35] Why "redeeming" – what is in need of redemption, and why the longing? If not, as the paragraph progresses, that this is a world only seeming to belong to "the good days when there was yet no evil in the world to forewarn of other evil things to come."[36] At this point the shepherds have not been identified and the land is replete with national, Biblical, passion: "quiet flocks were grazing, flocks from the days of Abraham, Isaac and Jacob."[37] By moving in to capture the shepherd, the soldiers show that the land will not bear its own lyrical burden. The violence tears into the opening lyricism and with it Zionism's sanctification of the land on which the Jewish claim to Palestine rests. This is from the "Declaration of Independence":

> Eretz-Israel was the birthplace of the Jewish people. Here their spiritual, religious and political identity was shaped. Here they first attained to statehood, created cultural values of national and universal significance, and gave to the world the eternal Book of Books.
>
> . . .
>
> Pioneers, ma'plim – immigrants coming to Eretz-Israel in defiance of restrictive legislation and defenders, they made deserts bloom, revived the Hebrew language, built villages and towns.
>
> . . .
>
> We appeal to the Jewish people throughout the Diaspora to rally round the Jews of Eretz-Israel . . . and to stand by them in the great struggle for the realization of the age-old dream – the redemption of Israel.

In "The Prisoner," redemption is a longing that will be powerless, we are more or less told on the first page, to redress "the evil to come."

One of the things the story most powerfully conveys is the pleasure of cornering the prisoner "like a trapped gazelle," "shivering like a rabbit": "What a laugh! What fun!," that is, the perversity of war.[38] There is no sign here – quite the opposite – of Israel's famous edicts or aphorisms: "purity of arms," "shoot and weep," with which to this day it insists on the ethical superiority of its army, and which have been so brilliantly laid bare in the writings of Ilan Pappe. The sergeant is "drunk with satisfaction," the soldiers whoop their way after the sheep "with wanton abandon."[39] "Our prisoner" – note the collective "our" – was "enveloped with dumbness, the silence of an uprooted plant – his misery so palpable that it flapped about his head in a rhythm of terror."[40] "Uprooted plant" is also noteworthy, because there is so little room in Zionist mythology for the image of the Palestinians as "uprooted" like the Jews. Zionism cannot justify its history in Palestine without the belief that the Jews have the monopoly of dispossession. There is, therefore, no place for empathy, still less for an identification that works to the humiliation of the victor as it does progressively in this tale. Nor for moments such as this one when the soldiers alight on the deserted Arab village: "Signs of the base, an empty Arab village . . . An abandoned anthill. The stench of desertion."[41] Hareven's Shlomek, remember, slipped past the Arab villages in the night. Here we are brought into the village, although we need to note the ambiguity: "The rot of humanity, infested, louse-ridden. The poverty and stupefaction of wretched villagers . . . They were revealed in their nakedness, impoverished, shriveled, stinking . . . Strangeness, hostility, bereavement. An air of mourning – or was it boredom? – hovered there in the heat of the day."[42] This could be seen as Orientalist writing par excellence. Except insofar as it at least allows that the desertion of the village is a cause of mourning, although only fleetingly. The abjection of the villagers sounds almost as if it is inherent or their fault. More than once the prisoner, whose misery is so palpable, is described as "repulsive." In fact, in these awkward moments, I think Yizhar is entering into the mindset of the soldiers, letting it hover, and then slowly but surely, as the tale progresses, condemn itself.

I started by saying the voice is what matters. If that is the case, it is because it moves from neutral to third to a form of first person in the final scene. Someone, we assume a soldier, in the back of the truck carrying Ahmed to the interrogation camp where he will surely be tortured, is asking himself whether he should not set the prisoner free. In fact the utterance splits between a "you" and an "I"; the soldier is arguing with himself, the first voice making the case for freedom, the second mouthing the platitudes of the State (the "you" is the most powerful as this is clearly what the soldier is telling himself to do, the "I" appears defensive and weak): "As for you, his little god, it's your duty to free him, even if he himself laughs at you, even if he (or someone else) sees it as a sign of weakness on your part, even if your friends make fun of you, if they try to restrain you, if they bring you up for court-martial, for twenty court-martials. It is your duty to break free of this habitual swinishness."[43] Gradually, and crucially, the range of the voice expands, to make a broader, more widely applicable, claim, issuing its challenge to the national imagination: "Let there be one person who is ready – even at the price of suffering – to get out of this heap of filth which was piling up in the days when we were good citizens and which is now the celebrated, the accepted, the official way of the world, embraced by those bearing the proud title 'soldier'."[44] "Habitual swinishness" – Yazhir is telling his reader that the army regularly, habitually, brutalizes itself – not, as the story announces, the "official," "celebrated," "accepted" view of the world. We can measure the force of this against the classical rhetoric – such violence is untypical, unsanctioned by the army or state – with which Bush and Blair have responded to the exposure of such violence in relation to UK and US soldiers in Iraq.

It would be impossible to overstate how counter-intuitive this is for the Israel Defense Force. Becoming a soldier was, and still remains for many Israelis, the induction process into citizenship, the way of becoming truly an Israeli Jew. Writing of the refuseniks in the introduction to her recent collection of their testimonies, *Breaking Ranks*, Ronit Chacham comments: "For these male officers, being an Israeli citizen and a man meant being a soldier, and indicting the Israeli army amounted to questioning an essential part of their identity. Military service is the path to full membership in Israeli society: the army seals the relations between the citizens and the state."[45]

The soldier doesn't act. He doesn't let Ahmed go. Lyricism returns: "The glimmering plain was a thin, bright foil."[46] But it is irretrievably damaged by what has happened, gnawed by doubt. These are the last lines:

> And yet behind us (but no one is gazing there) in the misty evening coming over the mountains, there, maybe, there is a different feeling, a gnawing sadness, the sadness of "who-knows?," of shameful impotence, the "who-knows?" that is in the heart of a waiting woman, the "who-knows?" of fate, a single, very personal "who-knows?," and still another "who-knows?" belonging to us all, which will remain here unanswered, long after the sun has set.[47]

In these lines, I see Yizhar flirting with the temptation of turning this into a purely personal, internalized dilemma – fate, a waiting woman – before, instead, acknowledging it as a collective responsibility: "another 'who-knows?' belonging to us all." Nonetheless, the rest of that final line, "belonging to us all, which will remain here among us, unanswered, long after the sun has set," is supremely ambiguous. It can either be read as a question that will go underground as the unanswerable dilemma of the nation (which I believe to be what has happened in Israel), or as a bland appeal to human weakness as recurrent and universal as the setting sun. A bit like, to permit for a moment an allusion to another historic drama unfolding at the same time, the famous last lines of Alan Paton's *Cry, The Beloved Country*, also published in 1948: "For it is the dawn that has come, as it has come for a thousand centuries, never failing. But when that dawn will come, of our emancipation, from the fear of bondage and the bondage of fear, why, that is a secret."[48]

It is not of course a secret, any more than "emancipation" in 1948 South Africa can justly carry the pronoun "our," as if there were not racial distinctions to be made, distinctions on which the rest of Paton's novel had so graphically based itself. It is of course, as with Yizhar, the classic liberal solution. Black and Arab, undesignated in the last lines of both stories, fade back into the shadows, their oppression disappearing into the dawn or the setting sun. And yet in the body of his story Yizhar has dismantled the army's, and – since they are so intertwined – the nation's, founding image of itself.

To end with one moment from his 1949 story, "The Story of Hirbet Hiz'ah," less well known and never completely translated into English, where Yizhar goes further, by allowing the challenge to the dominant ethos to seep into the constitutive moment of the state, bringing the dispossession of the Palestinians fully onto the page. Again a young soldier, this time engaged in the evacuation of an Arab village in 1948, finds himself slowly appalled by what he is doing. At a key moment, struck by the dignity of one woman with her child who refuses to break before their eyes, he recognizes a fragment of his own history that rises up to haunt him: "Something suddenly became clear to me in a flash. At once I saw everything in a new, a clearer light – Galut (the Hebrew word for exile). This is Galut. Galut is like this. This is what Galut looks like."[49]

Note the halting, partial, repetitions: "this is," "is like this," "this is what Galut looks like." These are the hesitant fragments of memory bearing witness to something that you will search in vain for in the dominant rhetoric of state: the recognition that the Israeli nation, in the founding, constitutive moment of its history, is exiling the Palestinians, and thereby repeating one of the repeated abuses against the Jewish people. In Yizhar's vision, exile, which the creation of Israel was meant to leave definitively behind, reinscribes itself into the nation's soul. The brilliance of this is its suggestion that, as long as Israel does not rectify the founding injustice of the nation towards the Palestinian people, the worst of its own history will still be trailing alongside it. It is a deeply counter-intuitive insight, since, in the dominant narrative, the continuing containment if not oppression of the Palestinians is the only way to save Israel from the continuous threat of a repetition of the worst of its own past.

My focus on Israeli writing has of course been part of a hope. First of all, to return to the start of this essay, to show that Israeli fiction, in its best moments, tears apart the seamless and destructive rhetoric of the nation-state. This has the utmost importance in a context where the struggle over language has played such a key role, as Edward Said always insisted it did, in the constitution of the nation's reality and its belief in itself.[50] I believe that to be especially true in the case of Israel where disputes over the history and meaning of Zionism continue to be at the heart of the nation's ongoing self-definition. The hope is of course that to point to these moments of creative dissonance is to show that the rhetoric is not as intransigent as it mostly seems to be; that the wall, to cite Michel Warschawski in a rather different context, will break.[51] "[C]ome to an end it would," Said wrote of the empire painted by Conrad, "if only because like all human effort, like speech itself – it would have its moment, then it would have to pass."[52] The political edge of fiction is its ability to undo one thing, so that we can imagine something other, something better, in its place. In the fiction of Hareven and Yizhar, Israel confronts its past as a first stage towards allowing itself to imagine another, more just, future, and thereby to secure the future for the Palestinians and for itself. Edward Said's generous vision of what writing could help us to do is needed more today than ever.

Notes

1 Ehud Olmert, Video Address to United Jewish Communities, 7 August 2006.
2 Edward Said, *Culture and Imperialism*, London: Chatto, 1993, p. 33.
3 Ibid. (emphasis original).
4 Edward Said, "Arabic Prose and Prose Fiction After 1948," *Reflections on Exile and Other Literary and Cultural Essays*, London: Granta, 2001, p. 47.
5 Ibid.
6 Ibid., p. 51.
7 Ibid., p. 53.
8 Ibid., p. 50.
9 Cited, Hareven, "Israel: The First Forty Years," *The Vocabulary of Peace: Life, Cultre and Politics in the Middle East*, San Francisco: Mercury House, 1995, p. 101.
10 Hareven, "The Witness" (1980), translated by Dalya Bilu in *Stories from Women Writers of Israel*, New Delhi: Star, 1995, p. 78.
11 Ibid., p. 82.
12 Ibid., p. 81.
13 Idith Zertal, *Israel's Holocaust and the Politics of Nationhood*, Cambridge: Cambridge University Press, 2005, and *From Catastrophe to Power: Holocaust Survivors and the Emergence of Israel*, Berkeley: University of Carlifornia Press, 1998.
14 Hareven, "The Witness," p. 73.
15 Ibid., p. 90.
16 Ibid., pp. 91, 92.
17 Ibid., p. 94.
18 Ibid.
19 Ibid., p. 98.
20 Ibid., p. 96.
21 Hareven, "The Man Who Descended into Inferno" (1990), *The Vocabulary of Peace*, p. 142.
22 Hareven, "Identity: Victim" (1986), *The Vocubulary of Peace*, p. 152.
23 Hareven, "The Man Who Descended into Inferno," p. 141.
24 Ibid.
25 In discussion with Idith Zertal at the *London Review of Books* bookshop on 24 October 2007, we decided to entitle the evening: "Zionism, the Holocaust and Israel: Past and Future." Zertal's argument was that Israel is trapped in a

traumatic past and messianic, apocalyptic vision of the future which leaves no space for the political responsibilities of the present.

26 Hareven, "Identity: Victim," p. 151.
27 Ibid.
28 Hareven, "Israel: The First Forty Years," p. 96.
29 Ibid., p. 116.
30 Ibid.
31 Hareven, "Identity: Victim," pp. 152–3.
32 S. Yizhar, "The Prisoner" (1948), in Robert Alter, ed., *Modern Hebrew Literature*, Library of Jewish Studies, New Jersey: Behrman House, 1973, p. 305.
33 Ibid., p. 298.
34 Ibid., p. 294.
35 Ibid., p. 294.
36 Ibid.
37 Ibid.
38 Ibid., pp. 295–6.
39 Ibid., pp. 296, 297.
40 Ibid., p. 297.
41 Ibid., p. 298.
42 Ibid.
43 Ibid., p. 309.
44 Ibid., p. 309.
45 Ronit Chacham, *Breaking Ranks: Refusing to Serve in the West Bank and Gaza Strip*, New York: Other Press, 2003, p. 8.
46 Yizhar, "The Prisoner," p. 310.
47 Ibid.
48 Alan Paton, *Cry, The Beloved Country: A Story of Comfort in Desolation* (1948), Harmondsworth: Penguin, 1988, p. 236.
49 Yizhar, "The Story of Hirbet Hiz'ah" (1949), translated by Harold Levy, in *Caravan: a Jewish Quarterly Omnibus*, edited by Jacob Sonntag, New York and London: Thomas Yoseloff, 1962, p. 330.
50 See especially, Edward Said, "Zionism from the Standpoint of its Victims", *The Question of Palestine*, New York: Times Books, 1979. I discuss this essay in "Continuing the Dialogue: On Edward Said," in Jacqueline Rose, *The Last Resistance*, London: Verso, 2007.
51 Michel Warschawski, *On the Border*, translated by Levi Laub, Boston: South End Press, 2005, p. 205.
52 Said, *Culture and Imperialism*, p. 28.

Part II

Speaking Truth to Power

3

Orientalizing the Orientals:
The Other Message of Edward Said

Fawwaz Traboulsi

In this contribution, I wish to make the case that Edward Said has in fact established two disciplines. One explicit, in *Orientalism*, amended, developed, and continuously enriched with an array of new contributions; the other implicit, and under-developed in the form of a contribution towards a critique of Occidentalism, i.e. the ways in which the West is represented in the non-Western world. Edward Said imagined the two processes to be intimately bound together, and warned very early on against a vicious circle in which Orientalism becomes complete when "the modern Orient . . . participates in its own Orientalizing."[1]

The main reason for this interest is partly due to the fact that Edward Said's critique of Orientalism (the discipline and the ideology) is tirelessly hijacked in the Arab world, as well as in the circles of the Arab intelligentsia in the diaspora, by all sorts of nativists or by social and cultural parvenus, who transform the critique of Orientalism into nagging about the way the Arabs are (mis-) represented in the West – the assumption being that Arabs/Muslims are "better," i.e. more civilized, than the way they are represented. Such complaints presuppose the existence of an Oriental essence, which is not correctly apprehended by a West likewise fixed into an immutable essence. Let me say, *en passant*, that too much effort has been invested in the fields of representation (the representation of the Arab in the cinema, the novel, the ads, what have you) at the expense of the production of knowledge in the Arab world, and by Arabs abroad, about both Arab and Western societies.

Said made it sufficiently clear, on many an occasion, that his critique of Oriental representations does not imply the existence of such an essence. His most recent argument can be found in the posthumous *Humanism and Democratic Critique*:

My critique [of Orientalism] was premised on the flawed nature of all representations and how they intimately tied up with worldliness, that is, with power, position, and interests. This requires saying explicitly that my work was not intended as a defense of the real Orient or that it even made the case that a real Orient existed. I certainly held no brief for the purity of some representations against others, and I was quite specific in suggesting that no process of converting experience into expression could be free of contamination. It was already contaminated by its involvement with power, position, and interests, whether it was a victim of them or not.[2]

Said's insistence is that Knowledge is always at the service of "power, position, and interests." Many among those who have not read any of his works besides *Orientalism* forget that he attacked Occidentosis – that pathological tick whereby all ills are blamed on the West – in addition to conspiracy theories (though colonial history reveals that real conspiracies greatly surpass the wildest imagined conspiracy theories!). Said also criticized the Arab regimes for their failure to resist imperialism and Zionism (despite the fact that he was rather "soft" on the oil oligarchies). And although he envisaged his critique of Orientalism as a cultural-political contribution to the anti-Zionist and anti-imperialist struggle worldwide, he was far from being complacent with certain ideologies which accompany liberation struggles, such as nativism (making nevertheless the distinction between nativism, nationalism, and nationality). His critique of Yasser Arafat and the PLO leadership, especially since the Oslo accords (which he brilliantly termed "the peace of the weak"), is in essence a critique of the *misreading* by a national liberation movement of US and Israeli strategies. Neither did Said spare Arab intellectuals from criticism – for example, those who supported Roger Garaudy's revisionism and denial of the Holocaust in *Le Monde diplomatique* (August–September 1998). An indefatigable writer explaining to his fellow Arabs the nature of US foreign policy and how it should be countered, one of Said's latest articles (also in *Le Monde diplomatique*) explained the new mechanisms of decision-making in the US, with the advent of the neocons to power and the rising influence of the Christian fundamentalists (though he also insisted on the great potential contained in the protest movement by the American people against the war in Iraq). One of the last messages by a man who saw himself both as Arab and American, was the call, at a commencement address at the American University of Beirut, for devoting more time and effort to studying the American society and state in the Arab world, rather than simply teaching Arab students from textbooks designed for American students.

Occidentalism

Occidentalism, for the purpose of this chapter, can be defined as a discourse nurtured by local versions of nationalism, a nativism informed by "conspiracy theories" and inflamed by anti-Semitic foibles imported from the huge reservoir of European and American right-wing literature. By Occidentalism, I don't refer to the definition used by Buruma and Margalit, as "The dehumanizing picture of the West painted by its enemies."[3] Theirs can be dismissed as a purely Orientalist and essentialist use of the term. My definition of Occidentalism also assumes that knowledge is at the service of power. In that sense, Occidentalism as a sum of partial, non-"knowledge" partly derived from the "power, position, and interests" of those who defend it, becomes a source of weakness, not only in the field of production of knowledge but also in the struggle for the liberation of the region from Western domination.

Against the "imperialism of our times", in the words of Aijaz Ahmad – globalized, security-driven, militarized, in which culture plays an increasingly greater role, as Said had predicted – Occidentalism is also a body of impoverished cultural and practical concepts that belong to an era of outdated anti-colonialism.

Universality and Development of Edward Said's Thought

Before proceeding further, let me make two additional comments. First, let me reiterate the universality and the development of Edward Said's thought. Any attempt to reduce Said's work to his remarkable and path-breaking critique of Orientalism overlooks the corrections he made to his initial theory as much as it ignores the different phases of development of his thought. Said's thought proceeds in a clearly dialectical manner (he would have preferred to call it "contrapuntal"). Much of the one-sidedness of Orientalism – with its Foucauldian influence, its implied East/West essentialism (the West begins with Aeschylus; Dante reduced to where he placed the prophet Muhammad in his Inferno, Marx to his views on India and Algeria, etc.) – was corrected partly in acceptance of many criticisms. Said admits in Humanism and Democratic Critique to taking into consideration James Clifford's criticism that Orientalism "sometimes appears to mime the essentializing discourse it attacks."

Culture and Imperialism was a corrective of Orientalism in more ways than one, not least in revealing the importance of resistances to imperialism, both cultural and practical, and in dealing with national liberation movements in a critical manner. On a more methodological level, Said took his distance from Foucault because the latter neglected classes, exploitation, economics, and revolution, and used in his critique the works of Fanon, Poulantzas and Chomsky among others.[4] There is a big difference between the critic who saw Marx only in terms of his comments on India and Algeria, lumping him together with the rest of the Orientalists, and the same critic who in his "late style" acknowledges the influence Marxism and Marxist authors had on him, such as Gramsci, Lukács, Raymond Williams, and others. He even came to speak of himself as an "undeclared Marxist." Finally, the East/West binary, with its domination, hegemony, and resistances, is subsumed in a call for the "discovery of a world not constructed out of warring essences." This revision expressed Said's commitment to *secular critique and a humanist outlook*, based on the belief that men make their own history and that the real world is the main object of knowledge.

Speaking Truth to Power

A second point refers to "speaking truth to power," a seminal concept for Said, which deserves more examination. In the era of the "imperialism of our times," I take it to refer to "all powers": imperial power as well as its local supports. The concept of power includes the economic, political, and cultural spheres in Said's argumentation. Though by all means, without making distinctions between those who hold power, backing one dictator or autocrat against another, or identifying with one on the grounds that he is being attacked by the "West"! The other key word here is "truth": it connotes a moral stance but mainly implies the production of knowledge that can contribute to subverting the powers that be and to changing power relations. All of this places Said in the tradition of the self-critical Arab intellectuals of the post–1967 period, a tradition that greatly contributed to creating the other "Said" whom the author of *Out of Place* speaks about, the Said we know.

Conspiracy Theories

Let me reiterate that *real* conspiracies by colonialist and imperialist powers concerning the Arab and Islamic worlds surpass the more phantasmagoric versions produced by the imagination of "conspiracy theorists." Two such flagrant examples of real conspiracies would be the Anglo-French Sykes-Picot accords of 1916 and the 1956 Tripartite Suez War against Egypt.

The Sykes–Picot Syndrome

The secret Sykes-Picot accords, and their implementation which led to the partition and colonial mandate of the Arab East, left an indelible mark on future generations. What I call the Sykes–Picot Syndrome is a fixation on only one aspect of colonial and imperial strategy: divide and rule. While the adage is supposed to imply that *dividing* is in the service of *ruling*, i.e. of colonial and imperial domination, to those who suffer from Sykes-Picot Syndrome, the reverse seems to be the case: *rule* is put at the service of *division*. In other words, rule has become the means, and division the end.

The most immediate connotation of the syndrome is the reduction of US strategies, usually called "projects," to basically one function: that of dividing the Arab countries both externally (from each other) and internally (the partition of each Arab country – for example, Iraq – into potentially a multiplicity of ethnic-sectarian defined cantons or mini-states). And all at the service of legitimizing the State of Israel by cloning it in the form of a myriad of weak and warring ethnic and sectarian-based statelets.

Even in old colonial times, dividing in order to rule – or to better rule – was always subject to colonial interests. In fact, the Sykes-Picot plan can be referred to as partition in contrast with the aspirations of the peoples of the Arab East to live in one independent and united Arab (nation-)state. But upon a closer look, the Sykes–Picot "partition" was itself a process of both partition and unification. While natural Syria was *partitioned* into five states in 1920, Iraq was created out of the *union/merger* of the three Ottoman provinces of Mosul, Baghdad, and Basra. The adding and subtracting of whole regions closely followed colonial interests both strategically and economically. Palestine (southern Syria) was wrenched from the French colonial mandate zone and added to the British area of dominion in the name of the Balfour Declaration, in step with a basic strategic British interest in controlling the eastern bank of the Suez Canal. The Mosul region was detached from Syria because of the discovery of oil. Despite the fact that France divided natural Syria into five statelets (Damascus, Aleppo, Druze, Alawite, and Lebanon) in order to weaken the anti-colonial independence movement, amputated Alexandretta in the North (ceded to Turkey in 1933), and ceded the oil-rich Mosul region to British-mandated Iraq (in return for a share in the Iraqi Petroleum Company), it nevertheless later reunited them into only two states (the Syrian Republic and the Republic of Lebanon) in preparation for retaining some influence in both republics after independence and under pressure from the nationalist movement in Syria.

One should add that imperial strategy may lean towards what is more dangerous, even fatal: dividing the people without dividing the political entity. The issue does not end here. Granted that imperial strategy was to divide a country along ethnic, religious, and sectarian lines, does that absolve the ruling classes and the political leaders and parties of said country from any responsibility even when they accept the division of their people along these lines?

Western designs for the partition of Iraq and for fostering sectarian and ethnic strife no doubt exist. But if Iraq is to be dominated as a whole, why bother to divide it? Nevertheless, the relevant question is: how to foil such designs? Certainly not by accepting the imperial identitarian geostrategic definition of Iraqis in terms of one ethnicity (Kurds) and two Muslim sects (Sunnis and Shi'as) in a "non-Arab Iraq" (as the oft-repentant neocon Kanan Makiya had wanted to build), and certainly not by building parties on those sectarian and ethnic bases.

Whom Do Conspiracy Theories Serve?

Conspiracy theories are not neutral. They usually reflect the material interests and class locations of dominant social and political forces, and very frequently play into the hands of colonial and imperialist powers. Many of them are mere imports from the intellectual arsenal of the European and American extreme right.

If the creation of the State of Israel and the European and American support for it has helped turn many Arabs against the West, there is no doubt that the opposite is also true. Zionist colonization and the existence of the Arab–Israeli conflict have also served to divert attention from Western colonialism and imperialism and from the Arab regimes themselves. Take the "Jewish conspiracy." In its Jewish-Bolshevik amalgam, it served the purpose of alienating Arabs from Communism and also absolving both Western powers and Arab regimes from responsibility for the Palestinian tragedy.

The Public Records Office (PRO) archives in London contain an interesting early specimen of this amalgam. It is allegedly a copy of a tract found on the body of one of the victims of the 1921 bloody clashes between Jews and Arabs in Jaffa-Palestine.[5] The tract is undoubtedly a forgery, as it takes the form of a letter, supposedly written in Arabic and dated 10 April 1921, addressed by Leon Trotsky, then Soviet People's commissar of Army and Navy, to Herbert Samuel, the first British high commissioner in Palestine. In it, "Trotsky" (described as "Minister of War for the Russian People") thanks the British because their project in Palestine has opened up Egypt and India to Bolshevik propaganda. "England, in confirming the Zionist question in Palestine, facilitates our way to the East," says Trotsky.

Not only that, but the Jewish immigration has been the occasion to send Bolsheviks into Palestine: "we have dispatched to Palestine those [Jews] who are bearing the Red Flag and the Bolshevik propaganda and are only a few. Millions of Bolshevists are still in Russia awaiting orders." After establishing the common Jewish identity of both the Soviet leader (Trotsky is made out to be the son of the chief rabbi in Russia, which of course he was not) and the British high commissioner, Trotsky makes it clear that in establishing a Jewish national home in Palestine the British serve the interests of Bolshevism:

> I am a Jew, as you are my friend: my father is the Chief of the Rabbi in Russia. I would not hesitate in hanging my father on the electric lamp [-post] near my office in the Karmelein [Kremlin], should he intend to establish a Jewish kingdom in the heart of Soviet Russia, but I will be glad to assist him with all my power should he demand of me to send the laboring Jews to any land for establishing a national home for them. I am sure that these laborers, wherever they are located, will not establish a National Home but they will establish Bolshevism.

Reiterating Soviet support for the Zionist project in Palestine, the Soviet commissar even offers to lend money to that enterprise if need be. The notion of "Moscow gold" had already reached the East!

The message is clear in its dual play: it fuses Zionism with Communism in the person of Trotsky, a Communist Jew, a Zionist who supports a Jewish state, on condition that it is not constructed on Russian territory, with the intention of transforming it into a Bolshevik state. Hence the message that the Zionist colonization in Palestine benefits neither the British nor even the Jews – not to speak of Palestinians and the Arabs! It will only establish Bolshevism, the common enemy of all concerned.

One variant of this is the idea of the "Jewish conspiracy" founded on both elements of power: money and revolution. One such propagator of this European anti-Semitic notion was Michel Chiha, ideologue of Lebanese nationalism but also fierce anti-Communist and defender of Arab conservative regimes. His writings invariably served the purpose of absolving Britain and the US from any responsibility concerning the creation and support of the State of Israel. In a series of op-eds in his daily, *Le Jour*, in the late 1940s, Chiha wrote that "the West is deceived" by the Jewish conspiracy as much as the Arabs are; he goes on to say that Britain and the United States are "prisoners of Zionism." It does not take much imagination to conclude that all "deceived" and "prisoners" should be allies against the deceiver and jailer.

Later, mainly after the defeat of 1967, British and American responsibility for the creation and support of the State of Israel were manipulated to the benefit of the US. If Western powers are responsible then they are most suited to find a solution to the Arab–Israeli problem. More recently the logic goes as follows: since the US has created Israel, it is the only party that can pressure it to withdraw from the Occupied Territories and achieve peace. These views were most popular at the time when Anwar Sadat claimed that 99 percent of the cards were in America's hand. This is the logic that led to the notion of the American "honest broker," with the results that we know.

Democracy or Imperialism?

The contemporary Orientalist/Occidentalist dichotomy is best expressed in the juxtaposition of democratization against resistance to colonial conquest and imperial policies. Partisans of democratization end up justifying colonial occupation (as in the case of the invasion and occupation of Iraq, presented as the necessary birth pangs of democracy); in contrast, opponents of colonial domination end up justifying Saddam Hussein's dictatorship. This echoes debates that erupted during the 1990–91 Gulf crisis and War when a certain Fred Halliday declared that if he had to choose between (American) imperialism and fascism, he would choose the former. Since that time, this Manichean choice has loomed over our heads like Damocles" sword. Raise the question "if you had to choose between Saddam and Bush, whom would you choose?" and you will find the majority of an Arab or Islamic audience defending the former. A few might opt for the latter, but rarely would a voice be raised to refuse the choice. It is also highly interesting to note how many Occidentalists share with the Orientalists the belief that democracy is not a natural product of Arab-Islamic societies: some welcome it as "salvation" imposed from the outside and others reject it as an "imported commodity."

In the 1920s, resistance to colonialism in the Arab East easily managed to mix the struggle for independence (and the evacuation of the mandatory armies) with the struggle for widening local political representation and the construction and defense of representative democratic institutions. There is no reason why a similar strategy cannot be adopted in our present times.

Talking to the "Other"

One other variant of Occidentalism is the age-old ploy by Arab elites of speaking to the "West" "in its own language." The many tribulations that this logic leads to are beyond imagination. If the amalgam between Zionism and Communism is an attempt to convince the "West" that backing Zionism serves the West's enemies, while its real interests lie with the Arabs, drawing analogies between Zionism and Nazism are attempts to speak to the West in its own language with an implied search for a similar affinity, establishing some identification between European resistance against Nazism and the Palestinian (and Lebanese) resistance against Zionism. "Just as you fought Nazism in the past, so we too are fighting Zionism today." The words come from a Lebanese legislator of Hizbullah addressed to Ségolène Royal, the French Socialist Party's presidential candidate, during her visit to Lebanon in December 2006. Royal's failure to aggressively react to the comparison triggered a political storm against her in France.

This analogic discourse is coupled, in many cases, with its opposite: a yearning for Nazism and a mimetic desire to identify with it in its persecution of the Jews. About the same time as Royal's visit (11–12 December 2006) to Lebanon, a "revisionist" conference on the Holocaust was being held in Tehran, attended by an assortment of well-known Holocaust-deniers and anti-Semites from Europe and Australia, such as Ku Klux Klan leader David Duke, but also by anti-Zionist ultra-orthodox rabbis, and many others. In a speech to the conference, Iran's president Ahmadinejad predicted that Israel would disappear just as the Soviet Union had, and the majority of the participants vied in denying the Holocaust, maintaining it is a myth, or putting in doubt the number of its victims. The Tehran conference epitomizes a kind of discourse on the Holocaust, Zionism, and the State of Israel in general, that has been in vogue among certain Arab (and Iranian) elites expressing their desire for mimesis vis-à-vis the Nazis. The unstated premise is: "Too bad he didn't finish them off"; a barely veiled mimetic desire to be associated with the Nazi crime or to complete a crime left unfinished by the Third Reich's "final solution"!

At times, that same antinomic discourse is found not only within the same political tendency (Hizbullah/Iran) but by the same author. Pierre Sadeq, the cartoonist of Lebanon's daily *An-Nahar*, commenting on Ariel Sharon's invasion of the West Bank and the Jenin massacre, published on 9 March 2002 a cartoon that shows a remorseful Hitler blaming himself for not exterminating Sharon: "How did I forget Sharon? how did I?" reads the caption. Of course, the only reason Hitler would want to exterminate Sharon is that he is a Jew. Yet, less than ten days earlier, on 28 February 2002, Sadiq's cartoon had pictured Sharon as a Nazi general, with the following caption: "A Failed Fascist"!

The Political Economy of Envy

During 12–14 March 2004, a big rally of intellectuals, experts, and NGO activists, from the majority of the countries of the Arab world, convened at the Alexandria Library under the banner of the "Congress of Arab Reform Issues: Vision and the Implementation." They produced a comprehensive reform project known as the "Alexandria Document." Apart from the fact that it pretends to plan reforms for 22 Arab states with some 270 million people, the document does not take into account such elementary things as the uneven development of those countries and the difficulties of imposing a common program; worse yet, it does not even try to find common characteristics to address. Oil is not mentioned once, in a region whose very definition, and not only its geo-strategic position and economic importance in the world, revolves around the fossil fuel. "Where there are Arabs there is oil," goes the current saying.

What the document identifies as a common denominator is that these peoples and countries do not conform to the neoliberal model of globalization and the injunctions of the International Monetary Fund and the World Bank. That is usually called bridging the gap between the Arab world and the "more developed" parts of the world. Of course, you will not find any reference to the control of natural resources as a means of development, assuming that development is the central issue, which is not the case. Only indicators of Direct Foreign Investment worried conference participants, in a region whose main function is to export petrodollars to Western metropoles! For some reason, the financial sector is considered the motor for Arab economies. While the Alexandria charter calls for the increase of production there is no mention of how this should happen (agriculture does not appear in the platform).

We are told that state monopolies should be abolished, but there is not a hint on measures to control private and corporate monopolies, even those inspired by anti-trust laws, following the American model. On the scale of political reform, everything concerning democratization is there except the principle of political and judicial equality of citizens. In the kingdom of freedoms, the press and the media are to be freed from state intervention, but no mention is made of the power of money in limiting the freedom of information. Presently, all the major Arab satellite TV stations and the pan-Arab press media are financially tied to – not to say completely owned by – a handful of Saudi and Qatari rulers. Is that to be considered state control or financial control? Here is a culturalist program par excellence with a post-9/11 US agenda aimed at producing a moderate form of Islam with an inflated emphasis on education. Concerning gender, the charter begins with the call for the empowerment of women and concludes with the call for the "liberation of woman's culture," which lays the blame on Arab women for their present inferior status.

Coupling technocratic mentality and neoliberalism, the platform is a masterpiece of the political economy of envy; a shopping list – exactly in the sense Huntington uses it – consisting of some 36 shopping bags, some containing up to a dozen articles of Western consumption. It happens to overlook a few minor details: 1) the means and methods (we dare not mention "struggle") required for the implementation of its "reforms"; 2) the articulation, periodization, and priorities of those demands; 3) the processes involved in the implementation, including the time limits required (where do we start? where do we want to reach within a set time limit?); and 4) what social, human resources should be mobilized in order to fulfill those tasks?

It is no wonder that this pure unadulterated intellectual product of our Orientalized Orientals led Jihad al-Zein, the op-ed editor of *An-Nahar*, to affirm that he could not see a single difference between the Alexandria Platform and the Reform Initiative proposed by the US Administration earlier that year. He concluded, however, that there will be no reform except from . . . the outside![6]

Needless to say, the signatories of the Platform never met again. Yet they may still be waiting for reform to come from the outside; waiting for the Barbarians.

Notes

1 Edward Said, *Orientalism*, New York: Vintage, 1978, p. 325.
2 Edward Said, *Humanism and Democratic Critique*, New York: University of Columbia Press, 2004, pp. 48–9.
3 Ian Buruma and Avishai Margalit, *Occidentalism: The West in the Eyes of its Enemies*, New York: Penguin Press, 2004.
4 See "Travelling Theory," in *The Said Reader*, New York: Vintage, 2000, p. 214.
5 F.O. 141/Box 433/File no. 10770, part 2. Lieut.-Col. Griffith (General Staff) – The Chancery, The Residency- Cairo, 26 May 1921. "Copy of a letter found in the pocket of a Jew killed at Jaffa in 'recent riots'. Letter stated to have been printed in Syria and circulated in Beirut and other towns."
6 Jihad al-Zein, "La Islah Illa Min al-Kharij," *An-Nahar*, 31 March 2004.

4

Edward Said and Palestine:
Balancing the Academic and the
Political, the Public and the Private

Rashid Khalidi

I happened to be living in Jerusalem doing research on a Fulbright fellowship in the summer of 1992, when Edward Said returned for his first visit to Palestine since 1967. It may indeed have been his first return visit since 1948. I often had the pleasure of accompanying Said and his family as they traveled around the country that summer. It was fascinating watching a man who by then had already written so much about Palestine – his books *The Question of Palestine*, *After the Last Sky*, and *Blaming the Victims* had all been published by this time – absorbing the new realities about which he knew and had written and spoken, but was in some cases seeing for the first time.

Edward Said was particularly interested in finding his family's old home in the Western part of Jerusalem. Even before he arrived that summer, at his request my wife and I spent some time trying to find it. After some searching, we discovered that the Said home had become the headquarters of the International Christian Embassy. There was an ironic touch there: in the wake of its confiscation by Israel in 1948, the home of a Palestinian Christian family had been transformed into an outpost of messianic, muscular Western Christian apologists for that process of confiscation. This trip, the first of several Said took to Palestine/Israel in the subsequent 11 years, seems to have affected him deeply, but though it was certainly reflected in his work, in my view it did not change it in any profound way. Indeed, what he saw only confirmed and deepened his basic human-istic approach to the question of Palestine that was already laid out in his previous writings.

As was noted by some of the many appreciations of his life's work, Edward Said's reputation does not rest mainly on what he wrote and said on

Palestine, important though it was. His long-term impact in the world of scholarship can be found elsewhere, in the fields of literature, culture, anthropology, history, and the other humane and social sciences. But his impact on Palestine, and the impact of Palestine on him, were surely both great. These impacts, and how Said balanced the demands of politics and academic life, are the main focus of this paper.

It has been said, invidiously and quite falsely, that "*Orientalism* could obviously have been written by no one but a Palestinian scholar with a huge chip on his shoulder and a very dim understanding of the European academic tradition."[1] Whether Edward Said had a chip on his shoulder is open to question; in any case, there can be little doubt that he had a far deeper understanding of the "European academic tradition" than do most of his critics (the author of that quotation included), as the continuing serious reception of this 25-year-old book across the academy to this day attests. But it is probably true that *Orientalism* could only have been written by Edward Said, and it is certain that his background and upbringing had a profound influence on all of his writings, including this book.

The impact on Said's work of his being a Palestinian, of his always feeling he was an outsider, and of his having been brought up as a colonial subject, is fully apparent from a careful reading of his gripping memoir, *Out of Place*. To me, this book is a key element in understanding the thrust of Said's life interests. This experience of being a *shami* (someone from the Eastern Arab world) in Cairo, of being an Arab boy in British colonial schools, of being a non-Muslim in a predominantly Muslim society, of being a young Palestinian Arab in American schools and universities, and the impact of the Nakba of 1948 (attenuated though that impact was in some ways for him and many other Palestinians of his class); all of these things contributed to producing the edgy perceptiveness, and the passion, that characterized Said's work. He was always both inside and outside of collectivities, a part and not a part of them. It was this complex, hybrid background that laid the groundwork for many of Said's great insights, whether in the field of literature and humanities, or in his more overtly political writings. I suspect that Edward Said's several visits to Palestine/Israel after 1992 reinforced these feelings, feelings that *Out of Place* tells us he had had since his youth.

Palestine had other effects on Said. He was profoundly affected by the Arab defeat of 1967 and the Israeli occupation of what remained of Palestine. This event had the consequence of politicizing him and members of more than one generation of Arabs and Arab-Americans, both in the United States and in the Arab world, myself included. The earthquake of 1967, experienced as it was in New York, where for most it had a very different meaning, had a serious impact on Said's work. It impelled him to write on a broader range of topics, including for the first time overtly political ones. As I have already suggested, however, Said's basic trajectory had already been determined by the experiences of his youth in Cairo, Jerusalem, and Lebanon, whether in the classroom, at home, or elsewhere. He was already out of place when this traumatic experience vastly increased his sense of alienation inextricably combined with a sense of belonging.

What seems to have struck Edward Said most forcibly, as it struck anyone living in North America and Europe who was familiar with the cruel reality of what the Palestinian people actually experienced, was how very little of that reality (or indeed of the reality of the Arab and Islamic worlds in general) filtered through in the West, especially in the United States. This was and is still due largely to the dark screen constituted by the American media and the American political system, a screen powerfully reinforced by sentiment, emotion, and widespread ignorance. Much of the evident passion that animated what Said wrote about Palestine thereafter derived from his realization of the enormous gap between the Palestinian reality and the distorted representations of that reality that was, and is, prevalent in Western public discourse.

One of Said's greatest contributions as far as Palestine is concerned probably lies here: in his making the quite large numbers of people who heard him speak in dozens of venues annually across the United States and in Europe, and the many tens of thousands who read his words in a score of languages, aware that there was another reality to Palestine than the distorted images purveyed by the mass media, and in most other representations available to people in the West. It is impossible to estimate accurately the impact that Said's writings and speeches on Palestine had in the West over the course of more than 35 years. But from a broad range of evidence, it seems to have been great, and it seems to be continuing even after his death.

This was a hard and lonely task, one made no easier by the fact that at the level at which Said spoke there was virtually no one else in the United States who could effectively and articulately portray these realities to an American audience. There have been a handful of other distinguished Arab-American scholars, most of them now dead or in semi-retirement, who could and did speak or write cogently, forcefully, and even eloquently, about political and historical aspects of the Palestine issue, and some of whom have had a great impact on audiences in the United States and the West. But none of them spoke from a universal humanist perspective rather than from within the fields of politics, history, and Middle Eastern studies, none of them was as eminent a public intellectual as Edward Said, and none had the impact he did on as broad a range of audiences.

The private price Said paid for doing this, and doing it so well, was far greater than most can imagine. It went beyond the crude threats of violence, and beyond the unceasing public vilification by small-minded, vicious detractors, vilification which has continued even after Said's death. This vilification affected his family, his private life, and his relations with colleagues and with friends, although he succeeded in surmounting these pressures to a remarkable degree. Most difficult for him perhaps was the constant sense of being misunderstood, whether willfully or otherwise, by those who in other contexts seemed so open-minded, so liberal, and so full of understanding, including colleagues, peers, and even sometimes friends. This was made far harder to bear by Said's extraordinary sensitivity to criticism. Such sensitivity may have seemed incongruous in one who appeared so supremely confident, but it was an essential part of Edward Said's character. Those who were taken aback by the occasional ferocity of his responses to those who attacked him cannot possibly have been aware of the unremitting nature of the attacks he endured, and of the toll these attacks took on him. Perhaps this was because the only apparent effect of these attacks was to cause him to redouble his prodigious efforts: to write more, to speak more, to work harder.

Beyond the difficulty of enduring the slanders and vilification of his detractors, some of whom denied his very identity (such as the ludicrous claim that he was not really a Palestinian), Said faced the constant necessity of balancing between the academic and the political, and of defending the work he did in the political realm from the snobbishness of some academics who looked down on any involvement with the real world, especially the world of politics. He faced finally the need to ensure that what was done in both spheres, academic and political, was done with the necessary rigor. Some would argue that all of Said's work in both spheres, the academic and the political, was of a piece, and that distinctions should not be made between the two types. While Said was of course *engagé*, passionate, and committed in all his work, I believe that even though they were deeply intertwined, a clear distinction can be drawn between these two spheres, and that Said would have accepted this. In any case, there can be no question that the virulent objections of some critics to Said's political activity and writings deeply colored their reactions to all the rest of his work, whether on culture, literature or music. This did not prevent Said, as a teacher and scholar, from being open to students whose beliefs and political stands were quite different from his own: such students found him in private to be open-minded, friendly, and generous with his time. Not surprisingly, they learned an enormous amount from him. Since I arrived at Columbia in 2003, the year of his death, I have met many former students of Said's of all political persuasions who still recall studying with him with fondness and affection.

Much of the impact Edward Said had in the United States and the West as regards the question of Palestine was well known to his friends and to others in the West. It could certainly be immediately deduced from the frenzied paroxysms his writings produced (and often still produce, even after his death) in his enemies. Much less is known in the United States about Edward Said's profound impact on Palestine and the Palestinians.

From very early on in his direct involvement with the Palestine question over 35 years ago, Said attempted to change the terms of Palestinian political discourse, in keeping with his beliefs about what was appropriate for Palestine, as well as his understanding of the world and his broad humanistic perspective. Together with many other leading Palestinian intellectuals, he was instrumental in moving the PLO and Palestinian public opinion during the mid to late 1970s towards acceptance of a two-state solution, involving an independent Palestinian state alongside Israel. He argued at the time that unjust though it was for one people, the Israelis, to keep 78 percent of Palestine, and for the other, the Palestinians, to get only 22 percent, this represented the only viable alternative to ceaseless war. While political leaders like Salah Khalf (Abu Iyyad) probably played the most important role in the evolution of Palestinian thinking and Palestinian politics in this direction, committed public intellectuals like Said were crucial in winning most of Palestinian public opinion over to these ideas by the 1980s. This effort was crowned by Said's central role, along with his friend, the poet Mahmud Darwish, and others, in the drafting in 1988 of the Palestinian Declaration of Independence, whereby the PLO formally accepted a two-state solution.

Just as important as these contributions, Edward Said was one of the first Palestinians to argue before Arab audiences for the humanity of the Israeli people, for their people-hood and their national rights, and for the absolute necessity of understanding the entire trajectory of Jewish history culminating in the Holocaust, if Palestinians and Arabs were to understand both what drove the Israelis and their own modern history. Having established his credentials as an advocate of greater understanding of the Palestinian perspective in the West, Said proceeded to use this position of eminence not to duck the hard questions and play to an Arab audience that idolized him, but rather to argue these unpopular and difficult positions. It was one of his greatest and most difficult achievements, and probably one of the most unappreciated by those many people who are ignorant of the impact that Said had on Palestinian public discourse.

These were not easy lessons to teach, and some in Palestine and the Arab world resisted them. This resistance may explain why *The Question of Palestine*, which embodies many of these insights, has still not been translated into Arabic. I was nevertheless constantly struck by the enormous respect with which Said was received when he spoke to audiences of Palestinian university students and others along these humanistic lines, even among supporters of Hamas and other militant groups who disagreed fundamentally with him. As I saw myself, at Bir Zeit University or Bethlehem University for example, when he went there in 1992 and afterwards, they listened, they argued, some were unconvinced, but all were affected. Most importantly, they learned that it was possible to feel the depth of the Palestinian tragedy, and at the same time to understand the position of the other, the occupier, the oppressor, the enemy. His example heartened those who understood these basic truths, and convinced many who had not previously agreed with him.

This was an aspect of Said's work that only grew in importance with time. In the 1970s he rarely wrote for Arab audiences, and where Palestine was concerned he devoted most of his energy to explaining the unknown aspects of the Palestine problem to American audiences. By the 1990s, however, Said was writing regularly for the Arab newspapers and magazines with the widest circulation, in both hard copy and on the web, and was speaking regularly via radio, television, and print interviews, to audiences all over the Arab world. When he spoke about Palestine, his focus was essentially humanist: this was a problem, he argued, that could not be solved in an annihilationist manner, a problem that admitted of no zero-sum solution, a problem that finally had to be resolved by both peoples accepting the humanity of the other. This was a message utterly at odds with the nihilism of the hard men of violence, and one that he never ceased to stress during the dark days from 2000 until his death in 2003, even as he forcefully castigated the futile and self-serving fatuities of the Palestinian Authority, the arrogant destructiveness of United States Middle East policy, and the serial war crimes of the Sharon government.

In light of these enlightened positions, put forward in a time of barbarism on many sides, it might be asked why Said's views drew such fierce responses from his detractors in the United States in particular. Very simply, it was because he complicated things for them: those who opposed him in the United States projected a one-dimensional caricature of what they saw their enemy to be, a picture that they had to keep trying to impose at all costs on a skeptical but virtually captive audience that was troubled by intimations that this image may not have been fully accurate. Said's complex, humanist, and thoughtful presentation of a reality that shattered this one-dimensional portrayal was far more difficult for his detractors to counteract than the effusions of militants on the other side whose views were sometimes just as one-dimensional as theirs were.

In the last years of his life, Edward Said began to realize that the two-state solution that he and others of his generation had pioneered several decades before was becoming increasingly unrealistic, as more and more of what was left of Palestine disappeared under acres of concrete and the treads of Israeli bulldozers relentlessly building settlements, bypass roads, and walls in occupied East Jerusalem and the West Bank, all of which were *always* designed explicitly to make a viable two-state solution impossible. He saw that these Israeli actions had begun to force the Palestinians in a direction that most of them would probably not have chosen voluntarily: living together with the Israelis in a single bi-national state.

Inexorably, events in Palestine/Israel seemed to be moving away from the tentative possibilities of two states coexisting in peace side by side. They now seemed to point to a new reality, the current reality, where only one state, Israel, existed between the Jordan and the Mediterranean, ruling over two unequal groups. On the one hand, there was a citizen population of 6 million – 5 million Jews and 1.2 million Arabs – who enjoyed rights in most of the country, albeit two differential sets of unequal rights, with the Jews enjoying manifold exclusive privileges and the Arabs at best second-class citizens in this self-described Jewish state. On the other hand, there was a helot population of over 4 million Palestinians with no guaranteed rights to speak of, neither national, civil, religious, political nor human, existing on sufferance and international charity, living under Israeli and international siege in increasingly appalling conditions, in an archipelago of ghettos, bantustans and prison camps in a tiny fraction composing perhaps 10 percent of the entire country. Outside the borders controlled by Israel, there existed a population of about as many Palestinians as those who lived inside under Israeli rule, refugees and descendants of refugees, most with no rights to speak of either.

Given this emerging reality of less than apartheid (parenthetically, this is a word which a broad range of Israelis from left to right appear to find no difficulty whatsoever in applying to what is happening in Palestine, but whose use in this context seems to cause fits among many otherwise apparently rational and calm Americans) Said and others began to consider whether, whatever its merits or demerits, a two-state solution was perhaps not being buried by its foes. In practice, these included the Israeli government, with its bulldozers, concrete mixers, walls, and checkpoints, the United States government with its blind support of any and all Israeli measures, and Hamas and its allies with their suicide bombs and Qassam

rockets (although, paradoxically, Hamas itself observed a unilateral ceasefire
– restraint that was not reciprocated by the Israeli military – and much of its
leadership came around to seeing the virtues of the two-state solution after
winning the January 2006 election). If that were the case, Said began to feel,
perhaps it was time to make a virtue of this necessity that had been imposed
by *force majeure*, and try to see how to deal with a nascent system of worse-
than-apartheid. I describe it as a system that was worse than apartheid, since
at least apartheid was codified in laws, racist though they were, and provided
clear and firm frontiers, unjust though they were. Neither of these things is
the case in the constantly evolving archipelago of vast open-air prison camps
in which the Israeli state has confined the 4 million Palestinians who have
lived under its military occupation for 40 years now.

And in this new world of monotonously repeated declaratory commitment to a two-state solution by the American and Israeli governments,
combined with the constant creation of realities on the ground which made
a viable two-state solution impossible, and where only one sovereignty exists
or will be allowed to exist, the idea of one state as the only possible outcome
seemed more and more inevitable. There remained fearsome difficulties,
among them the fact that neither the Israeli nor the Palestinian people
seemed or seems to want to live together with the other, and both were
attached to their own sovereignty and statehood, most Israelis to the existing
state they had fashioned at the expense of the Palestinians, and most
Palestinians to their dream of an independent sovereign state. But the
inexorable logic created by the bulldozers that have never stopped working
for nearly 40 years, whose progress Said saw on every trip to Palestine,
creating realities designed specifically to make a Palestinian state alongside
Israel unattainable, constantly weighed on his mind. At the end of his days,
this logic slowly drove him in the direction of a single bi-national state in
Palestine. He must have known that such an outcome, if it were ever
possible, could only come about after the indefinite prolongation, and
perhaps the worsening, of the intolerable current status quo of the Palestinians, and after even greater suffering for both peoples, and this must have
saddened him.

Perhaps it was that bleak prospect, and his disgust with the state of politics
in both Palestine and Israel, not to speak of the dogmatically unconstructive
policies of the United States government where Palestine and so much else
were concerned, which drove Said to spend more time in his last years with
his friend, the musician and conductor Daniel Barenboim, in developing the
West-Eastern Divan Orchestra. This is based on a summer workshop for
young Arab and Israeli musicians that started in Weimar in Germany in
1999, has spent several summers in Seville in Andalusia, and which took

place in 2007 in Salzburg. Out of it has grown an acclaimed youth orchestra that has toured Europe, the Middle East, and North and South America. Its name was derived from the poem by Goethe about the essential unity between East and West, and the Divan symbolized the ideas that Said always held about the essential humanity of both sides of this largely false dichotomy between East and West, and of both sides of the Palestinian–Israeli divide. It was to Seville that Said traveled on the last trip of his life in August 2003, to a city that symbolized coexistence between different peoples and religions and cultures, and where the apparently irresolvable political contradictions between the Palestinian and Israeli peoples could be briefly forgotten as young Arabs and Israelis collaborated in making music. The West-Eastern Divan Orchestra in some sense represents what was best in Edward Said's contribution as regards Palestine and much else: it was a contribution that was always didactic and educational, always humanistic, and always focused on the individual, and on recognition and acceptance of the other.

During this final phase of Edward Said's life, he continued to publish some of his most influential works of cultural criticism, and some of his most trenchant political critiques, while at the same time spending more and more time on a project, the West-Eastern Divan Orchestra, which he knew would take many years to reach fruition. This project was typical of Said's ability to excel in multiple spheres, and to balance between the academic and the political, the public and the private. The teaching function (an essentially private process which takes place partly in the classroom, partly in one-on-one sessions, and partly in the reading and annotation of papers and drafts of thesis chapters) was one of the central and less well understood tasks of Said's career. It was fitting that at the end of his life, Edward Said was deeply engaged in another mode of this teaching function, helping young Arab and Israeli musicians in the West-Eastern Divan Orchestra to expand their understanding of the conflicted Middle Eastern world which they have inherited from their elders, while at the same time learning to make beautiful music as a group.

It was an affirmation of hopeful possibilities in an exceedingly bleak time, an assertion that something constructive can be done even in a time of despair, and a typically Saidian assertion of optimism in the midst of pessimism. In the atmosphere of gloom that currently envelops Palestine, Lebanon, and most of the Middle East today, this last effort of Edward Said, together with his writings which continue to speak to us years after he left us, should serve as a beacon to encourage us to follow along the always humanistic path that he set out upon, and that it is up to us to follow.

5

Edward Said and the Style
of the Public Intellectual

Saree Makdisi

One of the primary concerns of Edward Said's work is the extent to which intellectuals are, in one way or another, directly involved in the manufacture of worldly realities, or are essentially – to borrow a phrase from Shelley – the real unacknowledged legislators of the world. The main argument of Said's best known book, after all, is that abstractions like "the West" and "the East" must be actively invented by scholars, artists, poets, and historians, and then gradually modified, adjusted, reinvented over time. According to Said, then, scholars and writers, and intellectuals in general, far from being merely the dispassionate detached observers they so often pretend to be, are complicit in the production of the very worldly realities that they claim merely to be faithfully representing. While such a proposition makes it difficult, or im-possible, to locate a single objective standpoint from which to accumulate knowledge and evaluate the truth, it also pushes us to consider the extent to which particular intellectuals are involved in either helping to maintain and extend various state policies – of conquest, brutalization, military occupation, injustice – or helping to contest them, and hence participating in the struggle to create an alternative world of freedom, equality, and justice.

Clearly, Said himself not only believed in but also actively demonstrated the ways in which an intellectual can play such an oppositional role. And in his book *Representations of the Intellectual* he elaborates the ways in which the intellectual ought to fashion him- or herself to play such a role.[1] His understanding of the intellectual involves something of a synthesis of the positions of Antonio Gramsci and Julien Benda, whom he discusses in the opening pages of the book. From Gramsci, Said accepts the notion that intellectuals compose a large and variegated social body, connected to classes, movements, and traditions and fulfilling all kinds of social roles, including the production and reproduction of official ideologies and world-views. But at the same time he finds deeply compelling Benda's much more restricted notion of the intellectual as a member of a small, embattled, morally driven group speaking out against prevailing opinions regardless of the consequences to themselves. Most intellectuals, according to Said, perform the social role ascribed to them by Gramsci; only a tiny minority are able and willing to elevate themselves to the heights prescribed for them by Benda, to become, in Said's words, one of those beings "set apart, someone able to speak the truth to power, a crusty, eloquent, fantastically courageous and angry individual for whom no worldly power is too big and imposing to be criticized and pointedly taken to task."[2]

What I want to question in this chapter is whether Said's radicalized version of the Bendaian intellectual, compelling and inspiring as it is, is as applicable to our own time as it so clearly was to the intellectuals of a previous age – the one in which Said received his own formation and formed himself in turn. For a number of reasons, as this chapter will try to explain, such intellectuals may no longer exist, or at least they may no longer exist in the way Said described them. And while we may still derive inspiration from Said's vision of the embattled intellectual, it may no longer be possible to model ourselves precisely along the lines that he prescribed.

There is, of course, no question that it remains possible for someone occupying what Gramsci considered the conventional social role of the intellectual – a teacher, a writer, an artist – to develop ways in which to critically consider, even to contest, social and political power, including the very power that endowed the intellectual with his or her sense of place and privilege in the first place. Such a public intellectual – one willing to speak up, to challenge prevailing social, cultural, and political norms and conventional wisdoms of all sorts – is, according to Said, "an individual endowed with a faculty for representing, embodying, articulating a message, a view, an attitude, philosophy or opinion to, as well as for, a public." This role, he continues,

> has an edge to it, and cannot be played without a sense of being someone whose place it is publicly to raise embarrassing questions, to confront orthodoxy and dogma (rather than to produce them), to be someone who cannot easily be co-opted by governments or corporations, and whose *raison d'être* is to represent all those people and issues that are routinely forgotten or swept under the rug.[3]

Said acknowledges, of course, that such an intellectual, while taking the side of the weak and downtrodden against enormously powerful social and political forces, is hardly free from social constraints him- or herself.

But while Said points out that it is difficult, if not altogether impossible, to speak today of a genuinely independent, autonomous intellectual, one not beholden to or constrained by various social institutions (universities, publishers, media outlets), he insists that the prime threat facing intellectual freedom of expression today comes not from these external forces but rather from a much more insidious pressure: the seduction offered by silence and compromise, or in other words what he distinguishes as the dark side of professionalism:

> thinking of your work as an intellectual as something you do for a living, between the hours of nine and five with one eye on the clock, and another cocked at what is considered to be proper, professional behavior – not rocking the boat, not straying outside the accepted paradigms or limits, making yourself marketable and above all presentable, hence uncontroversial and unpolitical and "objective."[4]

Said is neither romantic nor naive about the pressures of specialization and professionalization and the whole cult of expertise, but he argues that ultimately the most effective way to resist these pressures is to insist on also – over and above one's work as a professional – retaining a certain degree of amateurism.

What Said distinguishes as amateurism, however, involves only in part the capacity to allow one's work as a critical intellectual to be driven by care and affection rather than profit or specialization. For, as opposed to specialization, Said's version of amateurism also involves a willful transgression of institutional lines, which he identifies as *interference*, a "crossing of borders and obstacles, a determined attempt to generalize exactly at those points where generalizations seem impossible to make. One of the first interferences to be ventured," Said adds, "is a crossing from literature, which is supposed to be subjective and powerless, into those exactly parallel realms, now covered by journalism and the production of information, that employ representation but are supposed to be objective and powerful."[5]

Here I am quoting not from the book on intellectuals but rather from a piece I believe was Said's first sustained elaboration of the role of the public intellectual, namely, the essay entitled "Opponents, Audiences, Constituencies and Community," originally published in 1982. Here Said writes:

> It is my conviction that culture works very effectively to make invisible and even "impossible" the actual affiliations that exist between the world of ideas and scholarship, on the one hand, and the world of brute politics, corporate and state power, and military force, on the other. The cult of

expertise and professionalism, for example, has so restricted our scope of vision that a positive (as opposed to an implicit or passive) doctrine of non-interference among fields has set in.[6]

The problem here is not just that matters of public policy are left to so-called "experts" and "insiders" who are close to power, but also that academic professionals who insist on their own hyper-specialization end up folding in on themselves, confining themselves and their work to an increasingly withdrawn and remote constituency of fellow experts, and abandoning the wider world of what they regard as brute politics to others.

Said argues that such a withdrawal was particularly evident among intellectuals in the humanities after a certain kind of critical theory took hold of the academy in the 1980s; an event that seemed to prompt in some intellectuals ever further hyper-specialization, a process intensified by the proliferation of a formidable technical jargon, which, according to Said, led to a smaller and smaller circle of critics producing more and more books and articles for each other and seeming to care little about anything or anyone else;[7] so that, far from the non-specialized amateurism and border-crossing interference espoused by Said, the particular mission of the humanities seemed at that point to represent precisely a kind of *non-interference* in the everyday world; a non-interference that, as Said puts it, meant a kind of laissez-faire: " 'they' can run the country, we will explicate Wordsworth and Schlegel."[8] The larger point of Said's argument, of course, is that although academic professionals in the 1980s may have taken solace in their illusory separation from the ugly, worldly political realities of the Age of Reagan, that separation also helped make the Age of Reagan possible in the first place, because academics – especially those in the humanities, with their formidable interpretive, representational, and communicative skills – had abandoned the field to the political forces that brought Reagan to power.

Such willful non-interference – which continues in the Age of Bush, of course – takes many different forms, from the cloistered academic's naive sense of detachment from the social and political realities surrounding him or her to an even more deliberate fear of, or turning away from, political commitments. Indeed, if for Said the ultimate choice faced by the in-tellectual is not merely the one between interference and non-interference, but rather the one between being a professional supplicant or an unrewarded (if not altogether stigmatized) amateur,[9] nothing can be more reprehensible in his view than

> those habits of mind in the intellectual that induce avoidance, that characteristic turning away from a difficult and principled position which

you know to be the right one, but which you decide not to take. You do not want to appear too political; you are afraid of seeming controversial; you need the approval of a boss or an authority figure; you want to keep a reputation for being balanced, objective, moderate; your hope is to be asked back, to consult, to be on a board or prestigious committee, and so to remain within the respectable mainstream; someday you hope to get an honorary degree, a big prize, perhaps even an ambassadorship. For an intellectual these habits of mind are corrupting par excellence.[10]

The proper role of the intellectual, then, according to Said, is to maintain intellectual and political integrity, and to speak out, like one of Benda's lonely clerics, against all the odds, and despite all costs to oneself.

Speaking the truth to power – actively interfering with it – once one is in a position to do so is something Said saw as a moral obligation. Once one is comfortably tenured at a major university, say, and enjoying the freedom and relative security that go along with such a position, it would be, for Said, not just irresponsible but also a kind of moral failing not to speak out on public matters, especially the ones that urgently require intervention. Few intellectuals choose to take on such a public role, of course, much less to associate themselves with embattled or marginalized positions (by speaking out against imperial power or military occupation, or on behalf of brutalized and dispossessed peoples). Because being an intellectual in this genuine sense involves a deeply personal choice – a matter of ethics in the true, rather than the watered-down and fashionably depoliticized, sense of that term – Said argues that it is only the rare individual who possesses the integrity and commitment necessary to carry out such a cultural and political mission. Thus, given the individual pressures and commitments required – above all, the highly individual moral and political choice between deciding to remain critical of power, and hence paying the price associated with such criticism; or, alternatively, accepting the seductions and emoluments of power, and going along with it – the vocation of the genuine oppositional intellectual is by definition a solitary one.

Moreover, for Said, the genuine intellectual is an individual par excellence, someone who generally shuns participation in organized parties, organizations, networks. In the case of Said himself, such individuality was perhaps nowhere more visible than in the public positions he took against the official Palestinian leadership after it entered into the secret – and disastrous – series of capitulations to Israeli power beginning with the Oslo Accords of 1993–95. After Oslo, Said found himself battling not only the injustice of Israel's policies and the historical injustice of Zionism itself but also the corruption, ignorance, and poor judgment of the Palestinian leadership.

Perhaps it should come as no surprise, then, that being an intellectual involved for Said not merely being a lonely outsider and a consummate individualist – however committed to larger, more public goals, and however dedicated to a wider constituency and public – but also developing a deeply distinctive, even unique, individual style. In this sense, Said's elaboration of the role of the intellectual was profoundly modernist in its conception; it was, in other words, as much an aesthetic as a political project – so much so that it was virtually impossible for Said to imagine separating an individual's political positions from his or her unique personality, as much as it would be impossible to separate the literary or artistic creations of, say, Pound, Joyce, Eliot, Picasso or, for that matter, Miles Davis from the distinctive styles, mannerisms, and personalities of their creators. "When I read Jean-Paul Sartre or Bertrand Russell," Said writes, "it is their specific, individual voice and presence that makes an impression on me over and above their arguments because they are speaking out for their beliefs. They cannot be mistaken for an anonymous functionary or a careful bureaucrat."[11] That's why what he specifically singles out as the "personal mannerisms" of particular intellectuals are so important for Said.[12] In an impersonal age of anonymous functionaries, the genuine intellectual, with his or her distinctive charisma, not only can but also *must* claim a unique, individual style or signature, so that his or her work can be identified in precisely the same way that a sentence written by Conrad, a line drawn by Picasso, or a note played by Miles Davis can be instantly and unmistakably identified with, respectively, Conrad, Picasso, Davis.

Just as it is hardly a coincidence that so much of Said's work was devoted to modernist aesthetic figures like Joseph Conrad and Glenn Gould, it is hardly a coincidence that the intellectuals to whom Said refers most often are precisely charismatic modernist figures of this kind and, inevitably, men with whom Said identified himself in one way or another – Sartre and Russell, as well as C.L.R. James, George Antonius, Frantz Fanon, Antonio Gramsci, Jean Genet, Aimé Césaire – each of them associated with certain political and cultural positions, of course, but also with an extremely idiosyncratic personal style, a unique personal aesthetic, a profound personal presence and of course enormous charisma – the very features many of us so fondly recall when we remember Edward Said himself: his passion; his unflinching commitment to a forsaken people and their cause; his charm; his anger; and, yes, his beautiful Savile Row suits and hand-stitched English shoes.

Style for Said, in any case, is certainly something more than merely aesthetic, it is inherently political: it is a way not merely of asserting individuality but also of transgressing cultural and political norms, of resisting domination, ultimately of contesting socially constituted reality itself. This is especially true of what he identifies in his final book as the eponymous "late style," which, as he puts it, "is what happens if art does not abdicate its rights in favor of reality."[13] He is thinking in this context of Adorno's elaboration of the late Beethoven – the Beethoven of the Ninth Symphony, of the *Missa Solemnis*, of the final piano sonata, opus 111. In Adorno's directly aesthetic terms, such late style is evident when a great artist, fully in command of his form and medium, "nevertheless abandons communication with the established social order of which he is a part, and achieves a contradictory, alienated relationship with it." Being late here means not being at the end of one's career but rather in a more specific sense being at odds with one's own time;[14] or, as Said puts it himself, "late style is *in*, but oddly *apart* from, the present."[15]

Late style thus involves not merely what Ernst Bloch once famously called the synchronicity of the non-synchronous, but also a more explicit refusal of aesthetic compromise, as for example, when Beethoven refused to let opus 111 conform to the standard expected of the sonata form, refused to produce in his final piano sonata a pleasing but ultimately bankrupt summary of his successes to date; instead opus 111 marks a further opening out, rather than a conclusion, a closure, a form of easy satisfaction. But lateness in Said's sense is something far more than merely aesthetic: it involves, as we might recognize in William Wordsworth at his best – or in William Blake throughout his career – a refusal of co-optation, a refusal to go with the stream, a refusal to pledge allegiance, and a contrary insistence on heterodoxy, differentiation, unassailability, resistance. Late style expresses, in other words, not merely a certain cultural politics but a politics as such.

This is why Said urges us to recognize the style of the oppositional intellectual as such a central feature of his or her broader position. The genuine intellectual's style sets him or her apart: it registers not merely a unique differentiation from a surrounding present of ever-greater homogenization, specialization, and professionalization but also a refusal to accept the prerogatives, inducements, and pressures of power.

Here it may be worthwhile to recall Fredric Jameson's assessment of the personal styles of the great modernist writers and what he calls the sheer autonomy of their aesthetic, their refusal to go along with the tendencies of a modernizing economy – the very kind of refusal that Said intends in his discussion of late style. Jameson points out that such unassailability was often manifested in the modernism unto itself of the "isolated genius" and the great Work, and what Jameson identifies as the moment of the great demiurges and prophets – "Frank Lloyd Wright and his cape and porkpie hat, Proust in his cork-lined room, the 'force of nature' Picasso, and the 'tragic,' uniquely doomed Kafka."[16] But Jameson insists that we should disabuse ourselves of the lament that "from the hindsight of postmodern fashion and commerciality, modernism was still a time of giants and legendary powers no longer available to us." For, he adds, "if the poststructuralist motif of the 'death of the subject' means anything socially, it signals the end of the entrepreneurial and inner-directed individualism, with its 'charisma' and its accompanying categorial panoply of quaint romantic values such as that of the 'genius' in the first place." Seen thus, he concludes,

> the extinction of the "great moderns" is not necessarily an occasion for pathos. Our social order is richer in information and more literate, and socially, at least, more "democratic." . . . [it] no longer needs prophets and seers of the high modernist and charismatic type, whether among its cultural producers or its politicians. Such figures no longer hold any charm or magic for the subjects of a corporate, collectivized post-individualistic age; in that case, goodbye to them without regrets, as Brecht might have put it: woe to the country that needs geniuses, prophets, Great Writers, or demiurges![17]

It is in fact with Jameson's argument in mind that we must note a somewhat profound contradiction in Said's assessment of the intellectual. For while on the one hand he emphasizes the solitary, prophetic role of the intellectual not merely as non-co-optable but also as a kind of unapproachable, forbidding figure ("a being set apart, someone able to speak the truth to power, a crusty, eloquent, fantastically courageous and angry individual") – or, in other words, precisely the kind of demiurge or charismatic prophet whose disappearance Jameson says we need not lament – Said at the same time always insisted on the paramount urgency for an intellectual to be clear, accessible, non-specialized, serving and enabling a public, an audience, a constituency. After all, his argument against falling into an earnest circle of specialized critics who produce work accessible only to a narrow coterie of fellow initiates was precisely that they lock out everyone else. What, he asks in the 1982 essay that I quoted earlier, "is the acceptable humanistic antidote to what one discovers, say among sociologists, philosophers and so-called policy scientists who speak only to and for each other in a language oblivious to everything but a well-guarded, constantly shrinking fiefdom forbidden to the uninitiated?"[18] As we know, of course, Said's work offered us the very antidote to which he was referring: interference, transgression, a breaking out of the confines of tiny specialized disciplinary audiences, and speaking to a broader public. The question now is to what extent this openness and accessibility are consistent with – or at odds with – what I have been arguing is Said's highly modernist conception of the forbidding, charismatic, crusty, angry intellectual. Jameson's point, after all, is not only that our open, collectivized and post-individualistic age no longer requires the services of such a modernist giant but also, beyond that, that there is no room for such a figure in the contemporary world.

Jameson's argument prompts one to ask, then, how relevant Said's highly modernist conception of the intellectual with a unique and distinctive signature and personal aesthetic might be to our own jaded, image-driven age. Even at a single glance, it ought to seem obvious that the whole question of modernist style seems inappropriate to our own time. The politics and commitments of Genet, for example, may have been inseparable from his personal style or image, but that is because in his age, the personal aesthetic or image was just as inseparable from the underlying political position; it was not capable of reification, detachment, circulation, even commodification; the style and image of Genet in the 1950s or 1960s was inseparable from his underlying politics. Indeed, this absolute confluence of aesthetics and politics is, as I have been arguing, essential to Said's understanding of the intellectual.

It would, however, hardly be an original observation to point out that in our own postmodern age, not only has style become inseparable from image but also the production and circulation of images relies almost entirely on the separability of image from underlying political or cultural positions or associations. What this means is not merely that a personal aesthetic or image can circulate in a context entirely at odds with its original cultural and political associations. (Surely the most obvious evidence of such a disassociation is that practically universal image of Che Guevara, which is now used for all sorts of brands and marketing ventures, or simply as a commodified image in itself, rather than an evocation of what Che actually stood for politically and culturally.) It also suggests that success these days has at least as much to do with one's image – or even, in effect, brand – as with one's actual political or intellectual positions. It is worth asking, I think, just how possible it is for an intellectual to fashion him- or herself along the lines that Said prescribed in an intellectual, academic, and publishing marketplace increasingly driven by brands.

But there are other problems confronting the intellectual in the postmodern age. In fact, several factors must be taken into account in distinguishing the modernist intellectual as elaborated by Said from the postmodern intellectual of our own time.

There is, first of all, the question of publishing. The modernist intellectual could circulate his or her work in a publishing environment that was not entirely driven by and subject to commercial criteria. Specific publishing houses, journals, newspapers, magazines could be – and often were – identified with specific political or cultural issues or causes (*Tel Quel* is of course one classic example; the Beirut journal *Mawaqif* is another). By contrast, what little one can say about the distinctive political or cultural orientations of the publishing houses Pantheon, Random House, Vintage, Doubleday or Knopf is eclipsed by the material fact that they are all today nothing but subdivisions of Bertelsmann; and it goes without saying that Bertelsmann's primary commitment is not to ideas or positions – to which the giant global corporations like Bertelsmann, Disney, Time Warner or News Corp refer dismissively, if not altogether contemptuously, as "content" – but rather to revenues (17 billion euros for Bertelsmann in 2005) and the corporate bottom line. Indeed, it is unlikely that Edward Said himself would have achieved his global intellectual status had his books been published by an obscure and financially limited – however politically committed – press rather than by a transnational giant like Bertelsmann. Perhaps that's because even Edward Said himself had become – regardless of his own intentions – a kind of brand by the end.

The second urgent matter in this context is the virtual, if not absolute, disappearance of independent intellectuals. Susan Sontag's death may have marked the end of an era. There may be a few genuinely independent intellectuals left, but most intellectuals today are affiliated with, if not entirely beholden to, media organizations, think tanks or increasingly corporatized universities; indeed, the most powerful intellectuals today are, arguably, not even individual human beings but rather the giant global corporations themselves. None of this closes the door to free or critical thinking, of course; but the point is that the situation facing the intellectual today is hardly the same as the one at the peak of the modernist moment.

Finally, all of the institutions harboring intellectuals these days are facing not just mounting pressure but also in many cases a frontal assault designed to break them down and transform them beyond recognition. There is, for example, an unprecedented assault on academic freedom in the USA, and on the very institution of the university as we know it. (I will confine my remarks on the university to the USA, not because I think it is an exemplary case, but simply because it happens to be the case with which I am most familiar.) Much of this assault has taken on a right-wing tilt, but the process of undermining academic and hence intellectual freedom was initiated – and is today still most heavily orchestrated – by the sprawling network of individuals and organizations working to defend Israel's interests in the USA. The Israel on Campus Coalition, for example, whose aim is, in its own awkward prose, "to intelligently impact a pro-active pro-Israel agenda on campus," brings together under one umbrella 30 distinct organizations whose aim is to disseminate pro-Israeli propaganda and to suppress criticism of Israel on American university campuses; its members and affiliates include the formidable Zionist lobby organization AIPAC, the Israeli media-monitoring organization CAMERA, the Zionist Organization of America, the Israel Project, and the David Project.

Many of these organizations, particularly the David Project, were centrally involved in the upheaval in 2004 at Columbia University – Said's long-time home – in which three faculty members were singled out for attack by a coalition of media outfits, pressure groups, and politicians (including a member of Congress) largely because of their criticisms of Israeli policy. Under immense pressure from donors and lobbyists, the university president failed to stand up for his faculty members" academic freedom. In the end, the attack failed to accomplish its objectives – principally the firing of a vulnerable assistant professor – but it was a frightening example of the new atmosphere of political surveillance into which academic institutions have fallen. "Academic colleagues, get used to it," warned the pro-Israeli agitator Martin Kramer, who was involved in the attack on Columbia. "You are being watched. Those obscure articles in campus newspapers are now available on the Internet, and they will be harvested. Your syllabi, which you've also posted, will be scrutinized. Your websites will be visited late at night."[19]

One of the focal points of the campaign to monitor universities is the ongoing attempt to pass legislation at the federal level that would in effect not only impose state monitoring of academic programs all the way down to the level of classroom assignments and reading lists, but also make the academic mission of universities receiving federal funds subservient to the national security of the USA and Israel. It is striking, in fact, that in the congressional debates concerning the best known of these legislative packages, US House of Representatives Resolution HR 3077 (2003), the work of Said himself was exhibited in order to back up the spurious claim that, under the guise of poststructuralist and postcolonial studies, anti-Israeli and anti-American radicals had taken over the American academy, or at least all the major centers for international and Middle East studies. Here is the centerpiece of the congressional testimony of one of the bill's advocates, a Hoover Fellow ironically named Kurtz:

The ruling intellectual paradigm in academic area studies (especially Middle Eastern Studies) is called "post-colonial theory." Post-colonial theory was founded by Columbia University professor of comparative literature, Edward Said. Said gained fame in 1978, with the publication of his book, *Orientalism*. In that book, Said equated professors who support

American foreign policy with the 19th century European intellectuals who propped up racist colonial empires. The core premise of post-colonial theory is that it is immoral for a scholar to put his knowledge of foreign languages and cultures at the service of American power.[20]

The solution called for by this Kurtz and various defenders of Israel led by Martin Kramer and Daniel Pipes (another lapsed academic, who founded Campus Watch in the 1990s to monitor US universities for criticism of Israel) – and backed by the full strength of Israel's lobbying agencies in Washington – is the imposition of a state-appointed body to monitor international studies programs. Appointees would be political, not academic: they would be assigned by the leaders of the House and Senate as well as the Executive Branch, and would include two representatives from "agencies responsible for national security." With the ample backing of Israel's lobby groups, the bill passed the US House of Representatives by a wide margin in late 2003, only to die in a Senate committee. Its language was revived in 2005–6, however, and repackaged in new bills (Senate bill S1614, House Resolution HR609) that again passed House and Senate committees with comfortable majorities in 2006. The Republican-controlled Congress failed to bring the bills to a vote, however, and while it is not clear what the status of these bills will be in the new Democratic-controlled Congress, it is likely, given the persistence of their backers, that they will be re-proposed and perhaps passed; and if they do, the American university system will have crossed a threshold from which, in today's poisonous atmosphere, it is unlikely ever to recover.

In addition to the other somewhat more theoretical questions already mentioned, these added political mobilizations and pressures make it much more difficult to imagine the success today of the kind of modernist charismatic giant essential to Edward Said's conception of the intellectual – especially the public intellectual. Said himself frequently came under attack from powerful interests, of course. But he was already a giant when he came under attack; the question now is whether it would be possible for a new giant to emerge under today's altered circumstances or whether, instead, it would be better for us to create new ways of imagining the role of the intellectual, retaining the oppositional energies and ethical commitments championed by Edward Said, but tempering them with Jameson's assessment of the place (or lack of place) of yesterday's modernist giants in today's world and, as I've been trying to suggest, a sense of the unique challenges facing intellectuals in our altered social and political situation. The commitment, courage, and solidarity with the downtrodden and the dispossessed that Edward Said advocated are still, I believe, the indispensable requirements of the oppositional public intellectual today. But we should perhaps be wary of trying to fashion ourselves along the modernist lines advocated by Said himself.

Notes

1 Edward Said, *Representations of the Intellectual*, New York: Pantheon, 1994.
2 Ibid., pp. 7–8.
3 Ibid., p. 11.
4 Ibid., p. 74.
5 Ibid., pp. 81–2; Edward Said, "Opponents, Audiences, Constituencies, and Community," in *The Anti-Aesthetic: Essays on Postmodern Culture*, ed. Hal Foster, Port Townsend, WA: Bay Press, 1983, p. 157.
6 Ibid., p. 136.
7 Ibid., p. 140.
8 Ibid., p. 156.
9 See Said, *Representations of the Intellectual*, p. 83.
10 Ibid., pp. 100–1.
11 Ibid., p. 13.
12 Ibid.
13 Edward Said, *On Late Style: Music and Literature Against the Grain*, New York: Pantheon, 2006, p. 9.
14 Ibid., p. 22.
15 Ibid., p. 24.
16 Fredric Jameson, *Postmodernism: Or, the Cultural Logic of Late Capitalism*, Durham, NC: Duke University Press, 1991, p. 305.
17 Ibid., p. 306.
18 Said, "Opponents, Audiences, Constituencies, and Community," p. 143.
19 Michael Dobbs, "Middle East Studies Under Scrutiny in US," *Washington Post*, 13 January 2004.
20 http://republicans.edlabor.house.gov/archive/hearings/108th/sed/titlevi61903/kurtz.htm

6

From Auerbach to Said in Istanbul: Saidian Publishing in Turkey

Tuncay Birkan

In this chapter, my point of departure will be the intricate connection between Edward Said and Erich Auerbach. But before going into the details of this complicated relationship, I must issue a warning from the outset and try to clarify my own uneasy position. My text contains nothing by way of a rigorous analysis of Said's outstanding contributions to the various disciplines within the humanities. Instead I will focus on the experiential aspects of Said's intellectual stance that had an enormously strong appeal for non-academic intellectuals like myself, in both the West and the Third World. As a translator and editor I am an intellectual worker rather than an academician, therefore my primary focus will be not on "how to understand" but rather on "how to experience" Said's ideas in both our professional and political lives in Turkey.

From the scattered references in *Beginnings* (1975) to a separate essay in *Humanism and Democratic Criticism* (2005), Said himself repeatedly emphasizes his indebtedness to Auerbach's works, especially to his magnum opus *Mimesis*, written in Istanbul between 1942 and 1945. And much has been said about the "affiliative" connection between the author of *Mimesis* and the author of *Orientalism*. I shall dwell on just one relatively neglected aspect of the obvious connection between Said and Auerbach: That the "elective affinity" between these two great humanists has been established primarily via "Istanbul" which was nothing more than a signifier of exile, of distance from Europe for Said, but which, I shall argue, signified something uncannily "close" to contemporary Europe for Auerbach. Said almost always refers to *Mimesis* by explicitly underlining the fact that Auerbach wrote it in Istanbul, that is, away from his habitual (read: European) cultural environment. He practically elevates the descriptive phrase "Auerbach in Istanbul" to the status of a concept.

Let us remember what Said and Auerbach themselves said about being in Istanbul in the early 1940s before trying to understand this metaphorical concept. In the essay "Secular Criticism," Said first quotes Auerbach's own words in his epilogue to *Mimesis*:

> I may also mention that the book was written during the war and in Istanbul, where the libraries are not equipped for European studies . . . On the other hand, it is quite possible that the book owes its existence to just this lack of a rich and specialized library. If it had been possible for me to acquaint myself with all the work that has been done on so many subjects, I might never have reached the point of writing.

Said then poignantly subjects these words to the following eloquent analysis with his characteristic pathos and brilliance:

> That Auerbach should choose to mention Istanbul as the place of his exile adds yet another dose of drama to the actual fact of *Mimesis*. To any European trained principally . . . in medieval and renaissance Roman literatures, Istanbul does not simply connote a place outside Europe. Istanbul represents the terrible Turk, as well as Islam . . . Turkey was the Orient, Islam its most redoubtable and aggressive representative . . . The Orient and Islam also stood for the ultimate alienation from and opposition to Europe . . . To have been an exile in Istanbul at that time of fascism in Europe was a deeply resonating and intense form of exile.

And he goes on to add: "The book owed its existence to the very fact of Oriental, non-Occidental exile and homelessness."[1]

Said's point is clear. For him, Auerbach's exile in Istanbul was the condition of possibility of this extraordinary book, a condition that thoroughly determines its style and composition. But in Said's portrayal, Istanbul is not a real "location" with a present of its own; it is just a dislocationary symbolic space fully saturated with (and entirely situated by) its past as the capital city of the Other of Europe, an emblem of "cultural depravity" that denotes the impossibility of access to Western culture even from the "capital" of the Orient in the early 1940s.

It is irrelevant for Said's purposes that Istanbul, at that time, had been a republican city for nearly 20 years, and had invited some of the finest German scholars of Jewish origin seeking refuge from the Nazi terror to its universities in order to promote the cause of Turkish nationalism through education. In a perceptive essay, Kader Konuk examines the role these scholars played in a modernizing Turkey that tried to forge a new national identity precisely by attempting radically to break its bonds with its past as *the* Orient. As Konuk suggests, "having fled aggressive nationalism in Germany, the émigrés were functionalized in order to promote a new nationalism in their host country."[2] But Auerbach too seemed to be acutely aware of the role the new regime in Turkey assigned to the émigrés. Auerbach, who came to Istanbul in 1936 when the nationalist reforms of Atatürk were in full swing, had a subtle understanding regarding the nature of this nationalism and linked it not to Turkey's past as the Orient or the Other of European culture but to the "*present* international situation." In a letter to Walter Benjamin from Istanbul in 1937, he says:

> But he [Atatürk] had to force through everything he did in the struggle against the European democracies on the one hand and the old Mohammedan-Pan-Islamic sultan's economy on the other; and the result is a fanatically anti-traditional nationalism: rejection of all existing Mohammedan cultural heritage, the establishment of a fantastic relation to a primal Turkish identity, technological modernization in the European sense, in order to triumph against a hated and yet admired Europe with its own weapons: hence, the preference for European-educated emigrants as teachers, from whom one can learn without the threat of foreign propaganda. Result: nationalism in the extreme accompanied by the simultaneous destruction of the historical national character. This picture, which in other countries like Germany, Italy, and even Russia (?) is not visible for everyone to see, shows itself here in full nakedness . . . It is becoming increasingly clear to me that the present international situation is nothing but a ruse of providence, designed to lead us along a bloody and tortuous path to an International of triviality and a culture of Esperanto. I have already suspected this in Germany and Italy in view of the dreadful inauthenticity of the "blood and soil" propaganda, but only here has the evidence of such a trend almost reached the point of certainty.[3]

As we see, Auerbach regards Turkey not as the representative of a monolithic Orient but as an active part of a depressing and oppressive political climate he describes as "an International of triviality." His sense of homelessness seems to be rooted not in the fact that he had to work in an Oriental "non-space" without decent libraries, but in the fact that he felt alienated in a world which, he sadly observes, had increasingly been dominated almost everywhere by a shared and distinctively modern phenomenon: namely, "nationalism in the extreme." In other words, for him, Istanbul was not an Oriental fantasy-space providing an external vantage point to sadly contemplate the contemporary predicament of European history. On the contrary, it was an all-too-real and, in a sense, all-too-familiar environment, a concrete historical location having its specific share in this predicament.

Said was right in a fundamental sense: Auerbach was really in the grip of a sense of dislocation, a sense of being exiled from his habitual cultural environment, which is very effective in the composition of the book. But for Auerbach Istanbul intensified this feeling not only by its historical and "ultimate alienation from and opposition to Europe," as Said suggested, but by its contemporary and *uncanny resemblance and opposition to it* as well. In short, it seems that Said – who always alerted us to the dangers of reducing the complex history of any people to world-less texts and essentializing formulas like East vs West, urging us to pay due attention to "the actual links between the world of ideas and the brute facts of politics and state power" – surprisingly fails to do that as far as his entire conception of "Auerbach in Istanbul" is concerned, while Auerbach himself never reduces "Istanbul" to a symbolic status and sharply perceives the political situation in both Turkey and Europe. Nonetheless, and somewhat ironically, he does not seem to display a positive interest in the mundane life of Istanbul (as we know, in *Mimesis* the "reality" in the subtitle refers to the secular, everyday, mundane world that the works scrutinized in the book depict). In the book, or even in Auerbach's published correspondences, there is no mention of any significant exchange with dissident Turkish intellectuals or with those who were not completely pro-regime. I am sure he could have had illuminating and enriching conversations with Ahmet Hamdi Tanpınar, for example – a truly erudite intellectual with an extraordinary interest in Western literature who would go on to become arguably the greatest novelist, essayist, and historian of Turkish literature, through works produced in the 1940s and 1950s, and who happened to be lecturing at the same university. But such an intellectual encounter seems never to have taken place, between Auerbach and Tanpınar or any other Turkish intellectual within the university. And as far as we know, none of the students to whom Auerbach taught the basics of philology, nor the colleagues he worked with in Istanbul, seem to have been particularly inspired by his humanistic outlook.[4] Why?

First, let us remember the scene in Turkey at the time Auerbach was in Istanbul writing *Mimesis*. The majority of the few dissident intellectuals with any internationalist leanings (Islamists, liberals, and most importantly socialists) were subjected to serious persecutions. Nâzım Hikmet, one of the greatest poets of the twentieth century and a devoted Communist, was in prison; another important figure, the socialist novelist and storyteller Sabahattin Ali, was murdered as he tried to escape the country after receiving death threats. The printing house in which *Tan* – one of the few democratic newspapers of the time – was printed had been plundered and set on fire.

Although Turkey did not officially enter the war, most of the newspapers were barely able to hide their pro-Nazi sympathies and the others were heavily censored. An unjust and discriminatory tax called *varlık vergisi* was levied against all non-Muslim minority citizens. Universities, including Istanbul University, were systematically purged of all dissident elements during a special cleansing program. A linguistic purification-Turkification craze, started in the 1930s as part of the "rejection of all existing Moham-medan cultural heritage," reached its climax in 1942 when the great majority of Ottoman philosophical concepts were replaced almost overnight with newly coined "pure Turkish" versions established by an official commission. Somewhat ironically, the Turkish Ministry of Education began its great translation project in those years. Hundreds of classic works of Western literature and philosophy from Plato to Bergson, Sophocles to Proust, were commissioned by the state for translation and publication, even though the "newspeak" Turkish frequently used in these translations made it very difficult for contemporary readers to understand them, at least for the first 10 or 15 years.

These several factors may appear to suffice as an explanation for the puzzling lack of a genuine interaction between Auerbach and his Turkish counterparts or colleagues in the academy, but it still needs to be explained further. I would argue that the main reason for the lack was that most of the Turkish intelligentsia within or close to the academic circle were at that time unable and unwilling to take part as equal interlocutors in the conversation about the fate of the world because they had strongly identified themselves with the state's nationalist agenda and isolationist ideology. In this sense they were never "secular" in the Saidian sense of the word (as Bruce Robbins points out, "the term *secular* in Said stands in opposition not [only] to religious concerns or beliefs *per se* but to the nation and nationalism as belief systems [as well]").[5]

Most of the Turkish scholars allowed to work in and around the academy had no qualms about defining themselves firstly as "Turks" and only secondarily as "scholars." They sought to obtain knowledge not as the result of a collective, dialogic effort to get closer to an unattainable truth, but in order to reach *the* truth already obtained elsewhere, in order to find the "power" to fight the Europeans with their own weapons. One may ask: did not Nietzsche, Foucault, and Said demonstrate that the search for "objec-tive" knowledge and the will to power have always been intertwined to a degree in the "enlightened" West as well? Did not Said in particular emphasize the disturbingly strong links between the world of the academy, the humanities in particular, and the world of imperial power struggles? Yes, but because the search for knowledge had been so explicitly instrumentalized in the naked interests of power for such a long time in Turkey[6] – and because, thanks to the violent repression by the state, nothing like a strong tradition of "speaking truth to power" existed, whereby an independent, civil, and critical intelligentsia could emerge – the academy did not have even the relative autonomy enjoyed in the West.

In view of all of this, the pedagogical maneuvers of the state – inviting distinguished émigré scholars, translating Western classics – were fated to have no lasting effects on the younger generations of the republic for two general reasons. First, a whole society cannot go through a process of "Enlightenment" without an accompanying process of democratization: one cannot automatically become "enlightened" simply by "modernizing" the forms of education and translating European classics while the state simultaneously creates an official national ideology and heavily suppresses every kind of opposition to it. Second, the severe isolationism of the new republican and nationalist regime and the serious repression it exercised against any kind of internationalism prevented the formation of a worldly and secular consciousness, a sense of being-an-actor-in-the-world. As we all know, Turkey did not take part in World War II, despite maintaining close contact with the Nazis throughout. Following the War, in face of the perceived threat of Communism and the Soviet Union, the Turkish state joined NATO in 1952, becoming a loyal "strategic" ally, that is, a military partner of the West in general and the US in particular throughout the Cold War. So loyal in fact that Turkey was never officially interested in the anti-colonial struggles of the Third World – not even considering, for example, participating in the famous Bandung Conference of 1955.

The net result of these historical developments, relevant to our discussion here, was that Turkey as a nation never became a challenging "interlocutor" to the West. Said gives an insightful description of this concept in his wonderful essay, "Representing the Colonized: Anthropology's Interlocutors": "It was only when subaltern figures like women, Orientals, blacks, and other " 'natives' " made enough noise that they were paid attention to, and asked in, so to speak."[7] Until the end of the 1960s, when a civil and emancipatory social movement of leftist popular opposition started to take shape,[8] Turkish intellectuals in and around the academy could not have been a part of this "noise," this challenging demand to be treated as an equal interlocutor.

Jacques Rancière – who, in my opinion, is the greatest living philosopher of the political, of the demand for equality – supports Said in innovative ways that must be taken into account in evaluating why Turkey and Turkish intellectuals were unable to be an integral part of this political challenge for a long time. For Rancière, the fundamental condition of a critical encounter between the two parties of a power relation is that the weaker or "un-counted" party should go through a process of political subjectivization. The first requirement of this subjectivization is that it must never be "the simple assertion of an identity; it must always [be], at the same time, the denial of an identity given by an other, given by the ruling order of policy . . . Secondly, it [must be] a demonstration . . . a polemical commonplace for the handling of a wrong and the demonstration of equality."[9] That is, any given identity, and especially a national, communal identity (of course including such supranational identities as the European identity), cannot be the basis of a really emancipatory political practice. As Rancière adds: "the current dead end of political reflection and action is due to the identification of politics with the *self* of a community . . . The name of an injured community that invokes its rights is always the name of the anonym, the name of anyone."[10]

To return to our problem in light of these theses, we can see that if Turkish intellectuals and the Turkish democratic movement (like their counterparts in the world at large) were able to be part of a "polemical commonplace for the handling of a wrong and the demonstration of equality" at some point in history, it was because they were able to reject their given names, their identification with the state or nation or religion, and express a willingness to intervene in the affairs of the world by assuming names other than "Turk" or "Muslim": proletarian, revolutionary, socialist, communist, feminist, etc., in solidarity with all the "uncounted" of the world in their universal struggle for equality. It was first of all thanks to these political and internationalist leftist democratic movements of the 1970s that we in Turkey were able to break the spell of a deeply ingrained isolationism, and not because, as some liberals nowadays assert, the Turkish state was forced to abandon the long tradition of controlled economic autarchy and to join the neoliberal global economy in the 1980s.

On the contrary, the US-sponsored *coup d'état* on 12 September 1980 managed to implement this project of opening the country's economy to greedy corporate capitalism by actively destroying every vestige of the democratic and internationalist opposition. Political parties and trade unions were immediately closed down, thousands of political dissidents were imprisoned and subjected to torture. The media was heavily censored. The fact that the majority of Turks were Muslims was rediscovered and repeatedly emphasized: the so-called "Turkish–Islam synthesis" was actively promoted to isolate the possible divisive and confusing effects of the "Communists" who had effectively demonstrated that a significant portion of the people of Turkey can and must be considered to be more than simply Turks and Muslims. In addition to this heavy dose of Islam injected into the arteries of Turkish society, nationalism had to be strengthened as well, and this, in my opinion, was done mainly by heightening the long-standing tradition of oppressing the Kurds to an unbearable degree, thereby forcing them to form a nationalist resistance movement against which the blade of Turkish nationalism could be sharpened. (Of course, it would be a great injustice to deny any agency to the Kurdish movement itself and to reduce it to a completely reactive position. Needless to say, I have no such intention here.) And of course, almost all of the dissidents in the university were forced to leave the academy. Most sadly, for 25 years now we have been living in the shadow of the military's 1982 constitution and the oppressive laws enacted by the 12 September regime.

But just as it is utterly wrong to reduce a people to its ethnic and religious identity, it would be no less wrong to reduce the intellectual and cultural life of a country to a completely bleak picture of sheer oppression. As Foucault reminds us, "where there is power, there is resistance," and I shall argue that the main source of intellectual resistance and intellectual hope in the post–*coup d'état* period has come from the books and journals independent publishers have produced. If the younger generation of Turkey are able to keep in touch with critical and scholarly discussions on the political and cultural trajectory of the world, if there are still a remarkable number of young people who want to be part of the worldwide struggle to "create a better world," that is primarily thanks to the efforts of these publishers and the authors and the translators they work with, most of whom actively participated in the political and democratic struggles of the 1970s, violently interrupted by the coup in 1980. In the 1990s and the early 2000s, new generations of editors and translators joined them, whose political consciousness had been shaped mainly by reading the books the so-called "1978 generation" published and who could, incidentally, easily reach the critical/political literature of the social sciences and the humanities in the now much better equipped libraries of the universities. I will call them Saidian publishers, but before explaining why, I'd like to draw a general picture of Turkish publishing with the help of my dear friend and colleague, Müge Gürsoy Sökmen who has worked in the independent publishing sector for 25 years now.

In a speech Müge delivered in 2004, at the 27th Congress of International Publishers Association in Berlin, she succinctly sums up the specific situation of independent publishers in Turkey:

> With nearly 400 active independent publishers, Turkey sets a rare example. Independent in terms of finance and political affiliations; independent from the state or conglomerates. This of course is the result of a mixed blessing: The publishing market in Turkey is not stable enough to

satisfy big capital, so the market is left to independent publishers. Also, the decline of academic publishing after the *coup d'état* and the subsequent change of university law have made it possible for "lay" Turkish publishers to have very strong non-fiction lists. We also owe our survival to our young population, a youth quite political and eager to discuss.[11]

The number of active independent publishers has increased to 1,000 or more in the ensuing years. Turkey is now one of the countries with the highest percentage of serious nonfiction works in the total number of the titles published. Again, translated works generally constitute 30–40 percent of the total number of "culture books" published on a yearly basis.[12] I do not see this as a sign of intellectual dependence; on the contrary, this is, for me, a healthy marker of an authentic and politically motivated curiosity about what others think or write in other countries by way of science, politics, and literature. (If we remember that the equivalent percentage is only 3–4 percent in the United States, and that American readers generally do not have the chance to learn what is going on in the rest of the world through first-hand accounts, we may start to understand how this indifference about the rest of the world helps to create the aggressive, patronizing attitude and insolence US foreign policy makers easily assume.) In recent years, big capital has started to become seriously interested in the publishing sector in Turkey, following the commercialization of the printed word already begun some time ago by cheap, best-selling, easy-to-read fiction and pseudo-analyses of recent Turkish history that mainly concern secret plots by the Western powers to divide and rule Turkey – "analyses" that cater to the pathological needs of a rampant nationalism unfortunately fed by the double standards of EU powers.

University presses have started to revive, and to publish serious critical works in the fields of humanities and the social sciences. Yet most of the major radical thinkers of the last century are still being published in Turkey by non-academic publishers: Said, Williams, Jameson; Žižek, Foucault, Adorno, Benjamin, Rancière, Badiou, Guha, Karatani; these are just some of the hundreds of names whose works were first introduced to a larger Turkish audience by these engaged publishers over the last 25 years. While some may sell up to 10,000 copies, the average number of sales of these kinds of books is about 1,000–2,000, although most of them are read by a much wider audience than these numbers suggest through the common practice of borrowing from one another or, if one is lucky, from the libraries.

But let us ask the question Said himself asked the sales representative of a major university press at an MLA convention: "Who reads these books?"[13] He was implying that admittedly brilliant but highly technical books of literary criticism could not have a wide audience. The answer he received was that the people who write such books of criticism "faithfully read each other's books." This answer gave Said an excellent occasion to assault the hegemony of expertise and specialization, and the guild consciousness and hermeticism, the worldlessness this hegemony entails in the humanities. He concluded that the humanists'

> constituency is a fixed one composed of other humanists, students, government and corporate executives, and media employees, who use the humanist to assure a harmless place for "the humanities" or culture or literature in the society. I hasten to recall, however, that this is the role voluntarily accepted by humanists whose notion of what they do is neutralized, specialized, and nonpolitical in the extreme . . . the particular mission of the humanities is to represent *noninterference* in the affairs of the everyday world.[14]

And this is where the adjective "Saidian" in my title comes into play: the publishers I have been mentioning have a much larger and non-specialist audience in mind (and in reality) when they publish their own brand of difficult but always relevant books. They know that the senior academicians who make use of these writers in their lectures will not deign to read these translations.[15] In any case, they are not the intended audience for these translations. The Saidian publishers" constituency is a constantly changing and dynamic one, composed sometimes of students and the younger generation of academicians in the humanities with a serious concern for transforming the way knowledge is being produced or transmitted in the academy; sometimes political activists with socialist, anarchist, liberal or even Islamic leanings who need knowledge like their daily bread to broaden their sphere of influence; sometimes poets and men and women of literature; sometimes women and members of ethnic minorities trying to make sense of and change their subordinate status. In short, mostly young people with a keen political awareness who deeply desire to *interfere* in the affairs of the world.

This Saidian brand of publishing naturally requires a highly selective and politically motivated attitude in choosing titles for publication. You cannot be a Saidian publisher by simply name-picking and publishing every single title these names produce. A Saidian publisher must always ask him- or herself what it means to publish this or that particular title at a particular moment, and what possible uses might be made of it in the specific environment of the country's intellectual, cultural or political life. An author whose intellectual vision has convinced you to publish her previous works may write another equally interesting piece of work, but the Saidian publisher will be prepared not to publish it if it has become too entangled in the current jargon of a specialized field, preventing the author from addressing an audience beyond a limited circle of experts, or even worse if it has become too Eurocentric.

In fact, I myself have had to reject publishing several titles by a number of famous scholars, mainly for reasons such as these. I am sad to say that I encounter examples of unconscious ethnocentrism in the least expected authors with increasing frequency. To give just one instance, a number of important figures on the international left – including Badiou, Žižek, Critchley, Santner, and Eagleton – have in their recent works felt the need to probe the phenomenon of religion and grand questions concerning tragedy, freedom, and even the meaning of life. Because we too think it necessary to rid ourselves of positivist prejudices in order to understand why religion is so important to so many people – and that any critique of religion will be ignorant and empty unless it meaningfully addresses ethical and existential matters such as pain, death, sympathy, tragedy, and responsibility – we would have been glad to publish most of these works. But we could not. Because, with the possible exception of Critchley, they all sound too Judeo-Christian, and oblivious to other religious traditions. They sometimes seem to forget to exercise a "hermeneutics of suspicion" towards the Judeo-Christian tradition in particular and towards religion in general, and seem to attempt to understand it completely on its own terms. At times they write like devout Christians or Jews, failing to maintain the necessary secular distance towards religious discourse as a whole. By contrast a figure like Joel Kovel, who is barely known in his home country, has been able to find a quite remarkable audience in Turkey with his *History and Spirit* just because as a leftist radical he maintains this distance vis-à-vis both his own religious background and the whole institution of religion.

I think this example helps give a concrete content to what I mean by "Said in Istanbul." Said's works and his worldly and secular spirit have been "in Istanbul" for quite a long time, always alerting us to the dangers of lapsing unwittingly into unthinking identity-talk, or this or that version of ethnocentric parochialism, which is, I am sad to say, on the rise both in Turkey and in Europe. We Saidian publishers, translators, authors, and readers are acutely aware of this fact in Turkey and we try to fight back with all our might, if not to succeed, then at least to try to "fail better," as Beckett said. On the other hand, even our European counterparts, on the European left, frequently fall into a double trap. First, they readily identify themselves with Europe as a fixed and given identity, as the locus of an already-achieved universality. Second, they insist on naming us solely as "Turks" or

"Muslims," apparently thinking that we cannot assume another name, a name they may be willing to share in order to transform themselves as well.

Once upon a time, Turkey was one of the "developing countries" in the eyes of the Western intelligentsia and politicians. Then the industrialization paradigm fell out of fashion, followed by the collapse of the Berlin Wall, the rise of so-called "late capitalism," and the increasing emphasis on cultures, ways of life, and "identities." Hence public discussions began once again to be framed by such gross and reified entities as West vs East, or Europe vs Islam. As a result, Turkey, for example, has turned into a full-blown "Islamic" country which, with its terrible record in human rights violations, has the nerve to apply for participation in the "civilized" European Union. However, neither this admittedly awful human rights record, nor the fact that the majority of the Turkish population has always been Muslim, seem to have presented a problem, from 1952 to today, apropos accepting Turkey as an active member of NATO. It seems that for European politicians, Turkey as a military partner is OK, but Turkey as a cultural partner and potential beneficiary of the EU's economic resources presents a grave danger. In these circles hypocrisy is nothing unexpected. What is demoralizing is that an increasing number of leftist or radical intellectuals in Europe seem to be unwittingly subscribing to these same patronizing, essentializing attitudes towards "Islam" in general and Turkey in particular. Turkish cultural producers, e.g., writers, film-makers, academicians, are sick and tired of being treated by their counterparts in Europe as official representatives of the Turkish regime. They are tired of constantly being interrogated on the ever-same set of questions regarding the EU, the Kurdish question, women in Islam, the atrocities committed against Armenians in 1915, etc., and scolded for wrongs committed in the name of Islam or by Turkish state officials – as if they do not themselves fight against these wrongs and suffer the conse-quences of this fight on an almost daily basis, as if there cannot be any other subject about which a Turkish intellectual could or should say something worth hearing. But if we, as leftist radicals, really want to change the world we live in (including, of course, Europe) we must find ways to talk to each other as equal interlocutors, as friends, as comrades, regardless of our religious or national background, and act together to ease the common burden of history that has always been full of barbarism in every culture, as Benjamin taught us. It is very sad that even the left in Europe, in general, has seemingly become incapable of learning from others, of really listening to what they have to say without first putting them in the position of "victims," to use Alain Badiou's term.

Let me finish with a quotation from Rancière who puts the matter succinctly:

Twenty years ago we were "all German Jews"; that is to say, we were in the heterological logic of "wrong" names, in the political culture of conflict. Now we have only "right" names. We are Europeans and xenophobes . . . Objectively, we have no more immigrant people than we had twenty years ago. Subjectively, we have many more. The difference is this: twenty years ago the "immigrant" had an *other* name; they were workers or proletarians. In the meantime this name has been lost as a *political* name. They retained their "own" name, and an other that has no *other* name becomes the object of fear and rejection . . . If my analysis is correct, the question is not only "How are we to face a political problem?" but "How are we to reinvent politics?"[16]

I believe that Edward Said has much to say to all of us – Westerners and Easterners, Northerners and Southerners – who need to see that we can only reinvent politics together, and by leaving our given names and our given identities behind.

Notes

1 Edward Said, "Secular Criticism," in *The World, the Text, and the Critic*, London: Vintage, 1983, pp. 5–8.
2 Kader Konuk, abstract of her paper "Building Nations and Disciplines," at http://web-cygnus.sas.upenn.edu/~johannaj/nationalscholarship/ Abstracts.html#Kader_Konuk
3 Quoted in Karlheinz Barck, "Walter Benjamin and Erich Auerbach: Fragments of a Correspondence," *Diacritics*, Vol. 22, No. 3/4, Autumn/Winter 1992, p. 82.
4 A few months after I wrote the first draft of this essay, Martin Vialon, a serious Auerbach scholar from Yeditepe University in Istanbul, informed me in more detail about the intellectual relations Auerbach developed in Istanbul. As I understand it, Auerbach appeared to be in intimate contact with such leftist intellectuals as Abidin Dino, Sabahattin Eyüboğlu, and Bedri Rahmi Eyüboğlu during his Istanbul years, and he mentioned some of his pupils from Istanbul University with obvious affection even in some of the letters he wrote from the USA in later years. Vialon insists that Auerbach was acquainted with Tanpınar, though he admits that no serious intellectual interaction seemed to take place between these two great figures. While these details may seem to be at odds with my comments above, I think the argument is still valid insofar as there is no evidence that any of the people mentioned were particularly influenced by Auerbach's "humanistic" vision in their intellectual or artistic works, or vice versa.
5 Quoted in Aamir R. Mufti, "Auerbach in Istanbul: Edward Said, Secular Criticism, and the Question of Minority Culture," *Critical Inquiry*, Vol. 25, No. 1, Autumn 1998, p. 96.
6 Since at least the beginning of the nineteenth century, "ensuring the survival

of the state" has been the principal concern of the Ottoman/Turkish literati who were mainly bureaucrats working in the state apparatus.

7 Edward Said, "Representing the Colonized: Anthropology's Interlocutors," *Critical Inquiry*, Vol. 15, No. 2, Winter 1989, p. 210.

8 There were earlier leftist movements, of course. For example the TKP (Turkish Communist Party) was founded as early as 1920. But since the party was officially banned and its members severely punished by the republican regime, they had to work underground, and accordingly had limited access to (let alone a serious influence on) the general public.

9 Jacques Rancière, "Politics, Identification, and Subjectivization," *October*, Vol. 61, Summer 1992, p. 62.

10 Ibid., p. 59.

11 Müge Sökmen, "A Delicate Dance: Freedom to Publish in Turkey Today." Unpublished manuscript of a speech delivered on 21 June 2004 at the 27th Congress of International Publishers Association in Berlin.

12 Müge Sökmen, "Translating and Publishing Turkish Literature." Unpublished manuscript of a speech delivered on 1 June 2007 at the 1st International Symposium of Translators and Publishers of Turkish Literature in Boğaziçi University, Istanbul.

13 Edward Said, "Opponents, Audiences, Constituencies, and Community," in *The Politics of Interpretation*, ed. W.J.T. Mitchell, Chicago: University of Chicago Press, 1983, p. 10.

14 Ibid., pp. 25, 28.

15 Most of them would not even be aware that the books have been translated. They would mostly prefer to read the English originals or English translations of French or German originals. Again, most of them prefer to write their works in English rather than in their native Turkish (even though the problems dealt with in their books are Turkey's urgent problems) because they target a specialized audience: the other academicians in their field of work.

16 Rancière, "Politics, Identification, and Subjectivization," p. 63.

PART III

The Question of Palestine

7

The Saidian Fusion of Horizons

Ilan Pappé

Any assessment of Edward Said's intellectual legacy, indeed any tribute to the man and his work, has to move back and forth from his life involvement in the Palestine issue to his incredible presence in the more general debates about culture and power. This is easier said than done. On the very general and theoretical level, Said founded a school of thought and composed a whole area of studies, whereas his contributions on Palestine were very concrete, quite often simple narratives, with an accentuated political agenda. Even the mode of presentation was not the same: the stylistic flair and virtuous articulations on the general themes were replaced by focused, matter-of-fact descriptions and analyses on Palestine. It is no wonder that Said's theoretical works on literature and culture are quite often dealt with separately from his writing on Palestine. Said's books were indeed carefully written with this distinction in mind; in a way only his autobiography deviates from this division and fuses his local/emotional Palestine legacy with his universal/cognitive intellectual heritage.

This paper suggests that the fusion, so to speak, evolved with time and matured, affecting in particular Said's vision for the future of Palestine as a bi-national state and more specifically his engagement with Zionism and Judaism in the context of the conflict and its solution. An interesting phenomenon appeared in Israel where there was an attempt to separate Said the universal thinker from Said the Palestinian intellectual, and accept the former while suspecting the latter. I will argue here that this is impossible, and that such an interpretation of the man and his work exposes a tendency in the more critical circles in Israeli society – and indeed in the wider Jewish Zionist society abroad – to adopt a decon-struction of national mythologies and reject historical injustices every-where, apart from one place: Israel (very much like Eli Wiesel's inability to list, even once, in his enumeration of injustices in the wake of the

Holocaust, the one that occurred in Palestine and was perpetrated by the Israelis).

But it is not only in Israel that Said's journeys into Palestine's past are dealt with as a different subject matter from his books on literature, Orientalism, culture, and music. The multiple projects he pursued intellectually were inseparable in his life and only artificially compartmentalized in his writings. Over time, the division blurs and a dialectical relationship between the two avenues develops such that what seemed in the past to be two discrete trajectories, can be seen today, with the benefit of hindsight, as two parts of the same project that fused more clearly into one towards the end of his life. This nexus is used in a deductive rather than inductive way in his works. As such, the impact of his epistemological view on his Palestine studies is more evident than any influence his Palestinian background had on his theoretical probing into the question of power and representation. But they are present in both directions. Said's adoration for the exilic intellectual was the outcome of his Palestinian background, and in return his search for an exilic position as an intellectual placed him in a unique moral and political position on the Palestinian side towards Judaism and Zionism in general and towards a prospective solution for the Palestine question in particular. This distinct posture – an admixture of sorties into the Palestinian case and his reflections on nationalism in general – enabled Said to influence, and be engaged with, a specific section of the Israeli intellectual milieu, as will be described later on.

Said's interdisciplinary approach to knowledge focused on the cultural representations of one society by another in general, and more specifically on the particular era of Western colonialism and neo-colonialism. Even without reading a single book or essay by Said on Palestine, readers of his general critique immediately recognized that Palestine's history was, and still is, a prime example for such an inquiry. Once you read Said writing specifically on Palestine, you realize that his theoretical deconstruction of power bases of knowledge and exposure of the more sinister interests behind Western knowledge production on the Orient would have lacked impetus and zeal had they not been motivated by his struggle for the Palestine cause.

An illuminating example of this nexus is his anthology *The Politics of Dispossession*. It is a collection of short and lucid interventions, quite often articulated as immediate responses to recent crises or conjunctures in the life of Palestine and the Palestinians. As an overall assessment of Palestine's past they are the narratives of the people's physical dispossession, but analytically they are more concerned with the exclusion of the Palestinian narrative from the Western public mind. For Said, wiping the Palestinian catastrophe out of public memory is as much a crime as the expulsion itself. If one reads

Orientalism with *The Politics of Dispossession*, one has a complete picture of the universal mechanism of the Nakba denial and its dire consequences.

The Deductive Fusion: Said's Uneasy Dialogue with Israel

The universalized approach towards, and indeed the deductive prism used in, the study of Palestine did not at first win Said many followers in Israel. Noam Chomsky once described Edward Said as a man who was a target of constant vilification. The principal attacks came from the American Zionist establishment and later on, after the publication of *Orientalism* in 1978, from the Israeli Orientalists. The latter recognized correctly that the deconstructive theory applied almost more perfectly to them than to anyone else.

Indeed the beginning of the interaction between the ultimate articulator of Palestinian victimhood with the victimizer's society were troublesome. When Israelis first encountered Said it was through the Hebrew translation of *The Question of Palestine*; his first work ever to be published in Israel, by a low-budget, radical publishing house that did not survive the 1990s. The spirit of that book, no less than its factual basis, accompanied my own research in the early 1980s, when I was mining the archives and revisiting the history of 1948. I guess for some activists on the Israeli radical left, Said's historical perspective on Palestine highlighted for them, as it did for me, the relevance of the events of 1948 to the predicaments of the present Israel and Palestine, and to the need to locate the refugee issue at the heart of the Palestine problem. But this message, at that time, did not reach a wide audience either in Israel or in the Western world at large. Alas, during the Oslo days, leading Palestinian politicians seemed also to forget this incisive Saidian articulation of what the Palestine conflict was all about. Said's anger towards them was as fierce as his rage against Israeli crimes from 1948 until his death.

The Politics of Dispossession was not translated, although it included some of Said's clearest articulations on the question of memory manipulation and the dialectics between Jews and Palestinians. Said was calling for a better understanding in the Arab world at large, and in Palestine in particular, of the place of the Holocaust in Jewish history, but he demanded at the same time an end to the Nakba denial by the West and in Israel. The Israelis were not ready then, and are not prepared now, for the kind of soul-searching that would confront them with the crime against humanity they committed in 1948, and the war crimes they have perpetrated ever since.

This is why *Orientalism* was only translated into Hebrew more than 20 years after it was first published, and other works by Said which juxtaposed the Nakba against its denial in the West were not translated until today. But Said did transform the public mind in the West eventually, with his books and public lectures about Palestine. He did it by efficiently exposing the Western media's effort to sideline the plight and tragedy of Palestine in the public mind, if not altogether eliminate it. In the process, he lucidly associated the wrongs of the past with the tragedy of the present in the land of Palestine. This is where theoretical musings about power and representation were efficient tools for analyzing the Palestine tragedy in its current form. He was particularly heard from and looked for in the wake of the first Palestinian Intifada in 1987, and in 1988 when he was involved in formulating a new Palestinian agenda through the Declaration of Independence and the onset of American–PLO negotiations. It was only a short time before this new impact reached the more sensitive and open-minded sections of the Israeli cultural scene.

Said's intertwined interest in the world of subalterns in general and Palestinians in particular explains why he was sought after by the small, quite often politically insignificant, radical Israeli left. It was mainly his deconstruction of Orientalism that appealed to what I have termed elsewhere the post-Zionist movement of critique at work in the 1990s. This movement attempted to shake up the social and human sciences in Israel. It began as a modest attempt to revisit the 1948 Zionist narrative – an attempt that was named at the time the "new history" of Israel – and culminated in a scholarly Israeli deconstruction of the Zionist project as a whole and a severe critique in academia on Israeli policies since the creation of the state. The critical historians and sociologists focused in particular on the state's early policies towards the Palestinian minority and the Jews who came from Arab countries, the *Mizrachim*.

Already in the first phase of the post-Zionist critique, that of the "new history" of the 1948 war, Said's influence could be traced indirectly. The new history corroborated the major Palestinian claims about the 1948 war, notable among them the claim concerning the ethnic cleansing that took place in that year. Some of the "new" historians argued that it was only new archival material that had prompted their revisionist historiography – hence the "Paris catastrophe," when, in Paris in 1998, Said's attempt to bring together the "new" Israeli historians and Palestinian historians ended in deadlock. But it is very clear that they were influenced by the comprehensive shift in attitudes towards non-Western historical perspectives, to which Said contributed more than anyone else. The legitimization process meant accepting as professionally valid the Palestinian version of events, or at least part of it, while at the same time exposing parts of Israeli historiography as ideological and polemicist.

A decade later, it seemed that quite a few Israeli academics, media pundits, and general literati could not resist Said's desire, and ability, to engage with humanity. This propensity of his was displayed in the most elegant and intellectual way in his writings, but it was also evident in his enviable ability to delve into long conversations with anyone he met. I am sure I am not the only one who sat with Said in a coffeehouse in Paris or New York, only to find our conversation interrupted by inquisitive Saidian chit-chat with the waiter or an old lady sitting at the neighboring table.

On a much deeper level of intellectual curiosity, Said was reciprocated by his interlocutors" wishes to engage with his thought and views, including the more critical intellectual elite in Israel. As the 1990s passed on, more and more works in Israel referred directly to Said's influence. With his thoughts in the background, the post-Zionist critique deconstructed the mythological Israeli concept of the "melting pot" Zionist society, into which all the Jewish immigrants and the indigenous Palestinian population were to be integrated successfully to become one modern nation. This modernizationist notion was debunked with the help of Said's own deconstruction of Orientalism. This meant not only revisiting the actual policies towards the Palestinian minority and Jewish immigrants from Arab countries, but no less importantly critically examining the crucial role played by the local academia in sustaining and justifying these policies of discrimination and exclusion.

Said's work on Palestine, and his declared identity as a spokesperson for the Palestinian cause, gave a special impetus to the critical work of challenging Zionism in the Zionist state. The critique was born also out of the political developments that transformed the early scene, beginning with the 1973 October war and culminating with the 1993 Oslo process. Said's input provided a coherent intellectual way of articulating these challenges. Through his works it was possible to translate an emotional response in the face of historical and contemporary evils into an intellectual statement that questioned almost every foundational myth of the Jewish State.

Said was less influential in the political sphere. To be fair, neither in Palestine nor in Israel did intellectuals or activists draw the inevitable conclusion from his deconstruction. The need to search for a political structure where all these evil policies will have disappeared, or at least have been minimized, was never recognized in Said's lifetime. Very few even noticed the very clear Saidian vision for the future: there is a need for a state that will allow refugees to return if they wish to, and Arab Jews to remain loyal to their culture and civilization, while everyone else can enjoy basic human and civil rights. By 2000, Said saw the bi-national state as the only political arrangement that could contain these visions and hopes. Alas very few at the time, either in Palestine or Israel, were thinking in this direction.

Today with the disintegration of the Gaza Strip and the total destruction of the West Bank infrastructure, the relevance of this vision is accepted by more Palestinians than ever before, yet, while the small and courageous Israeli peace camp is moving in that direction too, the majority of Jews in Israel refuse to support any political structure that would force them to give up full control over most of Palestine with as few Palestinians in it as possible.

Although he was less influential in his political writing, Said enjoyed and encouraged his new position within the critical chattering classes of Israel. It seems that in his case, a position towards Israel and Zionism evolved as a result of his continued inquiry into the realm of culture and representation. It was the crystallization of his universal humanism that provided the potential common basis between him and a critical group of post-Zionist cultural producers in Israel, even after his death, by means of his works. When this dialectical association matured, alas only in the late 1990s, it allowed Said not only to elucidate, in political terms, a wish to bring an end to Zionist supremacy in Palestine but also to express a hope for a substitute political model far removed from the contemporary Arab nation-states around Palestine.

The critique of Arab politics, a very early motif in Said's public activity, was connected in his mind with the tragedy of Palestine, long before his renewed interest in Zionism and particularly the post-Zionists in Israel. When, in 1959, a friend of the Said family in Egypt, Farid Hadad, was murdered by Nasser's security forces, Said divorced Arab radicalism and socialism. His dismay at the more negative face of Arab nationalism was linked to his vision of Palestine as a different political entity – different from Egypt as well as from Israel. This association is touchingly illuminated by the dedication of *The Question of Palestine* to Farid Hadad.

In 1999, Said's relationship with Israeli academia reached a peak when he was invited as the keynote speaker in the annual meeting of the Israeli Anthropological Association. He came away with mixed feelings from that encounter. On the one hand, he witnessed in person how a deconstructive approach to Orientalism was gladly and enthusiastically employed by post-Zionist scholars (numbering at the time a few dozen, many of them present for his speech). On the other hand, he realized that the post-Zionist critics found it easier to employ his prism in relation to the cultural reality of Israel than they did to adopt in any meaningful way his political vision for the future of Palestine.

Following that visit, major publishing houses translated some of his works into Hebrew. *Orientalism*, although already a historical document by the time it was translated, appeared soon after, and his memoir, *Out of Place*, followed. This last book succeeded in touching chords and emotions in the post-Zionist, and even Zionist, intellectual milieu.

The Inductive Fusion:
The Exilic Intellectual in Search of a Homeland

In the last two years of his life, Said's political vision of a bi-national state and his very severe critique of the Oslo process was only faintly heard in Israel and made accessible only to that tiny portion of Jewish society that toyed with the possibility of shelling off the Zionist armor. He was invited in the last year of his life to make a rare appearance in the printed and electronic media. A long interview in *Ha'aretz* with the senior interviewer – who also challenged Said from a typical Zionist viewpoint, nonetheless with great respect and honor – was followed by an interview on television, in prime time, which was even more empathetic and forthcoming.

In both interviews, judging by letters to the editor and other responses, Said managed to strike a chord with his recurring theme that the Jews and the Palestinians were doomed by fate to share together a land – a destiny he admitted most of them disliked but he warned, in an atypically religious way, that one should not tamper with fate. This destiny to his mind required a mutual understanding of tragedies, national traumas, and collective fears. Alas, such an ability to contain and absorb was never reciprocated by any of the leading Israeli intellectuals of the day.

Said constantly referred to himself in all his last interviews, and in his memoir, as the only surviving genuine Jew – not as a religious or national identity but rather as denoting an intellectual personality. It was a continuation of his constant effort to find past examples of, and make room for, the exilic intellectual. Abdul R. Janmohamed was one of the first to try to present the late Edward Said as an exilic intellectual. For Said he coined a special term: the Specular Border Intellectual. There are two kinds of border intellectuals according to this view: the syncretic and the specular. In a very simplistic way, one can say that the former is an intellectual at home in two or more cultures, and thus busy fusing and combining hybrid inputs, while the latter is not at home with either, although immensely familiar with them, and is thus preoccupied with the deconstruction and critique of both.

Many who delved into the Saidian frame of mind found that exile and intellectualism were leitmotifs in his work and thought. In his later writing exile seemed ever to overshadow other concerns. I venture here that the idea of exile won prominence in his thought as part of a dialectic progress in the two fields of inquiry that attracted him most: Culture and Palestine. As discrete avenues of inquiry, when the two roads met, they quite often clashed. Where cultural studies produced a sharp critique of nationalism, love for Palestine had to be more tolerant towards the concept of nationalism. Exile coexisted more easily with both.

Indeed the centrality of exile as an epistemological construct is the product of time, and not only of principle. In his posthumous text, Said focuses on the theme of late style, undertaking a search into "the way in which the work of some great artists and writers acquires a new idiom towards the end of their lives – what I have come to think of as a late style."[1] Said was aware he was coming to the end of his life and this is why his own work began to transform not only idiomatically but also thematically. And this is where the discussion of exile is so mature. It is the maturation of Said's contrapuntal dialectical approach to harmonious and complimentary affiliations and values. He can tell Nubar Hovespian that he takes a lot of luggage with him because he fears he will never return – a sad reminder of his 1948 experience – and yet he recognizes that exiles like him are fortunate enough, unlike political exiles, to treat homes as temporary bases which allow freedom of thought and spirit. As a Palestinian, exile in the first instance is traumatic; as a universalistic intellectual it is an asset.

The exilic intellectual was able not only to suggest a path into a future liberated from both Zionism and Arab tyrannism, but also to confront head on the living symbol and leader of Palestinian exile – Yasser Arafat. Said's self-reconciliation, through his late-style writing between the narrow-mindedness of nationalism and the broader attitude of universalism, sharpened his criticism of Arafat, as well as of Oslo (the latter issue so preoccupied him that he published three short books on the subject). It was at the time a lonely position – Arafat's critics, who were also struggling bravely for the cause of Palestine, were mostly Islamists or hard-core leftists (loyal more to another variant of Arab nationalism than to internationalism). But on the other hand, it broadened his moral base and allowed him to fend off the last vicious attack from the Zionist establishment, before his death, and in the wake of 9/11.

Led by the pro-Israeli Orientalist establishment in America, the campaign against him this time was particularly venomous. It had two prongs: one was a pathetic attempt to present his autobiography as a falsification of the truth, especially the reference to his birth and childhood in Jerusalem. The second direction of the attack was to blame him almost solely for anaesthetizing the intelligent American community, by misrepresenting trends in the contemporary Middle East and by idealizing the evil enemies of the United States. He was heading a pyramid to which famous and less famous experts of the Middle East were linked, dominating American academia, disabling any counter-views, and reinforcing a dormant intelligence community.

This diatribe was forgotten a few weeks after it appeared, but it must have brought back bad memories from the1980s when the Zionist establishment in New York referred to Said as a professor of terror. The incident did inadvertently reinforce his connection with the post-Zionist academics he had so influenced in previous years. They sent a petition in his support that moved him, despite my attempt over the phone to explain some of the ulterior motives behind that petition. Some, though not all, of his supporters thought he was so important now that it was good to be seen, in an increasingly pro-Palestinian academia, as standing behind him.

After his death, he was assessed and remembered in Israel in a way that would have been unthinkable in the 1970s. He was still the most articulate spokesman of the enemy, but at least in *Ha'aretz* he was also portrayed as one of the great intellectual minds in the second half of the twentieth century.

But it is difficult to know how far and how deep his overall impact went. Post-mortem, it seemed that his intellectual influence was once more divided between the "general" field and the Palestine cause. Academics still employed his deconstructive approach, with a natural distancing and critique that time allows, but still finding it useful for looking at local cases of power and knowledge (although this trend too is waning in Israeli academia). In 2000, many of these critical voices in Israel subsided and the academics who produced knowledge relevant to political predicaments reverted back to eschewing a consensual interpretation of the present reality. For this reason, it is difficult yet to assess how significant or unique this chapter is in the Israeli history of ideas and ideologies. It may prove to be a passing phase, as alas it now seems, or the precursor of a more revolutionary future – if we are to take a more optimistic view on the chances for peace and reconciliation in the torn land of Palestine.

As for Said's Palestine, his vision, unlike the theoretical and methodological kits drawn from his general writings, has been planted away from academia and is nourished by a very small, but intriguing, group of political activists. One particularly interesting case is the Israeli NGO, Zochrot, devoted to remembering, recording and informing about 1948. Here and there, one can find the beginnings of experiments with the idea of a binational state, creating co-operation beyond the conventional meeting points of Palestinians and Israelis that were meant to partition the country rather than building a joint future.

Said the exilic intellectual, humanist and universalist, offers the Israelis, in his theoretical work, as well as in his writings on Palestine, a moral basis for living together with the Palestinians despite years of colonization, dispossession, and occupation. His search for the state based on universal values may be no more than an ideal type for the Middle East as a whole, but it conveys the message of restitution rather than retribution. It reflects the bewildering gap between the magnitude of the Israeli evil and the fragility of Palestinian revengefulness. It offers a political entity that is not Zionist, but is also a far cry from those of the Arab regimes around Palestine. Above all, it was visualized as a utopia by someone who regarded himself as the only remaining Jewish intellectual around, in contrast to the nightmare that another Jew from the same milieu, Theodor Herzl, inspired.

As Mariam Said suggests, Edward Said left it up to us to dot the i's and cross the t's in his vision, but he did ask us to allow all members of society, and not just its political classes, to partake in the process, including the refugees and not just the elite in Ramallah, the Palestinians in Israel and not just those in Gaza, the new Jewish immigrants to Israel and not just those who settled in the last century. For this we do not need to be giants, it seems, but just humanist human beings.

Notes

1 Edward Said, "Thoughts on Late Style," *London Review of Books*, 5 August 2004.

8

Analyzing Palestine:
Post-Mortem or Prognosis?

Raja Shehadeh

In an article in *Al-Hayat* newspaper Edward Said reflected on why I had termed my analysis of the Oslo Accords a "post-mortem." I had distinguished between the activist spirit in which I had written *Occupier's Law* in 1985,[1] when the possibility of affecting the course of events through exposing Israel's violations of international law seemed realistic, and the book written after the Oslo Accords which I described as having "the ring of a post mortem, rather than the call of an engaged activist."[2] In this chapter I want to reflect on the role of legal thinkers and strategists in the present profound crisis facing Palestine, and whether legal professionals or other intellectuals can at this point in the Palestinian struggle against Israeli colonialism influence the course of events or simply produce post-mortem reports about a lost cause. The same question can also be asked about other global conflicts and crises.

The failure of the PLO negotiators to avail themselves of the services of legal advisors in the course of their negotiations with Israel has been noted by Said among others. I want to propose that it was in fact an even more dire scenario: there was no role for a legal advisor in those negotiations because Israel had come to them prepared to impose on the Palestinians terms worked out long ago by its own legal advisors and strategists, while Palestinian leaders appeared to be seeking recognition at any price.

I am reminded of the numerous instances when I accompanied clients to meetings with military officers in charge of civilian affairs in the West Bank to argue their case against the refusal of the official to grant a license or withhold a certain permission necessary for my client's business, only to be told that the officer would not meet with me because he refused to deal with lawyers. In other words, there was nothing to negotiate, no legal case to be argued. If the military administration has the power to impose its will why should it tolerate legal challenges to its schemes? The same could be said of the Declaration of Principles signed by Israel and the PLO in 1993 that was "negotiated" in Oslo. Israel knew what it wanted and used its own advisors to draft the agreement. The Palestinians were left to make a few comments and answer interrogatories put to them by the Israeli legal advisor, as we learn from the book on the Oslo negotiations by Ahmed Qurie ("Abu Alaa"), one of the chief negotiators of the Oslo Accords.[3] Palestinian contributions were only tolerated if they involved details within the framework of the agreement proposed by Israel, not if they altered or violated it. Consequently the Accords that came to be signed were not the result of two adversaries sitting around the negotiation table attempting to arrive at a mutually acceptable middle ground through negotiations. Instead they represented the culmination of a process of legal developments which Israel had devised over the years of its occupation of the Palestinian territories.

Most of the elements of this scheme were already known to human rights activists living and working in the Occupied Territories, as well as to other analysts and activists working there before the two sides sat together in the Norwegian capital. Al Haq, the Palestinian human rights organization, had among others exposed these Israeli schemes of changing the law and administration in the Occupied Territories and had analyzed their legal and political significance. Two things were unusual about the Israeli occupation: it allowed the freedom for human rights organizations to operate and it published everything regarding legal and administrative changes affecting life and land in the Occupied Territories as well as the schemes for the settlement of Israeli citizens in them. There were no mysteries.

But the human rights organizations had no political power to influence the course of these negotiations. Nor for that matter did such important leaders as Faisal Husseini of Jerusalem and Haidar Abdul Shafi of Gaza. During the time they were negotiating with the Israeli Delegation in Washington from 1991–93, Arafat started a smear campaign calling them "the American gang." They were suspected by the PLO leadership in Tunis of attempting to make a separate deal with Israel and sidestepping the PLO. Arafat and the other prominent PLO leaders in Tunis were so suspicious as to shun any advice that those of us living inside the Occupied Territories were prepared to give, to avoid exactly the kind of tragedy that the Oslo agreements brought. What were these legal schemes?

Among Israel's undertakings in the Camp David Accords of 1978 was the withdrawal of the military government and the establishment of an "elected self-governing authority in the West Bank and Gaza."[4] Following the

Accords, and in order to subvert any genuine Palestinian autonomous control over the land, Israel began implementing a number of fundamental changes in earnest.

In the 12 years that passed between Israel's signing of the Camp David Accords and its acceptance of the Letter of Invitation to the Madrid Peace Conference,[5] Israel was able to carry out changes in the West Bank and Gaza that amounted to putting in place self-government arrangements for the Palestinians which would remain in Israeli hands administered by an Israeli colonel until Palestinian leaders were found to assume these civilian powers. The legal challenge facing Israel was to set these up so that they applied only to the Palestinians living in the West Bank while leaving out of their jurisdiction the Jewish settlers. In March 1979, in the wake of the Camp David Accords, Israeli Prime Minister Menahem Begin declared that "the Jewish inhabitants of Judea and Samaria [the West Bank] and Gaza will be subject to the law of Israel."[6] In other words, Israel wanted to annex the areas dedicated for Jewish settlements without declaring a formal annexation of the Occupied Territories, thus preserving the fiction that their final status was to be determined in future negotiations.[7]

The Civil Administration

In 1981 the Israeli military commanders of the West Bank and the Gaza Strip established what they called a Civil Administration for the Palestinians living in these areas.[8] This was headed by an Israeli army colonel who was given the responsibility of administering the affairs of the Palestinian inhabitants,[9] leaving the Jewish inhabitants of the settlements in the West Bank and the Gaza Strip subject to Israeli laws and Israel's direct rule. The significance of the distinction between military affairs and civilian affairs, which until the establishment of the Palestinian Authority were all administered by the Israeli army, became more apparent when the Oslo Accords were negotiated and civilian affairs pertaining to the Palestinian inhabitants of the Occupied Territories were transferred to the newly created Authority.

The separation of the civilian affairs of the Palestinian and Jewish inhabitants of the Occupied Territories was also accompanied by a deter-mined thrust to acquire for the Jewish settlements the largest possible area of Palestinian land. When the occupation began, the land owned by Jews before 1948 and administered by the Custodian of Enemy Property in the West Bank is estimated to have been 30,000 dunums (a dunum is 1,000 square meters) out of a total area of 5.5 million dunums, that is, 5 percent of the total area, mostly located in the Jerusalem metropolitan area and the Etzion Bloc in the southern part of the West Bank between Bethlehem and

Hebron. By November 1992, after the start of the Israeli–Palestinian peace negotiations, land held by Israel potentially for the use of Israeli settlers constituted more than 60 percent of the total area of the West Bank. The claim Israel made was that most of this was public land, a claim whose truth lay in Israel's illegal transformation of the definition of this category and the land that fell within it.[10]

By the time the occupation began in June 1967 the process of land registration that had begun in Palestine in 1928 had succeeded in registering only about a third of the land in the West Bank and East Jerusalem. Out of this an estimated 750,000 dunums was state land registered in the name of the Jordanian state. Israel proceeded to take all of this land and suspended the land registration process. When the British mandate took over the administration of Palestine in 1922 there was no Cadastral Survey in Palestine. Under the Ottoman System the title deed to land usually referred to a parcel of land the boundaries of which were stated without reference to a survey. This resulted in confusion of title to immovable property. In 1920 a Survey Ordinance was passed by the government of Palestine and the survey process began. Then in 1928 the mandate government issued the Land Settlement Ordinance which provided for the settlement of disputes over land and the registration of title to land on a system of recording of immovable properties on a territorial basis in blocks and parcels. The whole of Palestine was made subject to the provisions of the law and the process of land registration began mainly in areas where it was believed the Jewish state would be established. After the British mandate ended in 1948 and Jordan took over the West Bank, this process continued under a 1952 Jordanian law.[11] In 1983, when the law office of the present author wrote to the Israel military authorities requesting the resumption of the process, the request was refused. The justification given for this was to avoid "prejudicing the rights of the many absentees and the ownership rights of nationals of Jordan who have lands in the area but reside outside Judea and Samaria [the West Bank]."[12] But while suspending any further registration of land in Palestinian ownership, massive areas of land were being registered in the name of Israeli governmental and quasi-governmental agencies.

Under Jordanian rule and for the first 12 years of the Israeli occupation there was full public access to the land records. This access was then abruptly denied. I remember going one June day in 1979 to the Land Registration Department to carry out a search in the records on behalf of a client, as I often did, only to be told that I could no longer have access to the land records, since the rules had changed. From that day onwards the land records would be closed to the public.[13] This was done in an effort to keep Palestinians ignorant of illegal transfers of their land taking place on a large scale and to shield them from the knowledge of the status of these large areas. To further conceal the truth of what was taking place, lands acquired by the Israeli military as public land were not registered in the central land registry located in the West Bank city of Ramallah, but rather in an Israeli register especially created for this purpose under a military order entitled "Order Regarding Registration of Transactions in Special Lands."[14] This register eventually came to be merged with the Israel Lands Administration Authority, where Israeli state lands are registered. In this way, the Land Registration Department of the West Bank, which until 1967 served as the only register for West Bank land, came to be used as a register only for land owned by Palestinians, while the Israel Land Administration Authority became the register of West Bank land used and controlled by the Israeli government for the exclusive use of Jewish settlers. Commenting on this, Dror Etkes, head of the Israeli Peace Now's Settlement Watch, said:

> Regarding anywhere else within the State of Israel, the Land Registry is open for public viewing. Only in the territories of the West Bank is it defined as a state secret. The claim of land ownership anonymity is a means the state and its settler agents have created to limit the public and legal oversight of the phenomenon of land theft. This is an attempt to conceal conduct that can only be defined as a mafia state.[15]

This was one of the ways in which Israel managed to effectively annex land in the West Bank used to settle Israeli Jews.

In carrying out these changes, Israel aimed at achieving two objectives. The first was to enable it to transfer the administration of the West Bank Palestinians without having to transfer in the process the administration over West Bank Jewish settlers. Thus when in 1995 the West Bank Land Registration Authority under the Oslo Accords[16] came to be transferred to the Palestinian Authority, it had none of the lands dedicated to Jewish settlements. The second was to divide unequally the resources of the West Bank between Palestinians and Israeli settlers.

Other administrative changes also proceeded on similar lines. These included changes in land use planning and an Israeli-developed master plan for West Bank roads. Before the first agreement was signed with the PLO in September 1993, Israel had completed and obtained approval for outline plans for some 280 Palestinian towns and villages in the West Bank. Most of these consisted of plans crudely drawn by felt-tip markers on aerial photographs. The most outstanding feature of these crudely prepared plans was the boundary. Rather than define the area for which planning policies are to be prepared, the boundary identified the zone within which all urban development was to be confined. Meanwhile, outline plans for the Jewish settlements were made, followed by detailed plans which took fully into consideration present and future needs for the development of these Jewish areas. In this way development of Palestinian areas was restricted, Arab villages were prevented from forming larger units with other Palestinian settlements, while Jewish settlement blocs were encouraged. Through the implementation of Road Plan number 50 prepared in 1984, these were connected to each other and to Israeli centers bypassing Palestinian towns and villages. All these schemes were given statutory effect and became in fact part of the law of the land well before the first Oslo Accord was signed. It was these highly discriminatory and segregated town planning schemes concealed under the cloak of law which determined the unequal basis for the territorial division of the land between the Palestinian Authority and the Jewish settlements that the agreement signed between Israel and the PLO in Oslo ended up confirming.

According to the post-Oslo implementation legislation passed by the Israeli Commander of the West Bank, the Palestinian Authority established by the Declaration of Principles in 1993 became the successor of the Civilian Administration. Article 4 of Israeli Military Proclamation number 7, dated 23 November 1995, declared that "The Commander of the Israeli Army in the Area and the Head of the Civilian Administration shall transfer to the Council [the Palestinian Authority] and its agencies, powers and responsibilities exercised by them or their delegates including legislative, judicial and executive powers" as specified in the Interim Agreement.[17] Thus from the point of view of the Israeli authorities, Israel was the source of the powers enjoyed by the Palestinian Authority and of all residual powers not transferred. Following the establishment of the Palestinian Authority not only was the military government retained but the Israeli Civilian Administration created in 1981 was also not dissolved. It continues, to this day, to function in the Occupied Territories.

Prior to the Oslo Accords the role of legal scholars and human rights activists was to expose and challenge such schemes and indicate how they violated the provisions of local and international law applicable to occupation. They did so in the hope that such schemes would be stopped. It was in this spirit that I worked on my book, *Occupier's Law*, in 1985. As regards international law there were clear frameworks against which to assess Israeli action. The Hague Regulations imposed the duty on the occupying forces to take all the measures necessary to restore and ensure public order and safety.[18] The Fourth Geneva Convention prohibits the occupying power from transferring its own people to the occupied territories.[19] International humanitarian law provided recognized standards to use for developing positions regarding the rights and wrongs of the Israeli actions in the Occupied Territories. There was a common language between those activists inside and outside the Territories who worked on human rights issues. All this changed after the signing of the Oslo Accords.

As a consequence of the criticism by Said and others regarding the failure of the PLO negotiators to avail themselves of the services of legal advisors in the course of the negotiations in Oslo of the Declaration of Principles (DOP) of 1993,[20] the PLO invited legal advisors to assist in the negotiations of the Interim Agreement of 1995.[21] However, by then the Israeli framework for future negotiations as enunciated in the DOP had been confirmed. All future negotiations were to be confined to it. Much as Palestinian legal experts in the negotiations leading to the Interim Agreement of 1995 tried, for example, to expand the definition of powers and responsibility in the sphere of land registration that were to be transferred from the military government and its Civil Administration to the Palestinian Authority, they failed to extend that power beyond the territories specified in the DOP.[22]

The obvious question which troubled Edward Said was how it was possible for the PLO not to have known what Israel was preparing, given the availability of all this literature, and why they went to the negotiations unprepared. I will try to answer this below.

On 15 November 1988, at the historic meeting in Algiers, the Palestinian National Council declared a Palestinian state in the 1967 Occupied Territories. The Council also recognized "the necessity of convening the effective international conference on the issue of the Middle East and its core, the question of Palestine." Among the main aims of this conference was the achievement of "the annulment of all measures of annexation and appropriation and the removal of settlements established by Israel in the Palestinian and Arab territories since 1967."[23] But this resolution was not followed by any concrete plan or strategy as to how the PLO was going to achieve these aims given the nature of the changes Israel had implemented. Only three years after this important Council meeting, the PLO accepted the Letter of Invitation to the International Peace Conference in Madrid.[24] In this letter the aim of the conference was expressed in the following terms: "With respect to negotiations between Israel and the Palestinians . . . negotiations will be conducted in phases, beginning with the talks on interim self-government arrangements."

Clearly "talks on interim self-government arrangements" would avoid negotiations on "the annulment of all measures of annexation and appropriation and the removal of settlements" which were formulated as the main aim of the international conference at the PLO National Council meeting in 1988. So how was the PLO to achieve this aim through the limited scope of these terms? And were they serious about trying? It appeared that they weren't. In 1993 they signed the Declaration of Principles (DOP) that defined the jurisdiction of the Palestinian Authority as including the West Bank and the Gaza Strip, excluding a number of important matters among which were the Jewish settlements.

It was not as though the PLO was ignorant of the prevalence of Jewish settlements. What they seem to have failed to appreciate was the broader meaning of this development for the life of the rest of the territory. The notion that the settlements were enclaves within the rest of the Palestinian areas did not describe the reality. Rather, on the contrary, the Palestinian towns and villages had become enclaves within the larger areas reserved for the Jewish settlements. The Palestinian areas were restricted in their right to expand while maximum room for future expansion was reserved for the settlements. This inability to grasp the true nature of the developments Israel imposed on the Occupied Territories proved detrimental to the success of the negotiations between Israel and the PLO and the possibility that they would lead to a genuine peace and an end to the conflict between Israel and Palestine.

The justification offered by the PLO for accepting the DOP was that it was but the first step in the long march towards gaining political recognition for the organization, after which everything would be possible. But the DOP was a framework agreement drawn up mainly by Israel in fulfillment of its strategic objectives of preserving most of the territories occupied in 1967 and eventually annexing them to Israel. As has already been shown it was this framework which determined all future negotiations between the two sides. The negotiation process was launched by the "Letter of Invitation" to the Madrid Peace Conference. It was this document that initially set the limited agenda determining the scope of all future negotiations and in a profound sense doomed the prospects for a real peace by keeping out of the scope of the negotiations Israeli settlements established in the Occupied Territories. And yet despite its paramount significance little attention has been given in the vast literature that has appeared on the Israeli–Palestinian negotiations to the process of negotiating this important document.

In 1993 the PLO was feeling more vulnerable than at any other time in its history. There were two rivals, actual and perceived: the first was the Islamic resistance movement, *Harakat al Muqawama al-Islamiya*, the acronym of which is Hamas, an organization which the Israeli occupation originally encouraged in pursuit of the classic colonial tactic of creating a rival organization to the dominant resistance organization, the PLO.[25] Hamas emerged as a political wing of the Moslem Brothers dedicated to resisting the Israeli occupation. Prior to the emergence of Hamas the Brotherhood took the position that the liberation of Palestine was to be considered only after liberating the people socially, or only after returning them to the "right path" of Islam. Hamas differed fundamentally with the PLO, which was a national liberation movement that in 1988 had adopted the two-state solution. Hamas was not a member of the Palestine National Council, and was in principle against any compromise solution leading to the partitioning of Palestine. The second perceived rival to the PLO was the internal leadership headed by such figures as Faisal Husseini in the West Bank and Haidar Abdul Shafi in the Gaza Strip. In 1991, prior to the issuance of the Letter of Invitation to the Madrid Peace Conference, pressure was being exerted against the PLO. Available funds were becoming more scarce. They were being told that their lease in Tunis – to which they had relocated after their forced eviction from Lebanon in 1982 – was running out. They feared that unless they went to negotiations on whatever terms were being offered and made the concessions being asked of them, they would lose their standing as the sole representatives of the Palestinian people. Gaining the recognition of Israel and hence the US was the most important objective for which they were prepared to pay a heavy price. It was believed that this would give them a new lease on life. In his book *From Oslo to Jerusalem*,[26] Abu Alaa (Ahmed Qurie) writes: "It appears to be a characteristic of national liberation movements to regard the recognition by their enemy as a great achievement."

The desire by the Palestinian leaders in Tunis to hold on to power was so fundamental that they seemed to expend little time and show little interest in devising a strategy to fulfill the aims laid out in the 1988 resolutions concerning annulling settlements through these negotiations. I can say this out of personal experience because I was one of those who offered a legal strategy for tackling the issue of the illegal Jewish settlements when I acted as legal advisor to the negotiations in Washington, but the plan I presented was not even discussed in Tunis.[27] And I was not the only voice. Most of the members of the Palestinian Delegation to the Washington talks saw the refusal of Israel to suspend all settlement activities as a deal breaker. The respected head of the delegation, Dr Haidar Abdul Shafi, refused to attend the signing ceremony in Washington of the Declaration of Principles because it lacked such an undertaking by Israel.

It could be said that on the face of it the Oslo negotiations were not bound by the terms of reference that shackled the negotiations in Washington. But there are no grounds to make this assertion.[28] The negotiations there began from the same point that the Washington talks had started from, namely the restrictive terms which the PLO seemed to voluntarily accept. Being so anxious to win recognition they did not see themselves in a position to challenge the terms. Whereas in Washington they stalled on the issue of cessation of settlements, this was not a condition the PLO wanted to adhere to as long as they gained recognition. What transpired were negotiations on terms and according to an agenda determined by Israel. The leadership which Israel had been seeking to take over the limited powers of the civilian affairs of the Palestinian inhabitants of the Occupied Territories as defined in the Israeli Civilian Administration established in 1981 had finally been identified. In 1996 an elected Palestinian Authority took over those limited powers enumerated in the Interim Agreement and transferred by Israeli Military Proclamation number 7. But this did not mean that the military government or its Civilian Administration ceased their activities. They continued to exercise a free hand over some aspects of the life of Palestinians in the West Bank and to acquire and administer Palestinian land as a sovereign, using it to establish and expand Jewish settlements that to all practical purposes have been annexed to Israel.

Once the PLO succumbed to the Israeli scheme by signing the Declaration of Principles, everything changed. The structure that had determined the contours of the struggle in the past and which provided the common language between all the opponents of the Israeli occupation inside and outside of the Occupied Territories was destroyed. The life of Palestinians on their land in 2007, 14 years after the Oslo agreements, continues to be hostage to the Israeli annexation schemes. The US advocates easing a few barriers out of the 500 that now restrict the free movement of the Palestinians between the various ghettoes in which they have become confined, and avoids any talk about removing Jewish settlements or restricting their growth over Palestinian land.[29]

I remember Edward Said visiting us in Washington in 1992 when the negotiations were taking place and wondering what he could do to help. Nothing. A new phase had begun when the politicians were preparing to make deals with the occupier and were suspicious of anyone who could expose the paucity of what they were planning to accept. The same process continues at the time of writing.

A common response to criticisms of the Oslo deal is that it was dictated by the balance of power that existed at the time it was signed. The question that needs to be asked is if the PLO was unable to achieve the minimum that would place the Palestinians on the road to eventual phased recognition of their basic rights why did it need to conclude the negotiations with an agreement with Israel at any price? In 2000, the Israeli Prime Minister Ehud Barak left the Camp David talks in the US without agreement and was able to make political capital out of what he called the refusal of the Palestinians to accept his "generous offer." Surely Yasser Arafat could have mobilized Palestinian and non-Palestinian intellectuals and activists around the globe committed to Palestinian rights and to an end of the Israeli occupation to show the world how Israel was only proposing to end the conflict, not by ending its long-term occupation, but by forcing the Palestinians to accept an apartheid system? Instead, by going into secret negotiations, the leadership deprived the Palestinian cause of its main asset, the pressure of public opinion. Perhaps the explanation for this strange behavior can be found in the vulnerable state the PLO was in at the time. Unfavorable as the Oslo deal was for Palestine, it saved the PLO and sustained it for a number of years until the main faction, Fatah, was defeated in the 2005 elections for the Legislative Council of the Palestinian Authority held in the Palestinian Territories, with Hamas winning an overwhelming victory.

What Now?

The time of the Oslo Accords was an opportunity which Israel missed for resolving the conflict on the basis of a division of the land into two states. The Palestinians at that point had been waging their first Intifada which many had called the Palestinian War of Independence. Hamas, which rejected the two-state solution, did not yet have the power it enjoys today. The majority of those living in the Occupied Territories and many of those outside were willing to accept a resolution of the territorial conflict with Israel based on a partition of the land along the 1967 lines, with East Jerusalem as the capital of a Palestinian state established alongside Israel. Arafat had enough standing and power among the Palestinians to have been capable of convincing his people to accept such a historic compromise with Israel. But Israel lost this opportunity. It proved to be more interested in territory than peace and used the post-Oslo period to establish more Jewish settlements than at any time previously. Palestinians in the West Bank can now only access less than one-third of their land.

In 1979 Israeli Prime Minister Menahem Begin announced that he wanted to create a situation where the prospect of withdrawing from the Jewish settlements in the Occupied Territories would become politically impossible. Presently we have reached that stage. Both politically and geographically we are forced to deal with a Greater Israel that includes the Israel of the pre-1967 borders and the occupied West Bank in which a substantial Palestinian population is living subject to discrimination and denied the right to self-determination. Whatever solution is proposed would simply have to take all this into consideration. The Palestinians call the ethnic cleansing Israel was guilty of in 1948 their Nakba. My experience of life in the occupied West Bank leads me to believe that Israel has not stopped trying to drive the Palestinians out of their land through various practices and administrative maneuvers. The Palestinian Nakba is ongoing, as Israel implements policies in the territories it occupies that aim at making the life of Palestinians on their land so intolerable as to force them to leave.

The voices of those such as Hamas who fundamentally reject the Oslo Accords (even when they have taken office in a Palestinian Authority that came about as a result of this agreement), and who argue that the only way to bring about real change is through continuing the armed struggle, are now the most prominent in the anti-Oslo camp. Less vocal are those who believe in civil disobedience as a way to bring about change. Yet this is a growing camp. Within it are Palestinians and Israelis who have been waging a persistent battle against the partition wall Israel is erecting mostly in the West Bank on the Palestinian side of the border, and a growing movement towards divestment, sanctions, and boycotts as a means of non-violent resistance. What is tragically missing here though, is the resumption of a legal strategy to challenge Israeli maneuvers used throughout the occupation to acquire Palestinian land for the exclusive use of Jewish settlements, contrary to the Geneva Convention as has been mentioned above. Many diplomatic initiatives for the resolution of the conflict accept Israeli premises regarding the land on which the settlements now stand and do not challenge their legality, bargaining on the percentage of the occupied West Bank that can be turned over to the Palestinians. The legal strategists and human rights activists among the Palestinians have not succeeded in making their voice heard on such fundamental issues as the land acquired illegally by Israel or in influencing the political agenda through supplying politicians with legal arguments to support political positions. Even when the PLO obtained a favorable advisory opinion from the International Court of Justice at the Hague in the case against the wall, the politicians were utterly unsuccessful in making effective use of the outcome.

The point has often been made that failure to resolve the conflict between Israel and Palestine renders the whole region volatile and endangers world peace. But just as detrimental to universal peace and security is the negative example this conflict provides of the effectiveness of international law as a means for resolving disputes. No other conflict in human history has been more widely reported and none provides a better case of blatant violations of international law principles, yet for all that it has so far been brute military and political power that has proven the only real arbiter in this bitter conflict.

Notes

1 Raja Shehadeh, *Occupier's Law: Israel and the West Bank*, Washington DC: Institute of Palestine Studies, 1985, 1988.

2 Raja Shehadeh, *From Occupation to Interim Accords: Israel and the Palestinian Territories*, London, The Hague, Boston: Kluwer Law International, 1997, p. 2.

3 Ahmed Qurie ("Abu Alaa"), *From Oslo to Jerusalem: The Palestinian Story of the Secret Negotiations*, London: I.B. Tauris, 2006, pp. 156–7.

4 Article A.1.(a) of the Camp David Accords, a Framework for Peace in the Middle East Agreed at Camp David, signed between Israel and Egypt in Washington DC, 17 September 1978.

5 US–Soviet Letter of Invitation to the Peace Talks in Madrid, 18 October 1991.

6 Prime Minister Begin's autonomy proposals quoted in Meron Benvenisti, "The West Bank Data Base Project: A Survey of Israel's Policies," Washington and London: American Enterprise Institute for Public Policy Research, 1984, p. 39.

7 For a discussion of the legal mechanisms by which this was achieved see Shehadeh, *Occupier's Law*, pp. 65–8.

8 In the West Bank the Civil Administration was established by Military Order 947; for the Gaza Strip by Military Order 725.

9 For an analysis of this order see Jonathan Kuttab and Raja Shehadeh, *Civilian Administration in the Occupied West Bank, Analysis of Israeli Military Government Order No. 947*, Law in the Service of Man, West Bank Affiliate of the International Commission of Jurists, 1982.

10 An October 2006 report by Peace Now's Settlement Watch project ('Breaking the Law in the West Bank – One Violation leads to Another, Israeli Settlement Building on Private Palestinian Property," research and writing by Dror Etkes and Hagit Ofran, published at www.peacenow.org.il) has found that approximately 40 percent of Jewish settlements are built on land which even the Israeli military government acknowledges is private Palestinian land (p. 20). According to the report, the two largest settlements, Ma'ale Adumim and Ariel, are built on 86.4 percent and 35.1 percent of Palestinian private land respectively (pp. 112 and 50). Also reported by Yair Sheleg in "Study: 40 percent of settlements were built on Palestinian land," *Ha'aretz*, 21 November 2006.

11 Settlement of Disputes Over Land and Water Law No. 40, 1952, *Jordanian Official Gazette* 1113, 16 June 1952.

12 From a letter addressed to the law office of the author by the legal advisor of the area commander, dated 27 December 1983. The letter was published in Shehadeh, *From Occupation to Interim Accords*, pp. 255–6.

13 Circular from the Israeli Civil Administration Office in Charge of Land Department, Ramallah, No. 2-529 dated 14 November 1979. Full text is published in ibid., p. 257.

14 Dated 596, 17 December 1974.

15 Reported in an article by Akiva Eldar, "The Demolition Fast Track," *Ha'aretz*, 7 July 2007.

16 This took place by virtue of Article 22 of Annex III, Protocol Concerning Civil Affairs, of the Israeli–Palestinian Interim Agreement on the West Bank and the Gaza Strip between Israel and the PLO signed on 28 September 1995.

17 The full text of this order is published in Shehadeh, *From Occupation to Interim Accords*, pp. 273–7.

18 Article 43 of the Hague Regulations of 1907 annexed to Hague Convention IV on the Laws and Customs of War on Land. The article continues: "while respecting, unless absolutely prevented, the laws in force in the country."

19 The Fourth Geneva Convention Relative to the Protection of Civilian Persons in Time of War, Article 46.

20 Both Mahmoud Abbas in his book *El Tarik La Oslo* (Beirut: Sharikat El Matbo'at, 1994; English edition: *Through Secret Channels: The Road to Oslo*, Reading: Garnet Publishing, 1995) and Ahmed Qurie in *From Oslo to Jerusalem* justify the failure to use legal advisors on grounds of preserving secrecy in the negotiations. Abbas claims (p. 242) that "we did not initial the declaration of Principles on 20 August 1993 except after it was reviewed by the legal advisor Taher Shash who was called to Oslo for this purpose." In his book *The Confrontation and Peace in the Middle East: The Road to Gaza and Jericho* (Cairo: Dar Shurouk, 1995, in Arabic), Taher Shash, an Egyptian diplomat/lawyer who had been involved in the Camp David negotiations of 1978, writes,

> I was met [upon arrival in Oslo] by Abu Alaa (Ahmed Qurie) and Hassan Asfour very warmly and within minutes they put before me papers which contained a project for a Declaration of Principles. Hassan Asfour said that I had to review the project from a legal aspect and in terms of its drafting, explaining that I only had very little time to finish this work. I put the documents before me and began to write down my observations. More than once both Abu Alaa and Hassan Asfour came over to see me. It appeared that Asfour did not expect that my study of the project would require as much time as it was taking. I mentioned to them a number of observations that I had already noted but I noticed that the two were tied up by a previously set appointment which was about to be due. I then realized that my arrival to Oslo was one day too late and that there was nothing more for me to do but to make a quick reading of the project which was now in its final form. There was no possibility of making any amendments to it. After I finished reading the papers, I said that the project in light of the Washington negotiations can be considered a good project and there is nothing wrong in its drafting. We then moved to the reception room and it was minutes before Joel Singer, the Israeli legal advisor, arrived and shook my hands warmly . . . everyone was getting ready to dress up for the ceremony of initialing the Declaration of Principles (pp. 268–9).

21 Israeli–Palestinian Interim Agreement on the West Bank and the Gaza Strip, signed in Washington DC on 28 September 1995.

22 Article 22 of Annex III, Protocol Concerning Civil Affairs, of the Israeli–Palestinian Interim Agreement on the West Bank and the Gaza Strip, Washington, 28 September 1995 states that "powers and responsibility in the sphere of Land Registration in the West Bank and the Gaza Strip will be transferred from the military government and its Civil Administration to the Palestinian side. This sphere includes, *inter alia*, registration in the land registry of real estate transactions, first registrations of land, registration of courts" decision, registration of parcellations pursuant to the Towns, Villages and Buildings Planning law, No. 79, of 1966, and the administration of land registry offices and processes." On the face of it this formulation is clearly that

of legal practitioners who know the land law in force in the Occupied Territories. However, when read with other provisions of the DOP and Interim Agreement that restrict the territorial jurisdiction of the Palestinian Authority, this article fails to achieve its aim, which is to expand the jurisdiction of the PA over the land.

23 For the text of this resolution see *Journal of Palestine Studies*, Vol. XVIII, No. 2, Winter 1989, pp. 216–23.

24 US–Soviet Letter of Invitation to the Peace Talks in Madrid, 18 October 1991.

25 Interview with Avner Cohen in an article by Almog Boker in *Ha'aretz* on 22 June 2007. See Also Zvi Bar'el, "Lessons from Palestine," in *Ha'aretz* of the same date. The extent of Israeli support is contested.

26 Qurie, *From Oslo to Jerusalem*, p. 161.

27 'Proposed strategy for the Israeli–Palestinian peace talks," submitted by the author to Mr Yasser Arafat on 2 August 1992, is published in *From Occupation to Interim Accords*, pp. 267–72.

28 This was also the opinion of Hilde Henriksen Waage, in "Norway's Role in the Middle East Peace Talks: Between a Strong State and a Weak Belligerent," *Journal of Palestine Studies*, Vol. XXXIV, No. 4, Summer 2005, p. 9.

29 The result of one such effort by the US led, on 12 January 2007, to the publication by the government of Israel's Office for Coordination of Government Activities in the Territories of the briefing entitled "Key Measures for Easing the Daily Lives of the Palestinian Population." Like many similar promises, none of the measures described there were implemented.

9

The Role of Palestinian Intellectuals in the Collective Struggle for Palestinian Freedom

Karma Nabulsi

We have been celebrating the vast contribution Edward Said made in so many fields – in literary scholarship and the arts, and above all in public life as an engaged and brilliant intellectual. In these assessments one may capture fragments of that charismatic, restless, resisting *persona* one remembers so well in person, imbued with a remarkable presence, fastidious ethics, an immediacy and warmth, and a poetic sensibility to the essential commonality of human experience. Yet the sheer depth and quality of the work Said produced, and also perhaps the methodological vocabulary with which it is now studied and analyzed, has created near impenetrable thickets of professional formality in language and form, and systemic barriers of distance and height.

All of which tend to isolate from view that very precise, very precious context that served as a great source of passion and inspiration in all of these realms: the densely lived reality of the Palestinian struggle for justice. It was that precious collective experience, collective will, collective integrity, and imposing force gifted to him by his people that I would like to reintroduce here in this essay. As a first attempt to acknowledge the contributions of this extraordinary man to the Palestinian struggle, a crucial task, it seems to me, is to restore to his legacy some of that specific and timeless grandeur that was such an intrinsic part of him, and so little mentioned nowadays. Rather than touching upon one or several aspects of Edward Said's vital contribution to us in its many forms, I will explore here instead what the Palestinian people gave to Said.

During the period I knew Edward Said best, I was a young Palestinian representative whom he supported in a number of ways, employing a constant barrage of books, arguments, and encouragement. In that period, it was not Edward Said the intellectual, the academic, the musician, the remarkable individual (although one was aware he was all those things) who was among us; rather it was Edward Said the collective person: the activist among a huge circle of other activists, many of whom were also intellectuals. In that era he was surrounded, imbued, and effortlessly buoyed up – along with the rest of us – by the collective character and protean dynamism of that dazzling liberation movement we were all part of, and to which we had devoted ourselves. For Edward Said, as for most of us, the notion of universal humanism; the appreciation of the hard graft of struggle for liberation (rather than simply liberty or even independence); the determination to resist and never, ever give up; above all the raging, constant blowtorch of incandescent rage at the horrifying injustices inflicted every day on our people and society; and finally, the persistent quest for justice as the transcendent and binding glue that connected our people with other struggling peoples – all these were ideas that found their living articulation in the Palestinian liberation movement and found their way into the various kinds of work we all did.

Said wrote that Palestine meant many things for him; it was a homeland, a source of memory and a locus of both agony and hope. "Palestine is exile, dispossession, the inaccurate memories of one place slipping into vague memories of another."[1] But Said clearly understood – as did all of us in that common struggle – that Palestine had even a greater meaning as "an act of sustained popular will."[2] Preserving that clear will for liberation, persevering in its assertion, was (and continues to be) the essence of the commitment to our cause today.

Always sensible, even in those earlier days, to the failings and weaknesses of those who led our struggle, Said's writing on Palestine in the last ten years was increasingly haunted by the terrible fragmentation of the movement itself, and the accompanying inability of its people to resist. It signaled an awareness of a previous time when Palestinians had tried to restore themselves to some form of collective being and institutional framework, following the intense destruction and dispersal of 1948.

Less than two decades after the Nakba, the Palestinian body-politic was remolding itself; tens of thousands of young women and men heading the call for liberation from all over the Arab world where we had been dispersed by force. How can one even begin to recapture the dynamism of the time? Popular armies, guerrilla movements, unions, and associations were being formed. Hospitals, factories, kindergartens, a vast educative scout movement for youth, art galleries, and research centers were established in refugee camps and capital cities of the Middle East. Poems, novellas, and pamphlets were written, encyclopedias published, radio stations and newspapers founded, lectures were given and liberation films made, all Palestinian, and much of it from exile. Young Palestinians poured into Lebanon from the Gulf and the Arab world after 1970, and a flourishing audacity that nearly captured a collective will in action was forged. The force, the beauty, the promise of this collectivity had a lasting impact upon Said as it did on all Palestinians of his generation. Everyone had their place – the freedom fighter in Al Karameh, the worker in the Gulf, the New York intellectual; all joined in a common project, having similar thoughts and dreams, similar goals, speaking the universal language of liberty; they were all part of the Palestinian revolution.

Comparing Fanon's *The Wretched of the Earth* with Foucault's *Madness and Civilization*, Said noted the following:

> Fanon's text – the more significant of the two in my opinion – came out of an ongoing political struggle, the Algerian revolution. It is important that Fanon's book was the result of a collective struggle, as opposed to Foucault's work, which evolved out of a different tradition, that of the individual scholar-researcher acquiring a reputation for learning, brilliance, and so on.[3]

Edward Said's own early scholarly work was highly theoretical, but it became more concretized and universalized as he located himself as part of the Palestinian struggle. Most Palestinians were intrinsically and profoundly informed, in our various works, by the universality that was inherent to the Palestinian struggle, and Said was no exception. Yet what he did with it, the particular form it took under his hand, and the manner he connected it to both literature and culture in the West, was astonishing, formidable, and quite unique.

That universality was expressed in two realms, one historical and the other moral. Concerning the first, one need only evoke the huge number of liberation struggles the Palestinian movement interacted with, worked closely with, inspired, and in turn was inspired by. From 1917 onwards, Palestinians possess a rich international tradition of both practice and thought of international liberation. All Arab liberation movements without exception drew inspiration from the Palestinian cause, as well as practical, intellectual, and political frameworks, their outcomes also affecting its course. And more broadly Palestinians had a central place and role across the tri-continental world, their cause advocated by generations of progressive and anti-colonial leaders in the twentieth century, from Mahatma Gandhi to Nelson Mandela. Said wrote:

Some day the history of exchange and support between the PLO and such groups as the African National Congress (ANC), the South West Africa People's Organisation (SWAPO), the Sandinistas, as well as the anti-Shah revolutionary Iranian groups will describe an extraordinary chapter in the twentieth-century struggle against various forms of tyranny and injustice.[4]

Moreover, these struggles shared a moral universe that derived its commanding force from the actual experience of oppressed people, from their resistance and the nature that it took, in particular from the justice of their cause. In a sense, all of the principles, all of the moral lessons of the twentieth century, were distilled into the cause of Palestine. The experience of the Palestinian struggle gave Edward Said and countless others a grounding in the virtues of universalist humanism and a liberationist sensibility that pertained to a way of existing in the world, of connecting to it. That sensibility pervades his work from the 1970s onwards and is seen throughout books such as *Culture and Imperialism*. If Said's academic contribution can be seen as consisting (among other things) in providing a general theory of colonialism (as advanced by a prominent postcolonial critic),[5] without question his experience of the Palestinian struggle was the foundation for this work.

Palestine's place in Said's work is most tellingly portrayed in *After the Last Sky*, a powerful testimony of the aesthetics of Palestinian existence. To read it is to engage in a *sui generis* exercise in empathy. The reader is utterly persuaded, by Said's lyrical and mesmerizing text, to internalize the experience of Palestinian-ness: to attempt, if only for a moment, to think and feel from within it, without once fixing either a voyeuristic or distorted gaze on that existence. The prose does not refer to, or draw from, opinion pieces by commentators or the enormous "expert" literature on Palestine. Its source is, quite simply, the Palestinian people themselves – their images, their experiences, their stories, magically evoked in this book by the Swiss photographer Jean Mohr. Its extraordinary images were taken across Palestine and the *shatat*; they reflect our world; that is, the interstices between ourselves, our homeland, and among each other at given moments in time and space.

Said described this universe precisely and perfectly as "a secular world of fatigue and miraculously renewed energies."[6] The most extraordinary feature of that world was the sense of undying, absolute, and steadfast collectivity. That sense was not only evident in the shared Palestinian interiors Said eloquently described, but above all (and up until the signing of Oslo) it was embodied in the ongoing Palestinian processes of vibrant deliberation taking place in the representative institutions that Palestinians had fought so hard to create. In these representative spaces, general will was often (but not always) exercised, and the collective rights to self-determination and individual right of return were inseparably intertwined and united. In sum, our people's voice was both heard and represented.[7]

The Palestinian voice as a collective deliberating political will was almost completely lost with the advent of post-Oslo interim arrangements. Under huge international pressure, people became fragmented into disparate and competing sets of "interest groups" – town/village/camp, West Bank/Gaza, refugee/non-refugee, inside Palestine/outside Palestine.[8] The inseparable link between the two essential Palestinian principles, self-determination and return, was dramatically and dangerously severed. The Palestinian refugees became sidelined, and their rights made the subject of "final status" negotiations which have, some 15 years later, yet to take place. The Palestinian Legislative Council (PLC) elections in the West Bank and Gaza, by their institutional design, excluded Palestinian refugees from them, and no elections were held for our highest representative institution, the Palestinian National Council (PNC), a body that represents our people wherever they may be, both under occupation and in exile. The Oslo period not only witnessed an intensification of the Israeli colonial project, it was also a continuation of an ongoing assault against Palestinian representation and civic and political life whose destructive scope was profoundly experienced, not least since the 1982 Israeli invasion of Lebanon and siege of Beirut, and the total destruction of Palestinian social and political infrastructures.

Oslo filled Said, along with many other Palestinians (whether ordinary cadres and simple soldiers, who had devoted a life heavy with sacrifice, or prominent intellectuals), with rage. As the 1990s continued – each year weighed down with the acceleration of the practices of occupation, in particular the settlements policy and marginalization of core Palestinian aspirations – this despair was reflected in the collective national discourse. The common institutions that had once connected intellectuals to the movement and to the trajectory of the Palestinian cause were now lost, and the fragmentation of our people was now an obvious daily reality.

That reality was especially felt by Palestinian refugees. Channels of communication with the national representative now barely existed. Across the world and in various host countries, Palestinian conditions were unknown, refugee numbers unaccounted for, their presence ignored. Above all, there was no longer any national platform for them to speak from, and to make their voices heard. Meanwhile, the refugees were being *spoken for:* behind closed doors, deals were discussed in their name and they were turned into *objects* of countless projects and studies. The evident reality of the

Palestinian refugees being the key to any lasting and just solution was veiled by a discourse that presented their very rights as an obstacle to peace.

The task became obvious: to attempt to reinstate that voice. It was in this context, and from this analysis, that the Civitas project was initiated.[9] The quite simple concept underpinning it was to restore the primacy of our people's voice as the sovereign decision-making body, to be implemented through organizing public civic meetings in as many Palestinian refugee communities as possible, and providing a platform for Palestinian refugees to exercise their right to participation and to express their civic, political, and other critical needs. It gave members of refugee and exile communities an opportunity to define these needs for themselves, articulate their own platform, define the path ahead – most importantly, in their own words.

In the next few pages, I describe the process through which Civitas unfolded, using as much as possible the words of the organizers and participants themselves. Through this discussion I hope to draw attention to two things. First, that even in a time of fragmentation, there is a collective context to the opinions and experiences of Palestinian intellectuals – indeed I would suggest that the significance of a liberationist intellectual's work lies in the degree to which it reflects the aspirations and concrete concerns of the sort expressed in the collective endeavor described below. Second, by emphasizing something that transcends the limitations of the individual intellectual, the engine of civic process, one can find the real context to understand that work and its significance. Civitas is a robust example of a process which, initiated by thousands of Palestinian refugees, recovers something that was greatly missed by increasingly isolated Palestinian intellectuals of the last 15 years, in that it restores – for a transitory and transcendent moment – the deliberative and mobilizing tradition of the Palestinian cause which provided such a profound intellectual resource for Edward Said in his various writings. Civitas illustrated something that Said and other Palestinian intellectuals understood very well: that the Palestinian cause "concern[s] a community, not just individuals sitting on a chair somewhere saying, 'Well, this is what should happen.'"[10] The collective enterprise demonstrates that at the heart of that struggle for liberty and liberation lie the practices of mobilization, participation, civic deliberation, and the collective liberationist spirit that binds us together, still.

Civic Mobilization

Civitas was based upon the principle that Palestinian refugees are an indivisible part of the Palestinian body politic, and that the way forward for Palestinians was to create unity of purpose through constant, repeated creations of inclusive public space. This would reclaim, as an initial step, the democratic and participatory mechanisms that had been forcibly denied us by the current international arrangements, and was a return to part of Palestine's long tradition of associational and democratic life throughout its political history.

Mapping the communities was the first set of challenges faced. Creating public space, especially in such a fractured reality as ours, was a highly complex process. Hurdles set by government officials and the security services of various host countries, factional politics, stratifying practices, and logistical difficulties were some of the major constraints that had to be addressed.

The most exceptional aspect of the mobilization process was the creative and dynamic efforts of grassroots activists and community leaders in the face of various constraints imposed on preparing and holding the public meetings. The innovative methods undertaken by various refugee communities to overcome the enormous obstacles to political activism, particularly for Palestinians in the Arab world, highlighted a truly unique contribution Palestinians have made, and will continue to make, as a model of civic participation and organization anywhere in the world. In Iraq, for example, the security situation was a major constraint:

> In Iraq, the only obstacle is the security situation that requires us to move in secret or cancel one or two of the meetings, or hold it in one of the brother's houses. For example, a meeting was supposed to be held in New Baghdad, but as a result of the security situation it was canceled.[11]

A different type of logistical difficulty was encountered in Sweden, where a huge refugee community of more than 40,000 Palestinians, mainly from the Lebanon refugee camps, had been living since the mid 1980s, scattered in towns across the length of the country. A local organizer described the process of arranging the meetings, and the difficulties encountered, as follows:

> Some people appeared at almost every meeting ever since the project began. Initial meetings were held with the project director with the presence of the most active people. More information and clarification were provided until we received some written statements. This project created a discussion and a dialogue between people. We faced some obstacles toward acceptance of the project, perhaps logistical ones, i.e. obstacles that have to do with geography and nature of the country, the long distance between cities, and coordinating the meetings and dates.[12]

★   ★   ★

In addition to the constraints that would necessarily affect an unprecedented exercise such as this, there was a need to consider the procedural issues that would arise during the public meetings. These included the role and method of facilitation, maximizing inclusivity, and ensuring that the people themselves developed the questions around which public sessions could be organized. Accordingly, pilot meetings were held in Jordan and Lebanon at the inception of the work. Hundreds of people participated in these meetings, including workers and the unemployed, youth and the elderly, women's associations, political party cadres and independents, as well as service committee members, unionists, and refugee activists.

The early sessions anticipated many of the themes that were later expressed by Palestinian refugees across the world in the final-stage meetings, and began identifying the main issues people sought to raise and debate: above all it demonstrated the intrinsic connection between civil, economic, political, and social spheres, and that the complex realities of exile and dispossession meant all of these realms had serious dysfunctions. For example, the ability to obtain identity papers in a country was connected to the right to go to school, have a job, even get buried, and not just to the ability to travel, which was especially crucial for Palestinians as they lived with the devastating separation of families between borders. All of these terrible realities were combined with the political constants of Palestinian self-determination and return, so that these were pervaded with an urgency and immediate reality that was tangible and overpowering.

One of the constant issues raised was the fracture between inside and outside that occurred after the core elite of the PLO's political institutions resettled in Gaza under the terms of the Oslo Accords of 1993. As a refugee in Jordan explained:

> The absence of the institution is the cause of the problem. There is no Palestinian institution that works for me as a human being, as a Palestinian citizen. I do exist, and the germ exists inside me – and either I water it to let it grow, or I forget it and it will wilt. Before the peace treaties, Palestinian political parties were more effective, and we had a voice: we worked properly! We made our voice heard to the entire world. But the world now only hears the voice of the Palestinian president, and his prime minister. As a citizen, I no longer have a voice. His voice is enough. But before the peace process my voice was heard. If this peace will silence me then I don't want it![13]

Another issue discussed with great persistence and anxiety was the marginalization of the refugees in the negotiations process and in the structure of Palestinian representation:

I thank the moderator for holding this meeting, which is the first meeting of its kind as far as I know, and which should have been held long ago, because we, the camp's residents, know best how to talk about the Palestinian cause, and about our problems and tragedies. But unfortunately, our brothers who live in the cities or the fancy neighborhoods don't want us, and they even dislike the camps" residents lest they disagree with them on what they suggest . . . Among the important points we should discuss is the refugee issue and their return, which is something we should preserve. In Al-Baqa'a camp, about 100 or 150 thousand Palestinian refugees live in an area of one kilometer to two kilometers. I know people who live in small houses built with wood and zinc, you would cry if you saw them. What else shall I describe? What I am saying is that my friends and I loudly reject that someone would negotiate in our names. We are not against negotiations, but we won't allow anyone who lives in a villa and whose wife bathes in cologne while I can't get clean water for my children, to negotiate in the name of those who live in Al-Baqa'a camp, or to negotiate in the name of Jibreen, Haifa, and Yafa and to say that he represents the Palestinian people. Who gave him this right to represent us?[14]

Facilitating Civic Participation

Participatory methodology necessitated an approach different to that of current NGOs, rights campaigns, political platforms, or Palestinian civic associations and political parties. The methodology required that the public meetings themselves demonstrate what was important to refugees, by letting the refugees articulate these important issues, and accurately recording the views of the people in open meetings.[15]

But it was largely up to the small groups of volunteer moderators (relying upon the principles and facilitation method collectively devised) to imagine a practical way to convene the meetings, and this they did with great ingenuity and brilliance. Indeed, this project could not have seen light without the political sophistication and creativity of hundreds of Palestinian activists, who put forward unique and extraordinary models of democratic practices in different countries, operating autonomously, and under the worst of conditions imaginable.

Their overall aim was to be as inclusive as possible, involving as many sectors of their refugee and exile community as possible, regardless of factional belonging or political orientation. They also endeavored to be particularly aware of the need for women and youth to participate; indeed, it proved to be the case that the most dynamic and creative moderators active in this work were the women and the youth. The most inspiring and heartening parts of facilitating the work were witnessing and working with moderators, as they scrupulously organized and prepared meetings in a such a way as to ensure traditionally marginalized voices were heard.

Depending on their local political situation and institutional capacity, moderators choose to work along either a "maximum" or a "minimum" model of structuring the debates. The maximum model entailed holding preparatory meetings, syndicate meetings specific to certain sectors (e.g. women, workers, disabled, students, etc.), as well as the public meetings. The minimum model – applied in communities which faced constraints or difficulties with regards to mobilization (i.e. where holding such meetings was illegal under state law such as in Egypt, or physically dangerous such as in Iraq) – entailed holding as many meetings as possible under the given circumstances, always preceded by a period of extensive preparation, mobilization, and education within the community, using the literature that had been created and collectively agreed by the moderators and facilitators themselves. Lebanon was an example of a country were the maximum model was applied, in the end with great success. As a moderator from Lebanon explained after holding the meetings:

> The work team in Lebanon chose to implement the maximum model, by holding extensive meetings and discussion panels in different regions, and to return again to hold more extensive second meetings. We started the preparations, and advertised heavily and pushed towards discussions before holding the extensive meetings. In Lebanon, there are five main regions; each of them includes smaller gatherings. We started with the South, and an extensive public meeting attended by more than 225 participants was held. It included all the political powers, parties, youth and women unions, and the intellectual categories. This meeting broke both the actual and psychological barrier that could prevent people and all the parties in general – political, unions, youth and women – from participating . . . As a result, the first meeting, which was carefully and quietly prepared, was a great success. And it led to the success of the rest of the project's activities, since the project attained its legitimacy from the first meeting . . . We had our method, which was holding workshops about the project goals whenever we finished an extensive meeting in a certain region. These workshops addressed workers, women, and youth. We also held public meetings. This method of holding workshops and meetings proved later to be a big success. Three workshops were held for these diverse groups and spheres. We did the same in Tripoli, where the general meeting was

bigger and more extensive and attended by more people. The political groups, unions, and public participation were far larger. The number of attendants was between 350–400 participants, such that we even faced a big problem in trying to end the discussion in the same meeting. This was followed by six workshops, and three more in Al-Beddawi camp, and in Nahr el-Bared camp. All the work techniques previously agreed upon were also approved in these meetings . . .[16]

As the moderator went on to explain, the same model was applied, with great success, in Baalbek, Beirut, and Sidon. In Iraq, however, the minimum model was applied:

[A]lthough we would have liked to hold general extended meetings discussing the issue of Iraq, this was nearly impossible because of the security conditions. Consequently, the meetings were limited to some Palestinian activists in some of the Palestinian neighborhoods. These meetings were distributed as follows: two meetings in the university, and five meetings in different neighborhoods for the refugees living in Iraq.[17]

Deliberation

Said once contrasted Palestinian realities with a "literary, entirely bourgeois" notion of exile:

We think of the great paradigmatic figures like Ovid, Dante, Hugo, or Joyce; we reflect on the inner exile of various modern German or Italian writers; and in so doing we draw elucidation by analogy out of our own smaller-scale exile. But it is the mass of Palestinians dispersed throughout the Near East who, I think, really set the conditions for life in exile, and these are almost by definition silent, indescribable, utterly poignant.[18]

That utterly poignant silence was broken, over and over again, in the Civitas meetings, by the equally poignant articulation of Palestinian voices on the predicaments and sensibility of exile:

Palestine for us is not just a country on the political map. For us, Palestine is a history, identity, life texture, living, breathing; it is absolutely unique. You made me cry by remembering it. We no longer have relations with Palestinians. The Palestinian families that lived with us are scattered now. Some left and some emigrated. I always ask my father to tell me stories about it, because I can't even find a book with these facts. I started to seek my soul and my history, I no longer know where I am. I was watching a TV show when my father was telling me how the Zionists invaded. I no longer connect with this feeling. I feel that I am in a different world. The Palestinian youth lost their way. I won't tell you that they forgot their history but they made them forget it. I am searching very hard for something very difficult to find. I keep telling my friends that I am connected to things in an unusual manner, because I know that when you remove a plant from soil before it grows, it will forever remain wilted and it will never grow. They removed us from our land.[19]

The alienation that accompanies exile was also perfectly captured, time and time again:

When I think of myself as a member of a group, I wonder about my place within the group, and I feel like I'm sitting in a locked room watching people outside who don't see me, while I eagerly search among them for my family. I am talking about my internal feelings from an individual, as opposed to a wider cultural, perspective. I feel alone, we can be six people, but still we will feel alone. I don't even know the family next door. And I have no relation whatsoever with the neighbors. I feel that I am ignored even by the Authority. Therefore I am convinced deep inside that I am nothing, and that I have no rights in this life, I don't even have a land. I was born in Libya, and I heard that those who are born in Libya can't enter Palestine. I wish to visit Palestine, why can't I do that? If I can't enter Palestine to visit it, how would I dare enter it to vote? Did you know that they requested international supervisors, and I applied, not intending to vote, but just to observe? This is a great honor for me. I just wanted to observe as I did in the Egyptian elections. But the security service in Egypt refused because I am a Palestinian, and therefore I don't have the right to vote or to observe! Can you see the duality in standards? I don't even have the right to observe and at the same time I can't vote. I want to know: who exactly am I?[20]

Countless participants spoke about their experience of marginalization as refugees in host countries. Here, a young man from Gaza camp in Jordan:

I am from Gaza camp. I feel that I am not alive, as if I were a corpse without a soul. I see my close friends that are Jordanian, and who are the same age as me. They are exercising their right to vote, whether in municipal or parliamentary elections. And I wonder why I am deprived of exercising this right.[21]

Abandonment by Palestinian representatives was repeatedly discussed:

> There are two parties here. Those of us who are outside feel that the
> Authority does not care about them, and only cares about the Palestinians
> inside Palestine. The other party is the Palestinians inside who feel
> somewhat lost. Who are we? The Authority is busy with itself and its
> institutions, and the big question is: who represents the Palestinians in Al
> Shatat? [22]

Many immediate and concrete political demands were made in the meetings, often specific to the context of the local host country:

> I am a Palestinian, I want a Palestinian party. I don't intend to be planted
> in this country forever. I want to ask one thing: is the news we hear ever
> correct? Frankly I don't know anything about Palestine except when I
> hear the Ajial radio channel from the Occupied Territories, or going to
> the Dead Sea to catch the signal. There is no honest Arabic media. I am a
> refugee, and I am a Palestinian, I want a Palestinian party, I want a
> Palestinian youth assembly. [23]

Many interventions centered on the terrible and vital question of lack of
identity papers:

> If I could leave this country, I wouldn't hesitate. As a Palestinian who has a
> refugee document from Iraq, I don't have a chance to get further than the
> borders. There must be a common language between the Palestinian
> leadership and the current Iraqi leadership. [24]

The will to remember Palestine was mentioned in a hundred ways by
participants, often quite simply:

> Though I may be absent from my country as a Palestinian, whether I am
> absent or not, I mustn't ignore my country. I was forced to leave my
> country; myself and our parents and grandparents. [25]

In every meeting the will to return was expressed and the right of return
affirmed:

> Take me back and I will set up a tent on the beach and live in it, I don't
> want a house to live in, I will set up a tent and live, but let them take me
> back. [26]

I came here to affirm my right, even if I don't have any document; I still have the Right to Return. I came here to ensure that my desire to return is guaranteed and I will preserve it and fight for it, and I want to make sure that my voice is conveyed.[27]

Above all, everyone demanded that the Palestinian voice be restored:

We want to convey our voice to the whole world so that all people can know our cause, and so that we can claim our rights.[28]

The Civic Spirit of a People

The hundreds of meetings held by Palestinian communities in 25 countries throughout 2005 and 2006 were recorded, and these voices have all now been meticulously transcribed. Out of these thousands of pages of transcripts a beautiful document of their voices was produced – *Palestinians Register: Laying Foundations and Setting Directions* – in both Arabic and English. Many new links were established in the course of the project within fragmented communities and between fragmented communities. Most importantly, a return to traditional participatory practices of mobilization from earlier generations of the long liberation movement were re-established, and the founding principle of popular self-rule was reaffirmed. As Palestinian intellectuals, artists, and workers alike are aware – above all Said, an intellectual who was entirely imbued by this awareness – true sovereignty always lies within the wishes and will of the people.

The creative capacity and epic struggle of ordinary Palestinians inspired and continues to inspire all Palestinians; we are constantly pulled forward towards soaring humanist principles from the acute sensibility of those daily accounts of complex steadfastness and extraordinary resistance: of those being taken to prison, and of those who are struggling to stay free within the prisons of Israel, the host countries, and the military occupation. These acts gift us with a constant grounding in the tangible sense of the universalism of our fight for freedom, a constant connection to progressive forces, and to a unifying sensibility of liberation, regardless of the transitory fragmentation and dispossession we now find ourselves in.

Notes

1 Jean Mohr and Edward Said, *After the Last Sky: Palestinian Lives*, New York: Columbia University Press, 1999, p. 30.
2 Edward Said, *The Question of Palestine*, New York: Vintage Books, 1992, p. 5.

3 Edward Said and Gauri Viswanathan, *Power, Politics, and Culture: Interviews with Edward W. Said*, New York: Pantheon Books, 2001, p. 39.

4 Said, *The Question of Palestine*, p. x.

5 Robert Young, *Postcolonialism: An Historical Introduction*, Oxford: Blackwell Publishing, 2001, p. 18.

6 Mohr and Said, *After the Last Sky*, p. 37.

7 See Karma Nabulsi, "Being Palestinian: the General Will," *Government and Opposition*, 38 (4), 2003.

8 I describe this process of fragmentation in detail in "Justice as the Way Forward," in J. Hilal, ed., *Where Now for Palestine? The Demise of the Two State Solution*, London: Zed Press, 2007.

9 'The Civitas Project Report," *Palestinians Register: Laying Foundations and Setting Directions*, Oxford: Nuffield College, Oxford University, 2006, can be found in English and Arabic at www.civitas-online.org

10 Said and Viswanathan, *Power, Politics and Culture*, p. 404.

11 Moderator, Iraq.

12 Moderator, Sweden.

13 Participant, Women's Preparatory Meeting, Amman, Jordan.

14 Participant, Preparatory Meeting, Amman, Jordan.

15 Civitas, *Palestinians Register: Laying Foundations and Setting Directions*, p. 19.

16 Moderator, Lebanon.

17 Moderator, Iraq.

18 Mohr and Said, *After the Last Sky*, p. 121.

19 Participant, Meeting, Cairo, Egypt.

20 Participant, Meeting, Cairo, Egypt.

21 Participant, Preparatory Meeting, Amman, Jordan.

22 Participant, Women's Meeting, Athens, Greece.

23 Participant, Women's Preparatory Meeting, Amman, Jordan.

24 Participant, Syndicate Meeting, Hurriya shelter, Baghdad, Iraq.

25 Participant, Women's Meeting, Amman, Jordan.

26 Participant, Public Meeting, Uppsala, Sweden.

27 Participant, Youth Meeting, Dammam, Saudi Arabia.

28 Participant, Women's Meeting, Nahr el Bared camp, Lebanon.

10

Beginning with Edward Said

Joseph A. Massad

Deeply steeped in the literary tradition, Edward Said was a foremost analyst of the discourses of power and knowledge of modern Europe, especially as regards Europe's emergence as an idea articulated through its imperial expansion. His literariness and engagement with the discursive is what informed his analysis of how Palestine and the Palestinians emerged within European Orientalist thought and its Zionist correlate. But Said did not limit his investigations to the discursive, he was also informed by the visual register, whether in the imaginary dimension of thought and fantasy, visual representation in literature itself, or actually existing visual representations and artistic productions of the worlds that Europe constructed, including Palestine. In this essay, I explore the ways in which Said *saw* Palestine and the role he accorded the visual in relation to the Palestinians.

How does the visual begin to read the Palestinian situation for Said? Can the visual provide a venue to look at Palestine and Zionism from the standpoint of the Palestinians? It is in considering these questions that the centrality of the visual and its interpretation lies for Said when looking at the Question of Palestine. If, as Said saw it, Michel Foucault fascinated him because he began his historical and philosophical inquiries with the visible, the seeable, and then moved to the discursive, the sayable, Said began with the discursive and then moved to the visible. His book *After the Last Sky* is an introduction to the dialectics of seeing and blindness, and the role of the critic in appreciating and interpreting the visual. The book is in a sense an explication of how the visual would begin to read Palestine and how Said himself could begin again with the visual in relation to Palestine. But before we look at Said's visual beginnings, it is important to look briefly at the way Said began with the discursive.

Edward Said was born in Jerusalem. This biographical fact merely made Palestine a point of origin for him. Indeed, Said had much aversion to the idea of origins. For him, Palestine *became* a point of departure, or more precisely a "beginning" as opposed to an origin, a notion he associated with the theological, and which therefore had little purchase in his decidedly secular life. For Edward Said,

> beginning is basically an activity which ultimately implies return and repetition rather than simple linear accomplishment, that beginning and beginning-again are historical while origins are divine, that a beginning not only creates but is its own method because it has intention. In short, beginning is *making* or *producing difference* . . . which is the result of combining the already-familiar with the fertile novelty of human work in language . . . Thus beginnings confirm, rather than discourage, a radical severity and verify evidence of at least some innovation – of *having begun.*[1]

Palestine was a beginning for Said because it involved his active intention. For him "between the word *beginning* and the word *origin* lies a constantly changing system of meanings . . . I use *beginning* as having the more active meaning, and *origin* the more passive one: thus 'X *is the origin of Y,*'" while "'The beginning A *leads to* B.'" For Said, "ideas about origins, because of their passivity, are put to uses" he believed "ought to be avoided."[2] It is because of such uses that Said did not originate *in* Palestine but rather began with it. This distinction is crucial because, as he tells us:

> beginning has influences upon what follows from it: in the paradoxical manner, then, according to which beginnings as events are not necessarily confined to the beginning, we realize that a major shift in perspective and knowledge has taken place. The state of mind that is concerned with origins is . . . theological. By contrast, and this is the shift, beginnings are eminently secular, or gentile, continuing activities . . . Whereas an origin *centrally* dominates what derives from it, the beginning (especially the modern beginning), encourages nonlinear development, a logic giving rise to the sort of multileveled coherence of dispersion we find . . . in the texts of modern writers.[3]

How then did Said begin? How did Palestine begin for him? How did he begin in and decidedly with Palestine?

Although Said articulated his ideas about musical counterpoint as the basis of reading texts and analyzing historical events in a relatively late work, namely *Culture and Imperialism*, he had internalized this method much earlier in his scholarship, most eminently in his work on Palestine. For Said, to look at things contrapuntally is to "be able to think through and interpret together experiences that are discrepant, each with its particular agenda and pace of development, its own internal formations, its internal coherence and system of external relationships, all of them coexisting and interacting with others."[4] In *Orientalism*, Said had set out to do just that when he insisted that the history of European Jews and the history of anti-Semitism must be read in tandem with the history of the Muslim Orient and the history of Orientalism. If in an earlier work he had asserted that the "Palestinian Arabs, who have suffered incalculable miseries for the sake of Western anti-Semitism, really do exist, have existed, and will continue to exist as part of Israel's extravagant cost,"[5] in *Orientalism*, he would gesture towards the process through which Palestinians became linked to that very history of European anti-Semitism, indeed how the history of anti-Semitism is intimately connected to the field of scholarship known as *Orientalism*.

It is there that Said *intended* to begin with Palestine. He begins that interrogation by affirming that "what has not been sufficiently stressed in histories of modern anti-Semitism has been the legitimation of such atavistic designations by Orientalism, and . . . the way this academic and intellectual legitimation has persisted right through the modern age in discussions of Islam, the Arabs, or the Near Orient."[6] Indeed, the way Jew and Arab, invented as Semites in European philology as early as the eighteenth century, came to register in the West was best exemplified for Said in an astute aside by Marcel Proust, whom he quotes:

> The Rumanians, the Egyptians, the Turks may hate the Jews. But in a French drawing-room the differences between those people are not so apparent, and an Israelite making his entry as though he were emerging from the heart of the desert, his body crouching like a hyaena's, his neck thrust obliquely forward, spreading himself in proud "salaams," completely satisfies a certain taste for the Oriental.[7]

Said's interest here was not only discursive but insistently visual. In the wake of the 1973 war and the oil embargo, Arabs came to be represented, nay visualized, in the West as having "clearly 'Semitic' features: sharply hooked noses, the evil mustachioed leer on their faces, were obvious reminders (to a largely non-Semitic population) that 'Semites' were at the bottom of all 'our' troubles, which in this case is principally a gasoline shortage. The transference of a popular anti-Semitic animus from a Jewish to an Arab target was made smoothly, since the figure was essentially the same."[8] Here, Said begins again with the history of anti-Semitism to illustrate his findings about the history of the Arab, and specifically the Palestinian. To clarify what he means, Said states that in depicting the Arab as a "negative value" and as "a disrupter of Israel's and the West's existence . . . as a surmountable obstacle to Israel's creation in 1948," what Orientalist and anti-Semitic representations result in is a certain conception of the Arab that is ontologically linked to the Jew; and such a link is made in the visual register as much as in the discursive. Witness his description of this transformation:

> the Arab is conceived of now as a shadow that dogs the Jew. In that shadow – because Arabs and Jews are Oriental Semites – can be placed whatever traditional, latent mistrust a Westerner feels towards the Oriental. For the Jew of pre-Nazi Europe has bifurcated: What we have now is a Jewish hero, constructed out of a reconstructed cult of the adventurer-pioneer-Orientalist . . . and his creeping, mysteriously fearsome shadow, the Arab Oriental.[9]

In these remarks, what Said is gesturing towards is the endemic anti-Semitism that plagues all representation of Arabs today, indeed the very displacement of the object of anti-Semitism from the Jew onto the Arab. Thus, in light of Said's work, one cannot understand Orientalism, the Arab, and ultimately the Palestinian without understanding European Jewish history and the history of European anti-Semitism in the context of European colonialism, which made and make all these historical transformations possible and mobilize the very discourse that produces them as facts.[10] Equally important in this regard is that one cannot understand European visual and imaginary representations of Arabs and Arab geographies outside the modern European ontology of self and other and the European epistemology informing the imagination and the visual representation of these non-European objects of observation.

As seeing is not a simple photochemical response but a hermeneutical exercise, Said delved into the visual question of how he, a Palestinian, can see Palestinians through the eyes of a Swiss photographer. What is inside and what is outside, what is interior (and anterior) to the representation in a photograph and what remains outside it, is where Said located his intervention. While fully appreciative of the aesthetics of photography, Said apologetically justifies the role of the critic as a reader of the social text inscribed by visual representations. For him, Jean Mohr's photographs, around which *After the Last Sky* is constructed, demand an interpretation. In looking at pictures of shepherds, and of Palestinian women in the field, for example, Said explains how the process of interpretation begins:

> [The photographs] are all, in a troubling sense, without the marks of an identifiable historical period. And for that matter, they could be scenes of

people anywhere in the Arab world. Placeless. Yet all the photographs are of working people, peasants with a hard life led on a resistant soil, in a harsh climate, requiring ceaseless effort. We – you – know that these are photographs of Palestinians because I have identified them as such; I know they are Palestinian peasants because Jean has been my witness. But in themselves these photographs are silent; they seem saturated with a kind of inert being that outweighs anything they express; consequently they invite the embroidery of explanatory words.[11]

Said insists that his reading is one of many and that others can and do read them differently. Indeed, one of the first readings of a photograph is giving it a title, such as the one titled "Shepherds in the field." Mindful of his Western audience and the influence of Orientalism on them, Said explains:

and you could add, "tending their flocks, much as the Bible says they did." Or the two photographs of women evoke phrases like "the timeless East," and "the miserable lot of women in Islam." Or, finally, you could remember something about the importance to "such people" of UNRWA, or the PLO – the one an agency for supplementing the impoverished life of anonymous Palestinians with the political gift of refugee status, the other a political organization giving identity and direction to "the Palestinian people." But these accumulated interpretations add up to a frighteningly direct correlative of what the photographs depict: "alienated labor," as Marx called it, work done by people who have little control of either the product of their labor or their own laboring capacity.[12]

What Said is attempting in piling up possible interpretation upon possible interpretation is to demonstrate the centrality of hermeneutics in making possible not only multiple readings of aesthetic products and their social texts, but the instrumentality and inadequacy of hermeneutics as an exercise in dominating or in resisting domination. Thus he concludes the above paragraph by asserting that

After such a recognition [that of alienated labor], whatever bit of exotic romance that might attach to these photographs is promptly blown away. As the process of preserving the scenes, photographic representation is thus the culmination of a sequence of capturings. Palestinian peasants working are the creatures of half a dozen other processes, none of which leaves these productive human beings with their labor intact.[13]

Said is aware of the way in which certain readers of the visual want to insist on only one immediate meaning. Such visual fundamentalists can and often do marshal a theological approach to the visual in the interest of establishing facts and/or of propping up claims. *After the Last Sky* is an attempt on the part of Said and Mohr to begin again to view Palestinians differently, but Orientalism and Zionism had begun almost a century earlier in looking at Palestinians through other visual prisms. Said discusses that "most famous of early-twentieth-century European books about Palestine," namely *The Immoveable East* by the Alsatian Philip Baldensperger.[14] What struck Said as notable in this inaugural effort was that "it is magisterial in its indifference to the problems of interpretation and observation."[15] The same is true for Said of the work of Finnish archeologist and anthropologist Hilma Granquist. Reading them and "seeing their photographs and drawings, I feel at an even greater remove from the people they describe . . . What I think of as I read . . . Baldensperger is the almost total absence of Palestinian writing on the same subject. Only such writing would have registered not just the presence of a significant peasant culture, but a coherent account of how that culture has been shaken, uprooted in the transition to a more urban-based economy."[16] Said's own book, he felt, was beginning to register such a presence, uncomfortable as it is, both discursively and visually.

Understanding the status of Palestine as historical, Said never reified it:

> The fact of the matter is that today Palestine does not exist, except as a memory or, more importantly, as an idea, a political and human experience, and an act of sustained popular will . . . [It is the millions of Palestinians] who make up the question of Palestine, and if there is no country called Palestine it is not because there are no Palestinians. There are . . .[17]

Thus, for Said, to begin with Palestine is to begin with the understanding that "the struggle between Palestinians and Zionism [i]s a struggle between a presence and an interpretation, the former constantly appearing to be overpowered and eradicated by the latter."[18] Said demonstrated his hermeneutical skills as a critic to disassemble the web of representations that Orientalism and anti-Semitism mobilized through Zionism. His attempt to read Palestine from a Canaanite perspective contra Michael Walzer was deeply informed by his interpretative skills. It was not that Said posited some form of perspectivalism reduced to relativism, rather he began by repeating the logic of Zionism to retell its story differently. If Zionism insisted on playing some prehistorical archeological game, positing fantastically the ancient Hebrews as the progenitors of modern European Jews, Said smugly posited the earlier native Canaanites, conquered as they were by the invading foreign Hebrews, in ways reminiscent of the Palestinian experience.[19] Polemics aside, and he *was* a master polemicist, Said insisted on revealing that for Palestinians, Zionism constituted but part of the chain of historical invasions of Palestine from the Crusaders to the Ottomans, Napoleon, and the British. He insisted therefore on reading Zionism not only in its European environment but also from the standpoint of its Palestinian victims.

But if the struggle over Palestine is a struggle over interpretation, of what lies outside Zionist representations, both visual and discursive, and what lies within them, then the visual, given the apparent immediacy of its images, its apparent independence from the discursive where Said's expertise lies, can only evoke in the literary Said a sense of "panic," as he once told W.J.T. Mitchell in a now-famous interview in reference to the visual arts.[20] There, he reflects on his approach to writing *After the Last Sky*. First Said evokes his own subjectivity, the emotional responses that Jean Mohr's pictures provoked in him:

> I spent weeks and weeks making a selection of the photographs from his enormous archive . . . I wasn't really looking for photographs that I thought were exceptionally good, as opposed to ones that were not exceptionally good. I was just looking for photographs that I felt provoked some kind of response in me. I couldn't formulate what the response was. But I chose them.[21]

Said moved to group the pictures in four distinct piles, which ultimately set the stage for the four-chapter division that composed his book. For him, ultimately, the photographs provided a visual referent to a Palestinian narrative that Said wove around them: "I was really more interested in how they corresponded to or in some way complemented what I was feeling."[22] This is not to say that Said thinks the visual and the discursive – or as the interview puts it, "the seeable and the sayable" – are reducible to one another, or merely capable of symmetrical representations in different modes. Far from it. Said insists on the "correlative" nature of the seeable and the sayable, "not in the sense of interchangeable but in the sense of one doing something that the other can't do . . . and if you remove one, then something is missing in the other."[23] Indeed Said, as I mentioned earlier, was most impressed with Foucault precisely because the latter "would begin with the visible – in other words, it was the *visible* that made possible the sayable."[24] Said, however, did not think that the visual should be fetishized or made into an idol to be worshipped. Such fetishization was directly opposed to his secular commitments. Said's oft-repeated citation from the twelfth-century monk Hugh of Saint Victor is instructive in this regard:

> It is, therefore, a source of great virtue for the practiced mind to learn, bit by bit, first to change about invisible and transitory things, so that afterwards it may be able to leave them behind altogether. The man who finds his homeland sweet is still a tender beginner; he to whom every soil is as his native one is already strong; but he is perfect to whom the entire world is as a foreign land. The tender soul has fixed his love on one spot in the world; the strong man has extended his love to all places; the perfect man has extinguished his.[25]

This quote exemplifies both Said's resistance to nationalist belongings and his insistence on his central notion of "secular criticism' which allowed him to render sayable and seeable much that had been rendered silent and outside the visual frame in the Palestinian experience. Said's project was indeed to make the Palestinian narrative sayable and the Palestinians themselves visible to a world that insisted on not seeing or hearing them. That Said lamented the deafening silence of most American and many European intellectuals on Palestine was very much linked to his insistence that the intellectual must begin and begin again when reading a social, a literary, and indeed a visual text. For him, the justice of the Palestine Question would usher in a new beginning, discursively and visually, for global politics, not least because Israel is the last settler colony standing in Asia and Africa.

If Said began with Palestine, he would begin yet again after the Oslo agreement was signed. The importance of new beginnings for him is intimately linked to his aversion to origins. His insistence on the importance of what he called *affiliation* rather than *filiation* mirrored the distinction he drew between beginnings and origins. Thus while Said was filiatively connected to Palestine through the accident of birth, he would later intend willfully to affiliate with it. Hence his unwavering commitment to begin again from a new point of departure. For Said, affiliation offers a conscious choice of belonging that filiation simply imposes. While he affiliated with and belonged to the PLO when it represented the Palestinian people's interests, Said disaffiliated from it the moment it abandoned its mission following the signing of the Oslo agreement.

In this sense, Said's notion of secularism, understood as a refusal to believe in infallible gods, not least of which is nationalism and the nation form, is the organizing principle for his notion of beginnings and his rejection of origins as theological. Being exiled from dominant ideologies and cultures, including one's own, then, is what provides Said with the tools to be a critic, one who is inside Palestine and outside it, inside the West and outside it, and inside the nation and outside it. This is crucial to his project of being "out of place," physically and intellectually, and of belonging to certain intellectual and political traditions. Herein lies his sense of belonging to Palestine and Palestinian-ness, both filiative and affiliative.

This tension between the filiative and the affilative is what attracted Said to the brilliant work of Palestinian artist Mona Hatoum. In an essay that Said wrote for Hatoum's installation exhibit "The Entire World as a Foreign Land," an understanding that Said shared, he wrote:

> Her work is the presentation of identity as unable to identify with itself, but nevertheless grappling the notion (perhaps only the ghost) of identity to itself. This is exile figured and plotted in the objects she creates. Her works enact the paradox of dispossession as it takes possession of its place in the world, standing firmly in workaday space for spectators to see and somehow survive what glistens before them. No one has put the Palestinian experience in visual terms so austerely and yet so playfully, so compellingly and at the same moment so allusively.[26]

The importance of Hatoum's arrangement of different objects in her installation work, objects that are familiar and utterly unfamiliar at the same time, stem from the way they impress themselves on the viewer:

> In another age her works might have been made of silver or marble, and could have taken the status of sublime ruins or precious fragments placed before us to recall our mortality and the precarious humanity we share with each other. In the age of migrants, curfews, identity cards, refugees, exiles, massacres, camps and fleeing civilians, however, they are the uncooptable mundane instruments of a defiant memory facing itself and its pursuing or oppressing others implacably, marked forever by changes in everyday materials and objects that permit no return or real repatriation, yet unwilling to let go of the past that they carry along with them like some silent catastrophe that goes on and on without fuss or rhetorical bluster.[27]

It is this quality of Hatoum's visual art that makes it, as Said asserts, "hard to bear (like the refugee's world, which is full of grotesque structures that bespeak excess as well as paucity), yet very necessary to see an art that travesties the idea of a single homeland."[28] For Said, Hatoum's art speaks loudly, as his own writings do, against the ugly horrors of the Oslo capitulation, which American, Israeli, and Palestinian plastic surgeons spent (and continue to spend) countless hours in the operating room beautifying: "Better disparity and dislocation than reconciliation under duress of subject and object; better a lucid exile than sloppy, sentimental homecomings; better the logic of dissociation than an assembly of compliant dunces."[29] These words of Said are insistently correlative to Hatoum's visual assertions.

In insisting on new beginnings in reading literary and visual texts about Palestine and the Palestinians, Said offered a new language and a new vision, not only to non-Palestinians, but also and particularly to Palestinians, to speak about and see Palestine and the Palestinians from different historical angles and in different geographic contexts. Resisting his initial panic at the visual, Said pursued an engagement with it that uncovered layers of the Palestinian experience that his literary engagement did not permit him to *see*. In his literary works, Said's attention to the Arab and Western contexts in which the Palestinian struggle was waged was the hallmark of his approach. He insisted on reading the European Jewish struggle against anti-Semitism contrapuntally with the Zionist struggle to colonize and dominate the Palestinians, just as he insisted on reading the Palestinian struggle against Zionist colonialism alongside trenchant criticism of Arab regime politics and the politics of the Palestinian leadership. This analysis informed his study of visual representations of, and by, Palestinians, where everyday lived experience, as well as the overall political context of the Palestinian condition, were being revealed and concealed simultaneously through the power of the visual. In the context of photography, the camera thus dominates and captures Palestine and its native population while simultaneously showing them now to resist its power when they look back at it, challenging its attempt to capture them – or, when they look away from it – refusing the very terms of such representations. Indeed Said's own analysis of the visual is another Palestinian attempt to resist Orientalist and Zionist capturings. His literary studies of Europe and its culture constituted another way in which he turned the camera, or more precisely his gaze, back on the Western Orientalists engaged in representing and photographing the non-European. Said's method of contrapuntal reading then allowed him to contemplate secular solutions to the Question of Palestine that few others could offer. In seeing Palestine from the standpoint of Edward Said, it becomes clear that Said's indispensable legacy constitutes a new beginning for the struggle to see and speak about Palestine, to belong to the Palestinian idea, to be a critic of discursive and visual representations of the Palestinian experience. It is this legacy from which we can all begin again.

Notes

1 Edward Said, *Beginnings: Intention and Method*, New York: Columbia University Press, Morningside Edition, 1985, p. xvii. The book was first published in 1975.

2 Ibid., p. 6.

3 Ibid., pp. 272–3.

4 Edward Said, *Culture and Imperialism*, New York: Knopf, 1993, p. 36.

5 Edward Said, *The Politics of Dispossession: The Struggle for Palestinian Self-Determination, 1969–1994*, New York: Pantheon, 1994, p. 10.

6 Edward Said, *Orientalism*, New York: Vintage Books, 1978, p. 262.

7 Quoted in ibid., p. 293.

8 Ibid., p. 286.

9 Ibid.

10 On the transformation of the Palestinian into the Jew, see my "The Persistence of the Palestinian Question," in *Cultural Critique*, No. 59, Winter 2005.

11 Said, *After the Last Sky*, New York: Columbia University Press, 1999, p. 92.

12 Ibid., pp. 92–3.

13 Ibid., p. 93.

14 Ibid., p. 94.

15 Ibid.

16 Ibid.

17 Edward Said, *The Question of Palestine*, New York: Vintage, 1979, p. 5.

18 Ibid., p. 8.

19 Edward Said, "Michael Walzer's Exodus and Revolution: A Canaanite Reading," *Grand Street* 5, Winter 1986: 86–106, and Michael Walzer, *Exodus and Revolution*, New York: Basic Books, 1984.

20 W.J.T. Mitchell, "The Panic of the Visual: A Conversation with Edward W. Said," in Paul A. Bové, ed., *Edward Said and the Work of the Critic: Speaking Truth to Power*, Durham: Duke University Press, 2000, p. 31.

21 Ibid., p. 35.

22 Ibid., p. 36.

23 Ibid., p. 43.

24 Ibid.

25 Edward Said, "Reflections on Exile," in *Reflections on Exile*, Cambridge: Harvard University Press, 2001, p. 185.

26 Edward Said, "The Art of Displacement: Mona Hatoum's Logic of Irreconcilables," in *Mona Hatoum: The Entire World as a Foreign Land*, London: Tate Gallery, 2000, p. 17.

27 Ibid.

28 Ibid.

29 Ibid.

PART IV

Looking at Today Through Said's Lenses

11

Orientalism/Occidentalism: The Impasse of Modernity

Meltem Ahıska

Modernity is no doubt a highly contested term; indeed, to put it more strongly, a war is still being waged over its connotations. Debates on modernity mostly boil down to a political question concerning whether the "original' Western modernity could or should be a model for the "Others," with implications for shaping power regimes. As such, not only are there different theories of modernity circulating in academia, but being for or against Western modernity is practically invoked in political judgments and sentiments in different national and international contexts all around the world. However, my aim here is not to introduce yet another take on the term. Instead, I would like to pursue an immanent critique by attending to how modernity has been historically problematized in Turkey in the grip of Orientalism and Occidentalism. Revealing the impasse of modernity in this frame may contribute to a new understanding for appropriating the dubious "heritage of (Western) modernity" in its very process of liquidation today.[1] This is important if our aim is not only to separate and oppose, but also to connect and join – a perspective that Edward Said advanced in his critical quest for a secular human history.[2]

The concepts of "loss" and "sovereignty" seem to hold a central place in discussions of non-Western modernities: while "loss" renders the non-Western contexts extremely fragile in appropriating their "authentic" cultural past; "sovereignty" appears as a major problematic trope for crafting contemporary forms of modernity in "belated" non-Western contexts. I will utilize the concept of Occidentalism in this paper, together with Said's notion of Orientalism, to discuss questions of modernity and national identity with regard to forms of historical "loss" and "sovereignty" in Turkey. I will argue that Occidentalism is a conceptual frame that allows us to understand not only questions of identity and culture, but also operations of power in non-Western parts of the world. Occidentalism opens up a theoretical space for thinking about both opposition to and complicity with the power regimes in the so-called West in the shared format of the *nation*, which invokes the "loss" only to consolidate "sovereignty." Furthermore, by recognizing modes of Occidentalist thinking and politics, I claim we can reflect back on Orientalism to further think about its surviving hegemony, which is embedded in new forms of colonialism today.[3]

However, when one mentions the word Occidentalism one immediately steps onto the battleground and enters the debate over Western modernity. Therefore I would like first to clarify the way I define and employ Occidentalism, not only for purposes of delineating my position but also in order to refine the conceptual tool, making it more appropriate to convey my arguments that seek to go beyond the East/West dichotomy.

"Occidentalism" is indeed a highly charged term. Its most apparent connotation today is anti-Westernism. Yet beyond this popular meaning, the concept has also been employed in different academic contexts with different meanings, such that it remains rather ambivalent. The term has been popularized recently by Buruma and Margalit's book, *Occidentalism* (2004).[4] Since then, Occidentalism has usually been associated in the Western media with "dangerous" anti-Westernisms and specifically with Islamic movements after 9/11. But if Westerners regard Occidentalism as a threat to the core values of modernity, non-Westerners, on the other hand, have embraced Occidentalism as a response to the colonizing West. For example, Egyptian philosopher and Muslim reformer Hassan Hanafi elaborates Occidentalism as a "science," and as a necessary counter-discourse against the aggressive and declining West. Hanafi's project is to transform the Occident into an object as Westerners have done with the Orient, "with the purpose of recreating an independent Arabic intellectual tradition . . . Arabs must learn to dissect the West in the same way one does with mice in the laboratory."[5] According to Hanafi, Occidentalism involves a reversing of the roles: "The West becomes the Other, the Orient is restored to the Self."[6] While not simply pursuing an anti-Western political stance, Hanafi nevertheless defines the East/South as a distinct entity to be studied from a non-Western perspective, and which can be defined in national terms,[7] a critical vantage point that I shall problematize in this paper.

The popular accent on Occidentalism as anti-Westernism, most probably due to the present international political context, overshadows its previous meaning as simply "Westernism." Long before Buruma and Margalit's book appeared, Occidentalism had been employed to denote Westernism – for example, Xiao-mei Chen discussed Occidentalism in China,[8] ascribing a positive meaning to it as Westernism, which, in the author's view, provided a counter-discourse against the established regime. In another theoretical vein, the historical process of making and signifying the West was also labelled as Occidentalism, for example in the work of scholars such as Couze Venn, Walter Mignolo, and Fernando Coronil.[9]

I contend that the differing meanings of Occidentalism in different theoretical and political perspectives can be interpreted as a sign that testifies to the power of the concept rather than its inadequacy. Occidentalism is useful as a concept precisely because of the ambivalence of its meaning. The fact that Occidentalism simultaneously connotes both Westernism and anti-Westernism in existing literature does not, in my view, point merely to theoretical controversy or confusion, but reveals something very important: *the historical doubling of Orientalism and Occidentalism both in the West and the non-West*. The meaning changes depending on your point of view, but if we go beyond relativism, we may see that the discourse on modernity inevitably includes the entangled representations of the West defining the East, or the East reacting to the Western gaze (with changing contents and locations of East and West of course). I develop a conceptual frame for Occidentalism by appropriating its very ambivalence, and the shifting boundaries of the East/West divide in the Turkish context, rather than embracing the dichotomy as such.[10] I would say that Westernism and anti-Westernism are distorted mirror images of each other, despite the historically shaped hierarchy between what is designated as East and West.

But the reciprocity of the constructions of East and West should not mislead us in terms of the asymmetry in power relations. The half-acknowledged but still half-denied background condition of modernity is European colonialism. As Françoise Vergès argues, "Europe's colonial domination has been the subject of a profound forgetting. This forgetting should be seen as a system: it is vital, for instance, to place the history of slavery outside of the official story of modernity."[11] The Occidentalism of the West embedded in the historical context of colonialism and modernity generates the various Orientalisms and Occidentalisms as we know them today. Walter Mignolo suggests, in his *Local Histories/Global Designs*, that "'Occidentalism' was a notion that contributed to the self-definition of post-Renaissance Europe," and functions "as an overarching metaphor of the modern/colonial world" to define the limits of the modern/colonial knowledge and imaginary.[12] Drawing on the historical account of modernity/coloniality analyzed by Mignolo, it would be very important to say that a certain representation of the West (Occidentalism) was first fashioned by Western narratives and sciences in complicity with colonialism. In other words the geopolitical entity called "the West" was constructed in its consciously crafted representations, in which it mirrored itself in the rest of the world. Orientalism, then, is produced within the Occidentalism of the West enacting the categorical space of the Other located somewhere outside of *the present history* of modernity, but as a necessary constitutive outside defining the Western self.[13] In Mignolo's words: "without Occidentalism there is no Orientalism."[14] One then has first to deal with the question of the Occidentalism of the West before attending to the construction of Orientalism as a discourse of power. In a similar vein Fernando Coronil has suggested

> reorienting our attention from the problematic of "Orientalism", which focuses on the deficiencies of the West's representations of the Orient, to that of "Occidentalism", which refers to the conceptions of the West animating these representations. It entails relating the observed to the observers, products to production, knowledge to its sites of formation.[15]

If the Occidentalism of the West means the making and representing of the West, then the constitutive alterity to this definition would be the "East" as the Other. Yet despite the clarity of the projection at the level of representations, the category of the East is problematic in terms of its historical substance. Is the "East" a mere fantasy of the West enacted by the constructions of Western modernity/colonialism? Is it just a passive object that endorses Western hegemony? I would argue that we cannot and should not avoid the question of the agency, and the subject-constitution at a more analytical level, of the non-West. We cannot but ask the question of what happens when that externalized and supposedly silent Other, placed outside of history and doomed to chase Western values and targets without success, speaks and answers back. As I have argued elsewhere,[16] the Other is not only represented by the Western subject, within a discursive trope which Said brilliantly analyzed in his study of Orientalism. A historically simultaneous representation of the Other has been produced by the "Other" itself aspiring to fill in the subject position. I argue that the Other's inhabiting the space of the Other and speaking for itself produces the Occidentalism of the non-West, in which the locus of enunciation of modernity shifts from West to non-West with dramatic differences in its content and performance. Hence I argue that Occidentalism – and from now on I use it to mean the Occidentalism of the non-West – is a means of performing Western modernity while resisting its colonizing move. It is Westernism and anti-Westernism at the same time.

A second clarification concerns the subject status of the non-West. In contrast to accounts of Occidentalism which reconstruct the Other as the victim, and wage a war against the West in that respect, I argue that Occidentalism is not only a victim's discourse. Occidentalism may seek its legitimacy by mobilizing the resentment of the people against colonization, and hence refer to the non-West as the victim of Western modernity. But this is not the whole story since Occidentalism utilizes the victim status to create power. I depict and analyze Occidentalism as a discourse that attempts to build a certain power regime by investing in the victim status. The category of the Other is interpellated within Occidentalism to produce a "nativity" by which other Others are produced, judged, and marginalized. Then, the non-West as the Other is simultaneously a trope of political subjectivity that evokes and resists the "loss" due to Western modernity, but that also enacts "sovereignty" for sustaining a power regime, which opts for the restitution of the "loss" for being modern. By constantly pointing to what is lost, but also by denying coming to terms with it, and instead projecting it as a lack for which "others" are to be blamed, Occidentalism becomes a trope of both memory and violence.

Let me cite an anecdote to explicate the complexity of the above arguments and illustrate how Occidentalism works in the field. I borrow this story from a Turkish PhD candidate in York University, who conducts research on the wives of military officers in Turkey.[17] When interviewing an informant − a middle-aged woman married to a military officer who had recently died − she asked a rather general question about how the interviewee evaluated the social and political climate in Turkey. The interviewee first inquired about what the researcher wanted to hear: "What do you want me to tell you? I guess not the days of anarchy? No, no I won't talk about those days, *they* don't need to know" (emphasis mine). Then, she started out on a very positive narrative about Turkey's progress:

> I went to Diyarbakır recently to visit my son in the military. I was there only 15 or 20 years ago. But now, I saw a great city. The military houses were so developed, the new ones were very organized, had nice gardens, playgrounds. Interiors are large with nice kitchens and bathrooms; there is also a shopping mall. I saw with my own eyes that Diyarbakır has become a big city . . . I said to myself, that really Turkey is on its way to becoming a European country.

Her narrative halted when she was about to mention her husband's death. She said: "No I don't want to talk about that. *They* need not know how difficult a widow's life is in Turkey" (emphasis mine). When the interview was over and the tape was turned off, the interviewee added: "Do you know what, *in fact*, Turkey did not develop at all. Now that the religious people are in power we are getting more and more backward. I think you should stay in Canada, and not come back" (emphasis mine).

I believe this little story from the ethnographic field provides a perfect example of the working of Occidentalism in everyday life. It is impossible to give a full contextual interpretation in the limited space I have here,[18] but even if we take it as only an anecdote we can see that the story is significant for many reasons.[19] First of all, since the interviewee has a certain commitment to the military through her husband, she is in a position to defend Western modernity against, in her own words, those "backward" strata, such as religious people.[20] Second, her conception of modernity in Turkey is reflected through the imagined presence of the West, interestingly mediated by and embodied in the technology of the tape recorder. She censors her narrative for "them" not to hear. She designs her narrative according to what the imagined Western audience should know, so that Turkey will be accepted as a modern country by the Westerners, more specifically by the European Union. Finally, the "outside" of her narrative, her silences or her off the record comments, imply an inner truth that Turkey is in fact not modern. Her own experience as a widowed woman testifies to this. But the implicit truth is not only about self-deprecation. It also functions to establish an *intimacy*[21] with native fellows, as can be seen in her advice to the researcher to stay in Canada. Furthermore, the same intimacy provides a ground for judging who is and is not modern in Turkey. While in the interviewee's eyes both she and the researcher of course know what it is to be modern, those others, such as religious people, are cast off as barriers to modernity. The intimacy produced by Occidentalism thus becomes a ground for producing and judging others.

This little and seemingly naive story shows that the working of Occidentalism is indeed complex, but in all its complexity it produces subjects within a certain power regime. In this event, the Western gaze, or rather the imagined and projected Western gaze, is internalized as the ultimate authority of judgment about both personal and national conduct – as she tries to behave by saying the right words about Turkey into the microphone for the West to hear, she performs the role of proper national citizen. However, she is split in the sense that she can confess in an informal, intimate manner that this is all a staged performance needed to maintain power. The intimacy produced through the displayed form[22] becomes the medium for redefining Turkish "native" modernity and the dangerous others within – and of course Orientalizing them. This is a perfect example of Occidentalism as I understand and study it. The national subject is trying to perform Western-ness to claim a power position, enacting and reproducing at the same time her gender, ethnic, and class identities, while she reserves the inner truth for the sake of a more contingent yet more realistic intimate bonding. The intimate bonding may result either in an admiration for Westernism or resentment against it, in changing contexts given that the judging Western gaze is always already the ultimate criterion.

If we broaden our scale a little, we will see a similar Occidentalist dynamic within the recent pre-election "nationalist" demonstrations in Turkey.[23] The demonstrations started in Istanbul and spread to other cities and towns in Turkey with apparently the same aim of defending "core national values" against the threat of political Islam. The content and form of the seemingly spontaneous demonstrations resemble each other.[24] Thousands – millions as they would claim – of Turkish citizens, mostly women, wearing Turkish flags, shouted "creative"[25] nationalist slogans embodying Atatürkism and laicism, and pointing to Tayyip Erdoğan and his party as a major threat. They rallied against the prospect of an Islamic president and his veiled wife – primarily for the West to hear. In that respect they aspired to keep up the modern image of Turkey, prominently a gendered issue since modern Turkey has been symbolized through the visibility of a particular type of women, and the "veil" has been a symbolic political issue from the beginning of the *modern* Turkish republic.[26] But this endorsement of modernity bears in itself a strong resentment against the contemporary forms of Western modernity. This was apparent in slogans aimed not only against US financial domination over Turkey but also against the political vision of the European Union. The resentment against the West, and especially the European Union, which *still* does not accept Turkey as an equal peer, was voiced through "nationalism."

The demonstrators brought contradictory demands to the surface. For example, even if they were for endorsing a democratic and independent modern Turkey, they would still invite the military to be the guarantor of these principles. Furthermore, the protestors who aggressively performed as *laique* modern Turkish citizens were, in fact, Muslim at heart, which bred their Turkish-ness, and hence nationalism.[27] Modern, yet anti-Western; anti-Islam yet Muslim-Turkish. How to interpret these contradictory positions? They are indeed confusing at first glance. Which is why the slogans seemed enigmatic to most Western reporters of these events. For example, on its website the BBC introduced questions such as: "So is this a power struggle between Islamists and Secularists?" "Not exactly" was their answer. "Why is the Turkish army so determined to defend secularism, the separation of religion and state?" "Secularism is fundamental to Turkey's identity as a nation" was the answer.[28] The questions and answers don't offer much enlightenment. One fails to make sense of these events if the Western narrative of modernity is embraced as such.

The present mobilization of the so-called modern nationalists surely deserves a rigorous sociological analysis going beyond their apparent rhetoric of modern "laicism" (mostly and wrongly translated as secularism in Western sources). One can point to several social conditions that enable the collective expression of such strong yet contradictory sentiments. The conflicts of the new urban middle and lower-middle classes, and especially of women, who seek a sovereign national agency both enabled and threatened by the contemporary globalizing-modernizing economy,[29] are of course significant factors that should be cited among others for understanding these demonstrations. However, for my purposes in this paper, the very rhetoric is worthy of analysis because I find the way history is evoked as a hidden referent in the discourse of the nationalists very important in order to grasp the dynamics of Occidentalism.

As postcolonial theorists such as Dipesh Chakrabarty argue, the modern sense of history was embedded in the construction of a particular narrative of Western modernity, such that non-Westerners lack a sense of history. They are relegated to the timeless "waiting room of history."[30] Yet I would argue that history continues to play a role in the constitution of the non-Western political subject, akin to the unconscious in the Freudian self. In analyzing the *present* events in Turkey, the role of history – a repressed and denied history – should be acknowledged, if history is not an empty time but a ceaseless process in which the self attempts to center itself.[31] The discourses of nationalism and "laicism" embraced by the Turkish nationalists have long and charged histories informed by the colonialist practices of the West and Orientalist visualizations of Turkey. The present moment is very much infused with a past that has been repressed by the sudden rupture when Turkey stepped into "modernity." The "loss" entailed in that rupture is constitutive of modern Turkish subjectivity. The subject enacts the "loss" to re-center itself in the stage of modernity. In other words the past is kept alive by Occidentalism, which entails sedimented memories of the traumatic experiences in Turkish history. I would further argue that "loss" is the trope within which sovereignty is performed in order to create others and subject them to abjection. But before moving on to that discussion, let me refer to certain historical moments regarding the "loss."

One such moment is the dissolution of the "Turkish myth" in Europe in the late nineteenth century. Jale Parla, in her brilliant study of Orientalism regarding the Turkish myth, discusses its transformation in nineteenth-century Europe by referring to the writings of authors such as Byron, Hugo, and Lamartine.[32] She argues that the Turkish myth was constructed when the Orient was a fashionable theme in Europe and aroused curiosity – that is, when the "public was orientalizing," in Byron's words – and was mainly informed by a romantic search for self-identity through travels to the East, of course never independent of the will to power. The Turkish myth was coined in narratives, which staged repressed evil desires, sexual fantasies, and homosexuality dressed in Oriental costumes. However, Parla says, the Turkish myth declined[33] as the Ottoman Empire began losing its power, and started accepting Western tutelage and Western ways of life. What remained in the West was disappointment coupled with a derogatory, mocking attitude, and of course more manifest strategies to colonize the Ottoman Empire. The desired/feared "East" (as the Other unconsciously integral to the Self) was no longer the Ottoman Empire, which in its demise became an abject — a weakling that sought its savior and protector in the West.[34]

The transformation of the Turkish myth, when looked at from the viewpoint of the Other, is a story of "loss." The Orient is long lost in terms of its essential foundations of experience and knowledge. It is no longer a mirror that reflects Turkish identity. Turkey had to lose its past, its languages, its people, and above all of course its imperial power, in order to become modern. Nurdan Gürbilek, in her book *Kör Ayna, Kayıp Şark* ("Blind Mirror, Lost Orient"), gives a vivid account of this "loss" in the work of Turkish intellectuals. She discusses how, starting from the nine-teenth-century Tanzimat, they dealt with the growing invasion of Western culture and knowledge. Associating the East with spirit and the West with matter they have attempted different combinations for producing (gen-dered) syntheses. But there was a clear pattern of decreasing confidence and hope over time, marked by a narcissistic wound. For example, Peyami Safa, who was so keen on bridging East and West, would finally say in one of his articles addressing the imagined West: "Give it back! Give me back my spirit."[35] The intellectuals Gürbilek writes about can all be seen as Occi-dentalists in my view. Rather than living with the loss[36] and mourning, they invest in the loss in order to open up a space for claiming authentic nativity without totally renouncing modernity. According to one of the most intellectual Occidentalists in Turkey, Cemil Meriç (who first introduced Edward Said's *Orientalism* to Turkish readers before it was translated in the early 1980s): "we are watching ourselves in the distorted mirror that the West has built, or rather, we are trying to build ourselves upon that image."[37] The image (or the imago for the self) is distorted; but can one ever have recourse to the original image?

Interestingly, what I see as Occidentalism in intellectuals such as Peyami Safa or Cemil Meriç is itself in dialogue with an Orientalist depiction of the "Turk." They try to keep alive the fantasy of the sovereign Oriental intellectual, in fact aspiring to the Orientalist Turkish myth.[38] The loss is without any hope of restitution, yet the sovereign intellectual assumes the power position to decide on possible strategies for recovery. In doing so he reserves for himself[39] the capacity for making the best judgment on "authentic" culture and modernity, while declaring both the "West" and the "unconscious Middle Eastern people" to be enemies.[40] So, he assumes an Occidentalist position, since the subject imagines that he, as a sovereign intellectual, can combine the surviving elements of the Orient with the best parts of Western modernity/civilization.

Once tracked in the route of Western modernity, the Orient is to be reproduced within the grid of Orientalism and Occidentalism. For example, the paradox that in Turkey Orientalism has been regarded as useful for real knowledge to emerge about the Orient, and particularly Islam, is telling. Historian Halil İnalcık, among others, points to the need to institutionalize the European hermeneutical tradition of Orientalism in our universities for the sake of interpreting Islamic resources. He adds: "Orientalism is no longer in the monopoly of the West."[41] The paradox is even greater when one considers that Turkology – more specifically French, English, and Hungarian Turkology – as a branch of Orientalism inspired the first Turkish nationalist ideas in the nineteenth century. Bernard Lewis, as an Orientalist, proudly declares that the idea of Turkey as a country inhabited by a certain people and constituting a natural entity, and the idea of the Turks as a nation distinct from the Ottoman dynasty and empire, is owed to the European science of Turkology.[42] So the Orient as a reality cannot be signified without recourse to Western categories of knowledge ironically embedded in Western power.

As I have argued before, the evoked yet displaced loss is constitutive of Occidentalism. The discourse of Occidentalism opens up a subject position within which being simultaneously modern and authentic, as a way of both catching the time of modern history and recuperating the loss, seems possible. Occidentalism promises to restore the authenticity without losing the ground of modernity. But the promise is impossible to keep. Occidentalism offers authenticity in national terms only to deny the alternate possibilities within the past and the present as lived experience, and to order and control the realm of differences and social conflicts within society exposed to the destabilizing dynamics of modernity as capitalism. In other words, it provides the means of "overcoming modernity," in Harootunian's words.[43] According to Harootunian, attempts to overcome modernity in Japan, for example, define a specific time-space context – the realm of the national – by positing a culture exempt from the uncertainty of historical changes, and by embracing modernity and "capitalism without its social effects and periodic crises."[44]

Interestingly, Buruma and Margalit's book takes the same theme of "overcoming modernity," albeit in a very different way, as a prominent feature of Occidentalism defined as anti-Westernism. According to the authors, overcoming modernity is a form of hating the West and bears grave political consequences in non-Western parts of today's world.[45] The definition of Occidentalism in association with this "dangerous" tendency, and specifically with Islam in non-Western contexts, reproduces Orientalism in a new guise, namely for the sake of "understanding Occidentalism," which is politically urgent according to the authors. This view, while problematizing "overcoming modernity" in the non-West, helps to normalize not only Western modernity but its necessary counterpart: the superiority of Western nations.

But isn't "nation" the very form of overcoming modernity? As Harootunian rightly stresses, and as Balibar had discussed earlier,[46] the construction of national identity attempts to contain not only the temporal heterogeneity of native populations but also the unwanted consequences of capitalism, especially by colonizing the lives of the subaltern. National identity, as a fictitious organic and authentic community set against the fragmenting and centrifugal forces of capitalism, has been to a great extent the common denominator shared by both the "West" and "East"; a common format of power internalized by both Orientalism and Occidentalism. Consider what Bernard Lewis has to say on Turkish national identity. According to him the official campaign of Kemalists in the 1930s to write history anew – fabricating an authentic Turkish past, "a mixture of truth, half-truth and error" – cannot be derided as "the whim of an autocrat," namely Mustafa Kemal:

> One of the reasons for the campaign was the need to provide some comfort for Turkish *national self-respect*, which had been sadly undermined during the last century or two . . . It is difficult not to sympathize with the frustration and discouragement of the young Turk, eager for enlightenment, who applied himself to the study of Western languages, to find that in most of them his name is an insult.[47]

We should note the frame of *understanding* here, apart from the subtle irony. Orientalism is talking to Occidentalism and is in complicity with it, by evoking the most acceptable modern concept of political community, the nation, both as a particular-spatial category (which defines authenticity) and also as universal-temporal axis (nation as "unbound seriality," as Benedict Anderson would say[48]) which defines modernity.

I have argued so far that Occidentalism in the non-West has been dialogically shaped in relation to Orientalism, which is itself the product of the Occidentalizing of the world, or the Occidentalism of the West. But I have also stressed that Occidentalism in the non-Western context is a hegemonic discourse of power, which attempts to recuperate the historical loss and invoke authentic nativity in the form of the *national* as the ontology of being modern. However, it is very important to note that the term hegemonic is not only about the construction of consent and normality. Hegemony also means the policing of the boundaries so that the traversing of these boundaries entails various judgments, even punishments, as Judith Butler reminds us.[49] The hegemonic boundaries of Occidentalism, as a discourse of power, produce Orientalisms within itself. Historically, a most significant example would be the Orientalization of Arabs in the Turkish national discourse. Starting from Ottoman Orientalism,[50] we can point to several cases in which Arabic people and districts have been labeled as the "East," defined, denigrated, and subject to control by the "authentic" Western-ness of Turkish national culture. Occidentalism enables the fantasy of sovereignty for its historically privileged subjects, in terms of class, gender, and ethnicity/religion. I say "fantasy of sovereignty" because sovereignty is not only about being in a privileged position to decide on the exception, as Schmitt would define it, it is also about "mastery over non-mastery" in Bataille's sense.[51] In other words, reducing the strange and the unknown to known categories, such as the nation, offers certain subjects a designated and officially sanctioned stage on which to perform and enact power, as we have seen in contemporary nationalist demonstrations in Turkey. However, the Orientalizing produced by Occidentalism cannot totally make the unknown known, which means that a clearly demarcated object as the Other can never be fixed and stabilized. The obscure object of control, and of desire/ denigration in this frame, can only exist as an abject. Abjects, which belong to that zone of indistinction between East and West, are continuously being produced on the margins of Occidentalist hegemony in Turkey. They are either national but not modern enough or modern but not national enough. To the extent that they traverse the designated spaces and boundaries of public action and speech – the Kurd, the Alevi, the veiled woman, the non-Muslim, the transvestite, the urban poor, the dissident student, the non-loyal intellectual, etc. – all, in changing social contexts, have been violently turned into abjects, and rendered easily disposable in Turkish history. Occidentalism as a hegemonic performative discourse leads to a series of appearances and disappearances.

The boundaries also protect the domain of the visible and observable, hence in a way what is to be known. Orientalism has been a mode of making the Other visible in a particular way with a certain repertoire of clichéd images so that particular spaces and their histories disappear. When Edward Said wrote on Orientalism he made the power-oriented practices of the field of Orientalism visible; that is, he re-staged the image of the Orient from a critical political perspective to make the violence of colonization appear. I would suggest by way of conclusion that re-visualization, or re-staging practices and meanings beyond the scope of entangled Orientalisms and Occidentalisms, is an urgent political/scholarly task today. We need a *new image* for knowledge and politics, not only for criticizing, disrupting, and changing, but also for freeing ourselves from the worst parts of modern history sedimented in Orientalism and Occidentalism. The future is yet unwritten and we need hope more than anything else today.

Notes

1 Bauman employs the term "liquid modernity" to analyze the tendencies of the present-day state of modernity (*Liquid Modernity*, Cambridge: Polity Press, 2000). According to him all modernity has been a process of disembedding (melting solids) or dismantling the received structures, but the process of modernity also offered new ways of re-embedding. "Solids were not melted in order to stay molten, but in order to be recast in moulds up to the standard of a better designed, rationally arranged society." However, this is no longer the case in the liquid modernity, in which the bonds are loose, frail and transitory (see "Zygmunt Bauman: Liquid Sociality," in *The Future of Social Theory*, ed. Nicholas Gane, London and New York: Continuum, 2004, p. 19). Resulting in even more accentuated forms of polarization, these tendencies also liquidate the aspired forms and values of modernity.

2 Edward Said, informed by a musical term, advances the idea of *contrapuntal* criticism to rethink the exigencies of the cultural intercourse between the West and the rest of the world, which entails having "a simultaneous awareness both of the metropolitan history that is narrated and of those other histories against which (and together with which) the dominating discourse acts" (Said, *Culture and Imperialism*, London: Vintage, 1994, p. 59). The contrapuntal criticism allows one to speak of "overlapping territories, inter-twined histories common to men and women, whites and non-whites, dwellers in the metropolis and on the peripheries, past as well as present and the future; these territories and histories can only be seen from the perspective of the whole of secular human history" (ibid., p. 72). Hence his aim is not to separate but to connect, in order to show the interdependencies of cultural forms that are hybrid and impure.

3 Françoise Vergès focuses on the need to examine the new forms of colonialism in the world. Vergès speaks of "the drawing of new borders, new territories of colonization of those spaces which seem to 'fall' from the surface of the earth, away from our consciousness, even in our visual world: the *grey zones* [where] people who do *not* count live (the State no longer needs to collect taxes, to raise armies among them, does not need their children for its future or their existence

to construct its legitimacy), and where new routes of trafficking in human beings emerge" ("Françoise Vergès: Postcolonial Challenges," in Gane, ed., *The Future of Social Theory*, p. 194). Judith Butler, on the other hand, points to Europe itself as the very site of what can be called a new colonialism. The anti-immigration politics within Europe reveal "a very specific version of European modernity laying claim to the social as its privileged instrument, and being used in effect to cast the non-European or questionably European as the pre-social or anti-social" ("Judith Butler: Reanimating the Social," in ibid., p. 52).

4 Ian Buruma and Avishai Margalit, *Occidentalism: The West in the Eyes of its Enemies*, New York: Penguin Press, 2004.

5 Cited in Stein Tonnesson, "Orientalism, Occidentalism, and Knowing about Others," *NIAS*, 2 April 1994.

6 Kultur *Austausch* online, January 2005.

7 Hanafi argues that "Occidentalism defends national character, national culture and national life-style; it is a popular culture set against the elitism of Orientalism; an ideology for the ruled as opposed to the ideology of the ruler; a liberating device, similar to liberation theology, set against the dogma of the church" (ibid.).

8 Xiao-mei Chen, *Occidentalism: A Theory of Counter-Discourse in Post-Mao China*, New York: Oxford University Press, 1995.

9 See Couze Venn, *Occidentalism: Modernity and Subjectivity*, London: Sage, 2000; Walter Mignolo, *Local Histories/Global Designs: Coloniality, Subaltern Knowledges, and Border Thinking*, Princeton, NJ: Princeton University Press, 2000; and Fernando Coronil, "Beyond Occidentalism: Toward Nonimperial Geo-historical Categories," *Cultural Anthropology*, 11 (1) 1996: 52–87.

10 Rather than taking East and West as distinct and knowable identities, I have argued that the very distinction has been functional in forming communities and drawing boundaries both between and within national contexts (see Meltem Ahıska "Occidentalism: The Historical Fantasy of the Modern," in *Relocating the Fault Lines: Turkey Beyond the East/West Divide*, special issue, *South Atlantic Quarterly*, 102 (2–3) 2003: 351–79, and Meltem Ahıska, *Radyonun Sihirli Kapısı: Garbiyatçılık ve Politik Öznellik*, İstanbul: Metis, 2005. My work on Turkish Occidentalism was inspired by James Carrier's formulation that to simply criticize the essentialist constructions of the East and West is not enough; instead one should study "how that essentialist and selective vision arises, how it reflects people's social and political situations, how it affects their lives and works" (James Carrier, ed., *Occidentalism: Images of the West*, Oxford: Clarendon Press, 1996, p. 28).

11 Gane, *The Future of Social Theory*, p. 187.

12 Mignolo, *Local Histories/Global Designs*, p. 29.

13 In a previous article I addressed the significance of the temporal difference between the "model" and the "copy" in terms of the modernity that words such as "progress" and "backward" signify (see Ahıska, "Occidentalism: The Historical Fantasy of the Modern").

14 Mignolo, *Local Histories*, p. 28.

15 Coronil, "Beyond Occidentalism," p. 56.

16 See Ahıska "Occidentalism: The Historical Fantasy of the Modern" and *Radyonun Sihirli Kapısı: Garbiyatçılık ve Politik Öznellik*.

17 Mahiye Seçil Dağtaş, "Married to the Military: Family, Nationalism and Women's Political Agency in Turkey," York University, PhD dissertation in progress.

18 For example, her talking about Diyarbakır, a city associated with the "Kurdish question," has to be contextualized with regard to the ambivalent relations of the Turkish state to the European Union in the 2000s. While the armed conflict between the military and Kurdish political groups continues with devastating results on the local population, the Turkish state has been trying to adopt multiculturalist policies towards the "minorities," including the Kurdish, so as to conform to European Union demands. Yet Turkish politics regarding the Kurdish question dwells more on defining the states of exception than pursuing institutionalized and established policies.

19 Mustapha Marrouchi argues that the anecdote has a "de-idolizing" effect; it causes a disturbance that needs explanation, contextualization, and interpretation (see Marrouchi, *Edward Said at the Limits*, Albany: State University of New York, 2004, p. 3).

20 The military in Turkey has had the dual and interconnected role of both ordering and modernizing the society. (For a contemporary study on the Turkish military and its gendered impact on social life see: Ayşe Gül Altınay, *The Myth of the Military Nation: Militarism, Gender, and Education in Turkey*, New York: Palgrave Macmillan, 2004.) The connection of the army in Turkey to the "West" remains to be further interpreted. Said himself argued that the Orientalists were the "learned division of the army" (cited in Marrouchi, *Edward Said at the Limits*, p. 94); and one can likewise suggest that the Turkish army is the political division of the learned Occidentalists.

21 I employ the term intimacy the way Herzfeld offers "cultural intimacy as an antidote to the formalism of cultural nationalism" (Michael Herzfeld, *Cultural Intimacy: Social Poetics in the Nation-State*, London: Routledge, 1997, p. 14). Herzfeld argues that an adherence to a static cultural ideal, such as Western modernity in non-Western contexts, "provides some actors with a mask with which to conceal a variety of messages" (ibid., p. 21).

22 Intimacy is produced by the form, as Beatriz Colomina argues in the context of Vienna, a city with masks, "it is this obsessive concern with the surface that constructs the intimate. The intimate is not a space but a relationship between spaces" (Colomina, *Privacy and Publicity: Modern Architecture as Mass Media*, Cambridge, Ms.: MIT Press, 1996, p. 28).

23 The discourse on nationalism evoked in the recent demonstrations embraced the term *ulusalcı* as different from *milliyetçi* – associated with either the nationalism of "conservative" or "extremist" groups. The new discourse utilizes the minor linguistic difference (the former is a new word, the latter an old one) to distinguish the contemporary nationalists from worn-out and debased nationalist trends in society. The distinction is also significant for signifying a "laicist" political attitude as well as a class position.

24 Despite the hegemonic media claim, in line with the declarations of the army, that the demonstrations were spontaneous "reflexes" of the masses against threats to the ideals of the nation, it was apparent that certain institutions, including the army, some political parties, "civil society" organizations, and the media played an active role in mobilizing the people.

25 I find it very significant that the nationalist demonstrations made formal references through their slogans and props to the hotly debated funeral of Hrant Dink a few months before. The unexpected crowd at the funeral, the slogans "We are all Armenians," "We are all Hrant Dink," and the Hrant Dink masks that people wore to support the slogans had a shocking impact in a society within which Armenian identity has been cast and marginalized as Other, and in most cases associated with enmity against the Turkish nation. The nationalist demonstrations tried to counter the Hrant Dink funeral, by appropriating the same forms with a different content; hence there were Atatürk masks and slogans such as "We are all Atatürks."

26 See Nilüfer Göle, *The Forbidden Modern: Civilization and Veiling*, Ann Arbor: University of Michigan Press, 1996.

27 I have discussed before Turkish nationalism's implicit reference to Islam as its defining element, which manifests itself in several national policies and public actions against non-Muslim groups in "modern" Turkish history, as well as in the recent nationalist reactions to Hrant Dink's assassination (2007). It is also noteworthy that one of the slogans on the nationalist demonstration in Izmir evoked a well-known accusation that Izmir is a city of the infidel due to its Greek heritage. The slogan was an attempt to overcome the accusation in its nationalist context yet at the same time accusing the Islamic party in rule for not being real Muslims, hence appropriating moderate Islam as the identity of nationalists: " "Gavur" Izmir kadar Müslüman olun yeter" (All we ask of you is to be as Muslim as "infidel Izmir.").

28 "Defending the secular 'faith,' " Stephanie Irvine, "Q&A: Turkey's political crisis," http://newsvote.bbc.co.uk, 21 May 2007.

29 In our research on contemporary nationalism in Turkey, we discussed how the threat of the globalized economic and social regime provokes various nationalisms (that divide instead of uniting people) as tactics of survival, with reference to more than 90 interviews and focus groups held in different parts of Turkey (Ferhat Kentel, Meltem Ahıska, Fırat Genç, *Milletin Bölünmez Bütünlüğü: Demokratikleşme Sürecinde Parçalayan Milliyetçilik(ler)*, Istanbul: TESEV, 2007).

30 Dipesh Chakrabarty, *Provincializing Europe: Postcolonial Thought and Historical Difference*, Princeton, NJ: Princeton University Press, 2000.

31 Lawrence Grossberg, "History, Imagination and the Politics of Belonging: Between the Death and the Fear of History," in *Without Guarantees: In Honour of Stuart Hall*, Paul Gilroy, Lawrence Grossberg, Angela McRobbie, eds., London and New York: Verso, 2000.

32 Jale Parla, *Efendilik, Şarkiyatçılık, Kölelik*, İstanbul: İletişim Yayınları, 1985.

33 The "Turkish myth" finally came to an end with the Crimean War (1853–56), which was considered in the 1950s to be "the cold war in an earlier phase" due to purely European considerations concerning Russia rather than in favor of Turkey (Henry Gibbs, *Crescent in Shadow*, London: Jarrolds Publishers, 1952).

34 In the introduction to the 1955 edition of Robert Curzon's book *Visits to Monasteries in the Levant* – a product of travels in Egypt, Syria, Turkey, and Greece through the years 1833–34 – the editor notes "Curzon's East is no more." Interestingly, Curzon himself had made a similar statement already in 1865, in the preface to the second edition of his book. It is worth looking at

Curzon's comments in this respect. "The adventures which happened to me then are now never met with, and these pages describe a state of affairs so entirely passed away, that the account of them seems to belong to a much more remote period than the year 1833. Those countries were, however, much better worth seeing at that time than they are now; *they were in their original state, each nation retained its own particular character, unadulterated by the leveling intercourse with Europeans*, which always, and in a very short time, exerts so strong an influence that picturesque dresses and romantic adventures disappear, while practical utility and a commonplace appearance are so generally disseminated, that in a few years every country will be alike, and travelers will discover that there is nothing to be found in the way of manners and customs that they may not see with great ease in their own houses in London" (Robert Curzon, *Visits to Monasteries in the Levant*, London: Arthur Barker Ltd, 1955, p. 20, emphasis mine). Or for a vivid example that illustrates the derogatory attitude we can look at what Kinglake says in *Eothen* in 1896, arriving in Constantinople: "You go out from your queenly London – the centre of the greatest and strongest among all earthly dominions – you go out thence, and travel on to the capital of an Eastern Prince – you find but a waning power, and a faded splendour, that inclines you to laugh and mock . . ." (Alexander William Kinglake, *Eothen: Traces of Travel Brought Home From The East*, Oxford: Oxford University Press, 1982, p. 33).

35 Cited by Nurdan Gürbilek, *Kör Ayna, Kayıp Şark: Edebiyat ve Endişe*, Istanbul: Metis, 2004, p. 88.

36 Vergès argues that the idea of *métis* is a reminder "that one can live without a fixed genealogy, with a broken filiation but without experiencing lack. It is about living with loss" (Gane, *The Future of Social Theory*, p. 200).

37 Cemal Meriç, *Kültürden İrfana*, İstanbul: İnsan Yayınları, 1986, p. 68–9.

38 It is not at all coincidence that the semi-fiction books written on "Turks" by Turks, which have become bestsellers recently, such as *Şu Çılgın Türkler* ("Those Crazy Turks"), idealize the image of the Turk, which was once both an object of desire and fear for the Europeans. These narratives are an attempt to revive the Turkish myth.

39 These are mostly male writers; whereas women writers have a different relationship to the narrative of Turkish modernity. Jale Parla argues that women writers had difficulties in conceptualizing their self-development in positive terms, and produced narratives of "nightmare" that connected them to Turkish history ('The Burden and the Bildung: The Nightmare of History in Turkish Women's Writing', unpublished paper, International Symposium on the Centenary of Women in Turkey, Boğaziçi University, 12–14 April 2000).

40 Meriç, *Kültürden İrfana*, p. 68. "*Orientalism* is an explosive book, it both destroys and illuminates. Maybe not a calm light, but could one look for peace in thunder? You will read it and get furious with yourself. The enemy, the common enemy of all of us: Liar Europe and unconscious people of the Middle-East" (ibid.).

41 Halil İnalcık, "Hermenötik, Oryantalizm, Türkoloji," Doğu Batı, Oryantalizm-I, 20(1), 2002: pp. 13–39.

42 Bernard Lewis, *From Babel to Dragomans: Interpreting the Middle East*, New

York: Oxford University Press, 2004, p. 423. Even in Occidentalism as anti-Westernism, for example in Hanafi's texts or much earlier in Jalal Al-e Ahmad's *Gharbzadegi* ("Westoxication or Occidentosis") (1962), nativism is paradoxically sought in the light of Western civilization, by appropriating Western philosophy and sciences (see Mehrzad Boroujerdi, *Iranian Intellectuals and the West: The Tormented Triumph of Nativism*, New York: Syracuse University Press, 1996).

43 Harry Harootunian, *Overcome by Modernity: History, Culture, and Community in Interwar Japan*, Princeton, NJ: Princeton University Press, 2000.

44 Ibid., xxi.

45 Buruma and Margalit, *Occidentalism*.

46 "Class Racism," in Etienne Balibar and Immanuel Wallerstein, *Race, Nation, Class: Ambiguous Identities*, London and New York: Verso, 1991.

47 Lewis, *From Babel to Dragomans*, p. 427, emphasis mine.

48 Benedict Anderson, *The Spectre of Comparisons: Nationalism, Southeast Asia and the World*, London and New York: Verso, 1998.

49 'Mimesis as Cultural Survival," in Vikki Bell, ed., *Performativity and Belonging*, London: Thousand Oaks, 1999.

50 Ussama Makdisi discusses Ottoman Orientalism against the Arabs as an integral aspect of the process of nationalist modernization in Ottoman society: "the nineteenth century saw a fundamental shift from this earlier imperial paradigm into an imperial view suffused with nationalist modernization rooted in a discourse of progress. Ottoman modernization supplanted an established discourse of religious subordination by a notion of temporal subordination in which an advanced imperial center reformed and disciplined backward peripheries of a multi-ethnic and multi-religious empire. This led to the birth of Ottoman Orientalism" (Ussama Makdisi, "Ottoman Orientalism," *The American Historical Review*, 107 (3) 2002, pp. 768–96 at p. 769).

51 Michael Taussig, *Walter Benjamin's Grave*, Chicago: University of Chicago Press, 2006, p. viii.

12

Said's Antinomies

Harry Harootunian

Edward Said devoted a good deal of his intellectual life to navigating between two revolutions: one that had never happened, whose absent presence was inscribed in the cultural turn of the 1970s, marked para- digmatically by the appearance of *Orientalism* as a foundational text; the other, still continuing, unfinished, incomplete, powerfully present in the Palestinian struggle for national independence. With *Orientalism*, Said demonstrated an exemplary sensitivity to the figure of the discursive text and the aporetic status of representation, while his activity in the Palestinian cause made him its most persistently eloquent spokesman. The former – an abortive revolution – reflected a strategic diversion of the worldwide uprisings of the 1960s and thus their displacement to the culture of critique and the effort to find new enabling interpretative agendas promising to unveil the problematic claims of narrative coherence, unity, and closure. This particular reflex, as practiced by Said, recalls for us a specific historical conjuncture that willingly would supply the demand for new ways to look at history, culture, and politics outside of explicit political arenas and gener- ously offer new theoretical perspectives capable of fulfilling the new mission. But whereas others remained committed to the register of the cultural text, Said sought to balance this preoccupation with requirements of another revolution, still in the making, whose completion was yet to come, driven by a politicality not easily delegated to the humus of culture and a passed history. Resisting the seductions of displacement, this revolution vividly attested to a lived experience of struggle in the everyday against colonial domination, powerfully reminding us daily of the troubling consequences and disappointments of the postcolony after national independence. It revealed also how deeply the activity of politics was embedded in time and a temporalizing process. But Palestine was not yet even a postcolony, since its putative decolonization never exceeded the transfer of rule from one colonizing power to another. And the retention of the shadowy silhouette of national liberation shaped by Third World triumphalism in the 1960s was still capable of reaching to our present to force us to recognize its memory of a vivid moment, filled with promise, now passed into a past history. Because Said was, at the same time, actively participating in the plot lines of two different narratives, two antinomial (if not contradictory) moments constituting the structure of his intellectual practice, trying to align asymmetrical temporalities, his attempt to bridge them opened the path to rethinking the uncertain but more fundamentally antagonistic relationship between history and memory and to finding ways of refiguring the received hierarchy governing their order of veracity.

In this regard, Said's attempt to overcome the antinomies marking his project caught between representation and presentation – showing – necessarily required putting into operation a tactic, first enacted by Walter Benjamin, whereby the present telescopes the past, which polarizes the event in both an anterior and posterior history. History, as Benjamin proposed and Said showed, was as much a science, as such, as it was a form of rememoration (*Eingedenken*), as much experiential as facticity. What occurs in large measure is figured by the present since it is memory that establishes the facts. More recently, the French historian François Hartog has similarly forged the notion of "presentism" to describe a situation in which finally "the present becomes the horizon," one which, without future and past, will permanently engender the two – history and memory – according to its needs. While Said recognized that the appeal to memory invariably risks reducing experience to exceptional singularity, he also saw that the pitfalls of conventional historiographic practice – eschewing the subjective dangers of experience – was the impulse that transforms this singularity by resituating it as a refraction of the normative and familiar prism of history writing. In this effort to circumvent the protocols of conventional historiographic practice, the aim should rather be to inscribe the singularity of lived experience in the context of a global history yet to be envisioned. With Said, and especially *Orientalism*, the habitual Eurocentric paradigms, based on subordinating memory to (national) history, and thus taming its subjective excess, was permanently put into question when the explanatory models were finally derailed with decolonization and then the final parting of history and memory with the appearance of the subaltern classes as political agents. History was subsequently democratized in the wake of the shattered imperial borders of Western cultural unity and the de-monopolization of the dominant elites, whereas memory itself was freed from its exclusive dependence on writing (disciplined by historiography). The antinomial relationship between history and memory is thus reconfigured in such a way as to present it now in the form of a mutually reinforcing, dynamic tension which, I believe, was dramatized early and consistently by Said's practice. But fueling this tension was the figure of the momentary Third World triumphalism from the world of the 1960s, continuing to cast its shadow over his present, and demanding the necessity of articulating its singular experience in a changing global context. In this new interpretative strategy, memory emerges as the new site in the writing of history, inasmuch as history actually writes itself as daily experience in the everyday struggle to complete what had started long ago.

Hence, Said became the active participant simultaneously in a narrative driven by a politics of time and another fixed in the space of culture. If the latter resembled the colonization of space so prominent in cultural studies today, this prevalent cultural dominant would insist on inverting considerations of the space/time relationship – the mark of the political – to establish the primacy of a fixed spatial countenance announcing the "end of temporality." Yet it was, I believe, the temporalizing imperative required by the political and its associations with continuing the anti-colonial struggle of the 1960s in the present that often rubbed against the grain of Said's involvement in the cultural dominant – literary aesthetics, late style, and so forth, but which he managed, with often breathtaking skill, to bring together the different modalities by making each side of the antinomial structure into a mediation of the other, a form of a productive parallax and even, perhaps, a set of constitutive contradictions. Under the force of the current situation, he was able to successfully show how and why anti-colonial struggle and its memory – everywhere – was always the provenience of the present and the responsibility of history. Behind the forfeiture of the singularized experience embodied in memory and its exclusion from history, as Said recognized and the Palestinian cause daily dramatized for him, lurked the larger question it prompted of the prospect of what he described as the "unwritten histories and negated memories of violence." When describing the purpose of Israeli archeology and its obsession to restore and shed light on the millennial traces of the Jewish past in Palestine – creating a virtual national religion out of archeology, a new civic religion, perhaps – Said reports that the soil had been dug out with the same kind of relentless intensity as the bulldozer that plows under everything in its way and erases the material remnants of the "rich sediments of village history." Like other national narratives, watered down into lures of tourism, Israeli archeology has worked incessantly to extract from the soil a continuous Jewish identity, what Said calls a "dynastic continuity" cobbled together from dispersed fragments, despite evidence to the contrary disclosing the coexistence of ruins and traces that constitute an immense tableau attesting to a countrywide palimpsest of mixed cultures and their times, which are endogamous but non-Jewish. Here history, the national narrative, was able to enlarge its vocation to efface other histories, other's histories in the negation and denial of their memories. Sensitive to the Israeli expropriation of land in 1948, not really different from the French who came to Algeria and immediately settled on an already-occupied land, or the Japanese in Manchuria, Said was convinced that this act of dispossession (Israeli primitive accumulation at the expense of the Palestinians) was linked to the surrender of a memory and history culturally materialized in the sedimented soil. To this end, he endeavored to alert the present of the existence of these "unwritten histories" and negated memories, and to begin the difficult labor of restoring to the surface what had been bulldozed under, rescuing both the mixed temporalities embodied in Palestine's landscape from the flattened time of another's national biography, and making audible the distant echoes of its multiple voices.

In what is, perhaps, his penultimate book, *Freud and the Non-European* (2003), Said turned to speaking of the figure of other besieged identities and the compelling necessity of attending to it – thinking of an identity, as he put it, "outside the inside so often occupied by so many." Locating in Freud's *Moses and Monotheism* an instance of mobilizing the non-European past as the source of Jewish identity, Said was persuaded that this controversial thesis that placed Moses on the outside resulted in making Egypt into the non-Jewish antecedent of Judaism. This outside identity, constituted a "troubling, disabling, destabilizing secular wound, the essence of the cosmopolitanism, from which there can be no recovery, no state of resolved calm," but which still "wants to know if this psychological history has a real history that can be written," one capable of escaping history's own habit of simply coming after and writing over what happened – ideological superscripting – and repressing the "flaw." The problem Said discerned in Freud was how such a history might be grasped, written, and in which language might be the condition of a politics of diasporic life capture its unseen order. Yet, at the same time, Said wondered whether such a history could ever serve as the foundation of a bi-national state in which Israel and Palestine overcome their antagonism and come together in the form of a confederal political arrangement.[1] Said was optimistic and answered his own question affirmatively. But the possibility of realizing such a history – not the as-yet unwritten psychological history, but rather a real one requiring a strategy capable of avoiding the form of a national narrative and its habits – speaks against such hopefulness. It is important to recognize that the vocation of national history is to vocalize the singular and irreducible identity claimed by the nation, the collective singular – its triumph and completion, as it seeks to repress precisely what has enabled its modern achievement, which would necessarily entail finding another unit for organizing experience and event.

In this regard, Jacqueline Rose, in her response to Said's meditations on Freud, helpfully recalls for us Benjamin's conviction of the responsibility of every present to recognize the "image of the past" as its own concern, in order to forestall the fate of its forgetting and disappearance. Said's Freud, like the past Benjamin wished to retain in his time, is conjured by and for our present, just as we must today recognize how the present we live constantly works to expel and extinguish the troubling images of pasts that once commanded attention. If, as Rose observes, Said's reading of Freud constitutes a powerful political parable, it also appears before us as a profound historical allegory for all those experiences that have been lost and forgotten once they have done their job of enabling the formation of a particular identity. There is, in fact, a stunning symmetry between the founding of a Jewish identity on the outside and the inside claims of the nation-state and its effacement of the history – the outside – that had made its modern existence possible, whether it is the Palestinian struggle to keep that memory from disappearing, or the genocidal destruction of the colonized of Europe – what Aimé Césaire once described as producing the "highest heap of corpses in history" and which, he believed, ultimately prepared the ground for the later Jewish Holocaust. But this colonial instantiation of mass murder was also accompanied by the massacre of Armenians (too early for a postcolonial settling of scores and too late for realizing national aspirations because of World War I) which stemmed from the panic of a failing and receding empire, recently expelled from Europe, fearful of the peril of its own disappearance and the desperate effort of modernizers to retrieve it in the reduced shape of the nation-state, thus inaugurating the twentieth century's ambition for ethnic elimination and sending it on a "cleansing" mission on a scale never before reached in human history. If the near extinction of the Armenians in the Ottoman Empire inflected the imperial/colonial agency in the century's genocidal project, there are numerous examples closer to home and in our time testifying as to how the act of ethnic cleansing of minority populations and their elimination from the political body constitutes the source of the nation-state. It is, I believe, this history Said had warned against – the thrust of modernizing programs powered by the homicidal instincts of organic nationalism, whose own logic invariably leads to the killing fields of expulsion, extermination, and extinction of minority populations, since their presence constitutes a permanently obscene scandal and challenge to the imperative demanding centralization, integration, unification and the promotion of correlate economic conditions for the successful primitive accumulation of capital. In most of these modernizing episodes leading to forms of expulsion and extermination, the inducement of choice employed to gain assent and mobilize the ethnos as partners in crime is the promise of land and the expropriation of the wealth and possessions of the expelled. The Turkish example is almost paradigmatic since approximately 400,000 inhabitants were expelled from Europe after the Balkan Wars of 1912–13 and resettled in Anatolia, alongside historically embedded minorities like Armenians, Kurds, Assyrians, etc., now coexisting in an environment of diminished resources and scarcity combining to ignite competition.

This modernizing impulse was easily harnessed to the darker instincts of organic nationalism because the stakes are now seen as survival in a changing world of modern nation-states, each competing with the other, often making them synonymous with programs of ethnic cleansing and/or religio/racial purification promising the realization of phantasmagoric dreams of homogeneity. One group's dispossession and elimination is another's ticket to cash in on the prize of racial homogeneity and capitalist accumulation, whose achievement is seen as the fundamental condition of national survival in a modern and modernizing world dominated by nation-states. Long before Jean-Claude Milner proposed the somewhat outsized proposition that the destruction of Europe's Jews made possible the subsequent unification of contemporary Europe, calling it a "penchant," we have the examples of modern nation-state formations constructed on the banishing and vanishing of minority populations, on the genocidal event; a relationship which writers like Césaire, Fanon, Cabral, and Takeuchi had already incorporated in their critical perceptions of empire as the seedbed of race hatred that led to the removal of whole populations in Africa (who would deny that Leopold's depredations in the Congo were at the heart of the modern Belgian nation?), Asia (Cambodia, Indonesia, Timor, India, and Pakistan), Stalinist Russia, the United States and its reduction of native Americans, Argentina, Rwanda, Bosnia, Darfur, and more.

Said was cognizant of the history of this fearful record, which must have haunted his defense of the Palestinians' right to survive on their own land, and whose removal was already beginning to reveal the working out of a terrible equation of racial hatred and expulsion equaling the origins of the modern Jewish state. At the heart of this modernizing impulse calling for increased centralization and unification is the fictional figure of racial homogeneity, ethnos trumping demos. We also know from examples ranging from French Algeria to Japan's Korea and America's Philippines that modernization promoted by colonial powers was first a code for sanitation, cleansing, and purification – cleaning the place up and then acting as a model for class cleansing at home. As a process, modernization was initially understood as a forcible sanitization of society, cleansing the national body, ridding it of impurities which easily led to large-scale replacement of populations such as the Koreans of Eastern Siberia under Stalin, and ultimately removals like those of the Armenians, Greeks, and Assyrians in the Ottoman Empire, and to countless forced deportations in Africa and South Asia.

The modernizing process, like the modernism it often mimics, subsumes all of its antecedents, which demands the constructing of new narratives founded on self-invention and self-formation and forgetting. In fact, it was pioneer theorist of nationalism, Ernest Renan, who observed that nations invariably forget their origins as a necessary condition of achieving modern nationhood. But in the forgetfulness new narratives of origin and presence are constructed. This has meant that the nation has always existed – a presumed "fact" on which tourist brochures constantly harangue us, as in the case of Turkey, colorfully portraying the ruins of different cultures though their peoples are no longer visible, now available in trace only, scattered, dispersed, like random rock formations, over the Anatolian peninsula, all existing in an endless present that has managed to obliterate their own temporalities. These representations of ruins attesting to different temporalities marked by emptied churches and buildings resemble Orhan Pamuk's description of a scene in his novel *Snow*, where the protagonist returns home to Erzurum and passes through familiar neighborhoods still sprinkled with the spacious homes of wealthy Armenians, now long vacated, darkened, standing in mute attendance, waiting, perhaps, for a hint of recognition that will finally bring the relief of an uncomplicated retribution. But the sign of the longer and richer history of village life is not just absent in Pamuk's account, it has disappeared permanently from sight for a ghostly residence in the precincts of diasporic memory to secure a new but fleeting lease on life as the sole possession of the last community of survivors.

Here, it seems, is a clue to the logic compelling forms of denial on the origins of the modern past and its necessity, in the face of the immense violence committed to bringing into being the modern nation form. The Japanese today incessantly deny their own depredations in Asia during the Pacific War, blaming exaggerated reports by Koreans and Chinese. But this disavowal is very much aimed at concealing the wartime origins of contemporary society and the fateful history of fascism that drove Japan into imperial frenzy. Only the Germans, or at least some of them, have been able to own up to their responsibility for the destruction of European Jewry, even though most modern genocidal behavior involving the imperatives of ethnic cleansing of one group by another is passed over in silence and drowned in the din of clashing claims over legitimacy, as Said observed of nationalist agendas resembling each other in territorial contests. But even in this regard, there are still powerful revisionists like the historian Ernst Nolte, whose arguments have transmuted Germans from the figure of victimizers into heroic victims and the Holocaust into an instance of collateral damage. Nolte proposed that the Germans had only copied what the Soviets had done first, and that the killing of Jews was a byproduct of the titanic struggle to save Europe from "Asiaticism" – Soviet Communism – and its aim to destroy bourgeois civilization. The question of denial is pinned to presumptions of timeless, irreducible experience of belonging to an ethnic group as the principal condition for asserting the superiority of a singular identity and inclusion in it.

What cannot be acknowledged, and here Said's metaphor of the bulldozer is appropriate, are the violent historical circumstances enabling the formation of the modern nation-state. In the etiology of denial employed to counteract charges there is a first appeal to the "smoking gun" (Germans were obsessively concerned with trying either to show or conceal Nazi planning of the genocide); then there is the turn to a comparison that closes off all comparability by inviting critics to look elsewhere and usually closer to home, as Turkey did in relation to France recently (Japanese historians used to argue that Japan's fascism was not as bad Germany's!); then the tactic reverts to inverting the relationship between victim and victimizer, making the former occupy the place of the latter (Japan seized upon this device after the war, just as Turkey pointed to what Armenians had done to Turks and Kurds in Anatolia and in the former Yugoslavia, all of the contending parties constantly accusing the others as victimizers); then, there is the promotion of actual state legislation proscribing memory or mention of the violent origins of the nation form, which automatically licenses anybody who believes that a law of identity has been broken to make a citizen's arrest or commit worse acts like murder. In the United States there is still no legislation that even acknowledges the extermination of the native population, even though there is a museum devoted to the Holocaust, much less the existence of a monument commemorating the event and offering a place for mourning. But, in the end, the most consequential result of the structure of disavowal is the way the exceptualizing of ethnic experience, on which all presumptions of national identity must rest, works to singularize the negativity of the targeted group, making them both non-national and non-natural (as Carl Schmitt observed in his discussions on friend and foe), and whose elimination guarantees for the nation its purchase on modernity but also its reduction of the genocidal event to singular isolation, robbing it of a real family resemblance with the experience of other massacres. (Nolte, seeking to satisfy a historicist illusion, wanted to resituate Germany's destruction of the Jews as a moment in a wider history of both Germany and the world.) In our time, this effect may also be further mediated by the figure of the Holocaust itself and its elevation to unique and unparalleled status in the historical pantheon of global murder, at the expense of discounting and even dismissing other claimants to horror. Hence the doubly negative fate of the Armenian experience of ethnic cleansing, and others, which fail to measure up, produces an overdetermination of exclusions.

In this regard, it is hardly surprising that Jewish scholars like Bernard Lewis, after 1967, began to actively demote the Armenian genocide to the level of a "vivid ethnic imagination," fueled by the diaspora, even though many of them – including Lewis himself – once publicly acknowledged assent to and support for its claims. With Israeli scholars, there has simply been a studied indifference to its very existence, as if comparison would compromise the privilege accorded to the German extermination of European Jews. But there is an unwelcome symmetry between ceaseless Israeli appeals to the uniqueness of the Holocaust and Turkish denials of having inflicted a genocidal event. Even worse, the United States, along with the State of Israel, has continually reinforced this form of denial out of fear of alienating their combined national interests in Turkey, and have thus recklessly and irreparably banalized both history and memory in order to satisfy the demands of an expedient geopolitics, one which has already produced unimaginable destruction in Iraq. Under this circumstance, they have become complicit partners willing to legitimate and sanction the naturalization of race hatred and its most extreme consequences. Which takes us out of allegory and back to the actuality of Said's struggle for Palestinian liberation and the antinomial structure informing his intervention, which momentarily succeeded in bringing together allegorization and actualization into a lasting testament for any subsequent effort to resolve the knotted aporias of theory and practice, politics and culture, memory and history, home and dislocation.

Note

1 Edward Said, *Freud and the Non-European*, London and New York: Verso, 2003, pp. 54–5.

13

Said, Religion, and Secular Criticism

Gauri Viswanathan

In an interview with Tariq Ali, Edward Said makes a rare comment in which he links religion with dissent. In response to Ali's observation on the ominous rise of extreme fundamentalist Muslim groups, Said remarks that he sees them as "creatures of the moment [for] whom Islam is an opportunity to protest the current stalemate, the current mediocrity and bankruptcy of the ruling party."[1] While sharply disagreeing with extremism in all forms, Said, who as Ali himself notes was "totally secular and nonreligious,"[2] was able to recognize religion – at least in this one instance – as a site from which the failings of the ruling political order could be exposed. It is clear, even in this brief exchange, how important it was for Said to put pressure on cultural criticism as a means by which ideologies of power are made transparent and no longer serviceable to narrow, self-serving interests. That religion could be allied with critique opens an angle of vision on his uses of the term "'secular criticism'" that I wish to explore in this essay.

Rather than arguing that Said's subversive understanding of Islam in this context undermines his secularism and renders his practice of secular criticism unstable and incoherent, as some critics charge, I maintain that he was often tacitly aware of, without ever quite overtly acknowledging, the densely packed meanings in the word "'religion'" itself, covering over a history that includes both orthodox and heterodox elements. At one level Said has been criticized for inconsistencies in his approach to religion when he discusses Islam. William Hart maintains that "Said's hostile critique of religion stands in sharp contrast to his defence of Islam,"[3] a view that is patently contradicted when one probes Said's efforts to salvage Islam from the homogenization that reduces it to an abstraction and cancels out important variations of Islam, heterodox in some cases, which might provide more rounded insights into a rich and multi-layered religion. Indeed, those heterodox elements in religion permit Said to speak of Massignon's views on Islam thus:

Islam is therefore a religion of resistance (to God the Father, to Christ the Incarnation), which yet keeps within it the sadness that began in Hagar's tears . . . Within Islam, Massignon believed he was able to discern a type of countercurrent, which it became his chief intellectual mission to study, embodied in mysticism, a road towards divine grace. The principal feature of mysticism was of course its subjective character, whose nonrational and even inexplicable tendencies were towards the singular, the individual, the momentary experience of participation in the Divine. All of Massignon's extraordinary work on mysticism was thus an attempt to describe the itinerary of souls out of the limiting consensus imposed on them by the orthodox Islamic community, or Sunna.[4]

This is an extraordinary passage to my mind, one that shows Said to be particularly responsive to those charismatic elements in religion that resist consensus and authority. This passage is all the more striking when one considers that, for Said, secular criticism is a centerpiece of intellectual work, defined in opposition to religious criticism which, in *The World, the Text, and the Critic*, he repudiates as steeped in arcane mysticism. At the same time, certain turns in his work, like the one quoted above, suggest that he had a much more complicated view of secularism: he tacitly acknowledged that, for secular criticism to be directed towards an ethical basis for justice against oppression, the source of ethical knowledge or values would have to be clearly defined. Whether that source led him to religion or not, whether he acknowledges religion as a source of dissent – a place from which to speak truth to power – remained unspoken in his work. In this essay I examine Said's complicated understanding of secular criticism from the viewpoint of recent scholarship on secularism and cultural criticism, which might shed some light on why Said may not have been entirely able to disentangle his notion of secularism from its religious forebears.

But first I want briefly to allude to Said's single most important influence in developing the idea of secular criticism, namely, Vico. From Vico, Said derived the conviction that only humanly attained knowledge can promote human freedom, and this remained a fundamental tenet of his secular criticism. Vico's opposition of sacred (Hebraic) to worldly (gentile) history was of fundamental importance for Said because of its pivotal shift from divine to human history as the basis of knowledge. Though Vincent Pecora, among others, sees Said as the direct heir of Enlightenment rationality, in the tradition of Diderot seeking his ethical impulse in rational tolerance, the more immediate influences on Said represent transitional moments in religious history when notions of time are defined in terms of genealogies of human development and progress. Such genealogies do not necessarily exclude Christian ethical humanism, as I hope to show later. While it is convenient to see empirical reason as constituting a principal challenge to religious doctrine, the mistake (and it is one that Said also makes at times) is to homogenize religion as a unitary concept and understate the degree to which it comprises competing beliefs, some of which were historically marginalized, others totally obliterated, and still others assimilated to a dominant religious system. To conceptualize religion in opposition to reason, therefore, misses the role of oppositional, so-called heretical discourses like Gnosticism, Manicheism, and Hermeticism in defining what Karen King calls "the boundaries of normative Christianity."[5] That Gnostic beliefs were rendered equivalent to Oriental heresies furthered the aims of colonialism in propagating Christianity as the only true authentic religion.

The standard argument about the Enlightenment as a vehicle for secularization, in which conceptions of divinely inspired history are replaced by the idea of history as a product of human agency, pays little heed to religious heterodoxies in the secularizing process. These oppositional knowledge systems challenged canonical tenets and initiated skepticism and resistance to official, state-sponsored doctrines. Furthermore, at least one of these knowledge systems – Gnosticism – called for a return to inaugural moments in the rise of religion when the mysteries of life, while being an object of religious thought, at the same time represented a moment of "existential experience of human alienation."[6] The attempt to turn such experience into theodicy, offering systematized explanations for suffering that eventually put in place doctrinal religions, was a prime target of heterodox thought falling outside the canonical mainstream. I wish to argue here that it is in his literary readings that Said captured something of the oppositional nature of heterodox religions.

Saree Makdisi, in his contribution to this volume, noted two contradictory perceptions of the intellectual in Said's work: one, the idea of the intellectual as a solitary, forbidding, inaccessible, and charismatic prophet; and the other, the idea of an accessible intellectual speaking to a community at large. In what follows, I offer a reading of Max Weber in order to show how he helps us understand why there were two contradictory views of the intellectual in Said, and how that contradiction underwrites Said's ethical humanism. It is interesting that Weber, notoriously credited with having institutionalized the notion of the "disenchantment of the world" as a secular outcome of religion's decline, has received far less attention for several arresting passages in his work tracing the genealogy of the intellectual to theodicy. For, according to Weber, the modern intellectual – the ultimate product of a secularized world – has been paradoxically consumed by the need to understand the causes of pain and suffering in the world. Weber offers what to all intents and purposes is a theory about the religious origins of the modern intellectual. From ethical guilt and unjust suffering, the intellectual develops a compensatory ethics that ultimately seeks not to reject religion but to *rationalize* it. The compulsion to explain seemingly random, pointless, and meaningless suffering is accompanied by a conviction that there must be just recompense for unjust suffering. That compensation is found in ethical meaning. Suffering, for Weber, is the key starting point for rationalization of the world. His argumentation does not follow a straight-forward path and, indeed, works obliquely to link compensatory meaning with loss of mystery and human alienation (I am purposefully refraining from using the word "disenchantment" at this stage in order to unpack the semantic possibilities encrypted in this word). Weber argues, for example, that the more one seeks to find meaningfulness, the more the world itself is devalued. But conversely, the more the world is devalued, the more its value is sought . . . but in what, exactly?

Marcel Gauchet, writing on disenchantment, draws attention to Gnostic thought as refusing any kind of rationalization: "At one extreme lay gnosticism's great rejection, the irrevocable devaluation of this world in favor of the unimaginably other to which the soul aspires."[7] At the other end are proto-secularist efforts to "reintegrate the order here-below with its source in the beyond, the theocratic attempt to put worldly life on the same footing as life directed toward the beyond."[8] If Gnosticism represents one extreme, radical in its total rejection of rationalization, we find Weber struggling to break out of a bind that kept the intellectual in the grip of religious rationalization, despite the apparent worldliness produced by intellectual moves: "For the more intensely rational thought has seized upon the problem of a just and retributive compensation, the less an entirely inner-worldly solution could seem possible, and the less an other-worldly solution could appear probable or even meaningful."[9]

Reading Weber, I am reminded of Simon During's suggestive analysis of literary history, in which he observes that the more literature is devalued, the more it breaks off from its institutional affiliations and enters the fantasy spaces of wonder. Wonder, unlike tradition or orthodoxy, has no institutional home, no anchoring mechanism that channels its expression in determinate ways. It does not require a structure of reference and inter-textuality to construe its meaning – indeed it thwarts all identification with systematized forms of knowledge. It would seem Max Weber makes an uncannily similar move by opening up the possibility that the "existential experience of human alienation," to use Karen King's phrase, initiates a search for value in an as yet indeterminate space. The fact that this search results in rationalization, which in turn perpetuates the repetitive cycle of devaluation and revaluation of the world, does not take away from Weber's characterization of the intellectual enterprise as shot through with motivations akin to those driving theodicy.

Furthermore, Weber's understanding of rationalization follows a peculiarly dialectical progression. I quote an important but under-glossed passage from his essay "Religious Rejections of the World and Their Directions," which I believe has considerable relevance for Said's critical practice:

> The less magic or merely contemplative mysticism and the more "doctrine" a religion contains, the greater is its need of rational apologetics . . . The more religion became book-religion and doctrine, the more literary it became and the more efficacious it was in provoking rational lay-thinking, freed of priestly control. From the thinking laymen, however, emerged the prophets, who were hostile to priests; as well as the mystics, who searched for salvation independently of priests and sectarians; and finally the skeptics and philosophers, who were hostile to faith.[10]

Strikingly, Weber's account of intellectual activity following upon religious rationalization brings the anti-clerical, antinomian intellectual closer to Gnostic ways of knowing than to Enlightenment rationalism as we understand it. Here is another quote from Weber: "Every religion in its psychological and intellectual sub-structure . . . has taken a different stand towards intellectualism, without allowing the ultimate inward tension to disappear. For the tension rests on the unavoidable disparity among ultimate forms of images of the world."[11] This is clearly not a triumphalist narrative of reason's ascendancy over belief but a subtle reading of religion's oppositionality as being internal to it – an oppositionality that embraces different dissenting traditions.

Most importantly, Weber recognized the bonds that kept the intellectual tied to rationalizing processes in religion: "Redemptory religion will see nothing but the intellect's desire to escape its own lawful autonomy. Above all, religion sees all this as a specific product of the very rationalism that *intellectualism, by these endeavors, would very much like to escape.*"[12] Weber sees rationalization as a trap that the intellectual can escape only by, paradoxically, taking recourse in what Simon During, describing literary subjectivity, calls "the fantasy space of wonder." If this is the inevitable but startling trajectory of rationalization, then its outcome in spurring resistance to rationalism speaks to the oblique routes through which we would need to trace not only the pathways of intellectual activity but also secularism itself. For if the irony of rationalization in explaining irrational experiences like suffering and pain produces equally irrational concepts like original sin (the example Weber gives), then true acts of intellection *must* go in opposite directions, short-circuiting the compulsions to rationalization. So perhaps more than he may have intended, Weber brings the skeptic and the intellectual closer to the dissenting knowledge systems that posed heterodox challenges to mainstream doctrine by questioning the very premises of religious rationalization.

Rudyard Kipling was a writer much admired by Said, as evident in his memorable introduction to the Penguin edition of Kipling's novel *Kim*. Said treats the religious figure in the novel, the Tibetan Buddhist lama, with comical affection, respecting the spiritual figure's mystical search, without seeing it as having any significant effect on the real world of British India. Yet it was also Kipling, particularly in the short stories, who presciently honed in on the unstable relation between secularism and religion, and was especially sensitive to the crucial role played by history in linking narratives of linear development found in Judeo-Christian traditions to secular rationality, indeed even anticipating it. The distortions of time suggested by ideas of recurrence, repetition, and cycle in metempsychosis and reincarnation – themes that engrossed Kipling throughout his writing career – simply do not fit into the narrative scheme of the historical traditions, supported to a great extent by Judeo-Christian history. A sneaking suspicion that secularism retains aspects of religious ideas remains just below the surface of Kipling's works, sometimes exploding in shocked recognition of the multiple orders of time that render secularism's relation to religion unstable at its very core. Such instability, working against religious rationalization, dogs the work of even the most skeptical and rational intellectuals such as Nietzsche, Weber, or Habermas. To this list one might also add Said, who was encouraged to read literature's oppositional energies as a form of dissenting theology.

One need only turn to the recent writing of Marcel Gauchet to see how contemporary scholarship on disenchantment and secularism, which purports to be revisionist, accepts the powerful hold of the Judeo-Christian tradition on the thinking of modern intellectuals, indeed, a far greater hold than is generally acknowledged. The new revisionism is captured by Gauchet's insistence that Christianity is a *precursor* to modern secularism because it introduced ideas of rational and moral progress fundamental to conceptualizing modernity. Following Gauchet's argument to some extent, Vincent Pecora's recent book *Secularism and Cultural Criticism* maintains that the Western intellectual can never escape reverting to the deep relationship between the secularized Judeo-Christian tradition and Enlightenment notions of truth and progress. However, Pecora's aim is not so much to affirm that Christianity is secularism's precursor as to question gaps in memory and knowledge of secularism's own history persisting in contemporary criticism, particularly about secularism's religious origins.

Pecora's book offers a useful point of reference in understanding how secularism is brought within the frame of Christianity's ethical imperatives, even as secularism's derivation of messianic trajectories of progress and redemption from Christian tenets becomes a fundamental point of contention in cultural criticism. Recognizing the effects of such a bind, Löwith and Blumenberg adopted the most radical and uncompromising approach: In seeking to dismantle secularism's Christian edifice, they distanced themselves from secularism's putative moral trajectory, arguing instead that history is contingent, cyclical, mechanical, and purposeless. Their effort to disentangle secularism from Christianity was so pronounced that it led to their conceiving of human action as mechanistic and random, without any sort of anchoring in principle or redemptive promise. No doubt, the conception of secularism as a materialistic, mechanical philosophy puts into question the commitment to principles of distributive justice and equality that post-religious societies strive for, in place of the hierarchical structures preserved by clerical or priestly authority. The cold logic that underwrites the mechanistic reinscription of secularism brushes aside the ethical implications of such a position, insisting that secularism must be extricated from its religious antecedents if it is to have any consequence.

Notwithstanding a significant critical move to disavow secular culture's evolution from religious origins, taken to its most uncompromising limit in Löwith and Blumenberg, we would do well to ask how and why religion lingered even in the work of skeptical intellectuals, who were haunted by the challenge of explaining where a concept of the good comes from if religious belief no longer supplies codes of behavior and action. Is religion so inextricably tied to modern secularism that the latter cannot be conceived without its predecessor? There is a strain of thought in Western philosophy and social science that cannot altogether dispense with the legacies of Christianity, and this is marked in Said's work as well by a turn towards ethical humanism. By way of comparison, we might refer to Habermas'' conflicted theories of modernity, which Pecora examines brilliantly to locate the precise points at which secularism has been rendered most vulnerable when unmoored from its religious foundations. For example, art objects that have ritualistic religious significance, blending the sacred and the secular in their iconic status as instruments of both worship and aesthetic appreciation, become problematic when placed in museums, where the pre-existing balance between secular and sacred elements becomes disrupted, contributing to an inherent instability in the identity of secular culture. Is this a sign of modernity's incomplete project, as Habermas claimed? If modernity's projcct is incomplete, the reasons may well lie with secular philosophy's inadequacy in translating "all the *politically significant* religious and Judeo-Christian concepts into a viable public and universal discourse."[13] Pecora's inclusion of the words "politically significant" to characterize the ongoing relevance of religious precepts raises the stakes for the creation of a pluralistic society. Is political significance measured in terms of a common denominator across all religions? Is there indeed a unifying point of reference in religions that yields a public and universal discourse? Or is cultural and religious difference so incommensurate that there is no common ground for a universal and shared discourse?

If rupturing secularist discourse from its religious antecedents jettisons the theological baggage encumbering secularism, unlocking it from universalizing narratives of progress, this radical move still assumes that secularism *succeeds* religious culture. This linear chronology automatically sets up the definition of secularism as a post-religious development and prevents alternative questions from being asked along the following lines: Was the idea of secularism always there, preceding the rise of religion? To what extent can various forms of "paganism" be considered secular? Can Greek philosophy and mythology be regarded as proto-secular in their representation of human agency contesting divine will? Does the answer to religion's hegemony consist not so much in creating a *future* condition in which its influence is curtailed and privatized as in returning to conditions *before* religion? To raise these questions is also to draw attention to the processes by which mainstream religions acquire their dominant status through the absorption, elimination, or adaptation of sub-sects and heterodox strains.

These questions, however, rarely find their way into the contemporary scholarship. Indeed, whatever revisionist turn the scholarship has taken is directed towards probing secularism's relation to Christianity, which has had a restrictive influence on our ability to engage with a long view of history. The view advanced by Habermas, and taken further by Gauchet, that Christianity paves the way for secularization by emphasizing rational thinking and moral progress forbids the secularist narrative from being conceived outside Christianity's moral and social teleology. This is one of the main dilemmas Pecora probes in his book, though he stops short at the point of exploring the prehistory of secularism, appearing even to propose that, if Christianity enables secularism, then what precedes Christianity remains outside the realm of secular thought. On the other hand, if Löwith and Blumenberg had their way, secularism would have to be defined outside the salvific rhetoric of Christianity, in which case, instead of moral progress and individualistic will and action, there is only mechanistic movement, cycles, contingency, and non-deliberateness. In neither case is there a conception of a prehistory for modern secularism outside the reference point of Judeo-Christianity.

At first glance Charles Taylor appears to hint at such an absence when he refers to the subtraction theory of secularism, by which he means that secularism is achieved by removing God from the picture. A set of truisms governs the logic of the subtraction theory: you cannot be modern unless you discard the old beliefs; it is impossible to live fully in the modern age and still believe in God; if you still believe, you cannot be modern; therefore, the death of God is the starting point for a modern outlook. But in contesting the subtraction method of attaining a secular society, Taylor takes his argument in a surprising direction, which in fact preserves aspects of Judeo-Christian ethics in the quest for re-imagining secularism from the standpoint of human goods. For Taylor the appeal of materialism lies in its offering a moral outlook, rather than in the fact that science drives away religion. Arguing against the "death of God" narrative as a negative model and an inadequate account of modernity, Taylor goes on to propose, as a possibility, that Western modernity might be sustained by its own original spiritual vision, not one generated out of the transition from a religious to a secular worldview. Importantly, Taylor does not deny the secularization thesis, but he objects to it being played out as a subtraction theory, in which modernity requires the jettisoning of religion for its own self-definition. Rather, he sees secularization as motivated by an internal shift within Christianity, which leads towards a value-laden humanism. Taylor makes a startling move that salvages Christian history as the basis for a new social order shorn of its transcendent content, and capable of being embraced outside a religious framework:

> If we no longer rationally believe in God, the starting point is the ethical outlook of the modern age . . . Our public life in societies which are secular is exclusively concerned with human goods . . . Some people see no place in this kind of world for belief in God. A faith of this kind would have to make one an outsider, an enemy of this world . . . Thus one is either thoroughly in this world, living by its premises, and then one cannot really believe in God; or one believes, and is in some sense living like a resident alien in modernity. Since we find ourselves more and more inducted into it, belief becomes harder and harder; the horizon of faith steadily recedes.[14]

In many respects, Taylor turns towards an older understanding of humanism as an outgrowth of Christian civility, indeed even coming to define Christianity in terms of civilizational criteria. The humanist intervention paved the way for what Taylor calls "the modern moral order." This belief in a moral order of socially responsible individuals is not a construct of human will but is instead continuous with divine purpose. Taylor's recuperation of Christian humanism is particularly interesting because of the expansive possibilities he sees in it as at once an instrument of reason and right conduct *and* dissent against notions of providence. Christian humanism is thus all-inclusive enough to admit skeptics and detractors (like Voltaire, Gibbon, and Hume) as well as devout believers. Strikingly, according to this argument, even dissent coheres entirely with divine purposes. What makes Taylor's argument so intriguing is that he ascribes the moral mandate of secularism to transformations within Christian history. In this reading, secularism constitutes a perfection of a flawed Christianity, which began to correct itself by moving in the direction of reason and civilization as the highest expressions of Christian thought. A drastically scaled-down providential, divinely sanctioned order in which human activity is the centerpiece is the key entry point to modern secularity. Far from being a subtraction of religious influence, secularism is an enhancement of its intended trajectory.

This argument is reaffirmed, though in a more critical way, by Vincent Pecora who observes that "secularism becomes the paradoxical path to a more profound, because more rational, sense of the religious than had existed before."[15] Far more interesting, however, is Pecora's explanation for secularism's affinity to the religious culture it supposedly replaces, which he explores in terms of the imaginative energies religion makes available (through the exercise of belief), and which secularism salvages as a key resource in resisting mechanical, rote thinking: "The will to secular rationality in modern culture . . . preserves the imaginative rudiments of its religious traditions, not merely as a kind of strategic resistance to the irrationality of capitalism's 'iron cage.'"[16] Of course, the central paradox is that the oppositional logic of secularism paradoxically preserves religious elements in its own self-definition. And the means by which such preservation is ensured is art, which refines its own non-rational propensities of imagination into a resistant rationalism fighting against the deadening effects of modern capitalist bureaucracies. Of course it was none other than Adorno who "inadvertently ended up arguing on behalf of a resistant art that, by becoming pure form, preserves a dissenting theology that resists instrumental rationality."[17] What Adorno called "dissenting theology" Said called "hedonism" in literature, "the freeing oneself of one's past attachments and habits and alliances," for him a strategic form of knowledge.[18]

However, the freeing of oneself from the past, in a dissenting gesture, never meant for Said that wrongs could or should be forgotten, nor that suffering can ever be rationalized. The religious language of atonement pervades his description of Edward Thompson's powerful call, in his 1926 book *The Other Side of the Medal*, for Britain to recognize the harm it had inflicted on the peoples it colonized. It is not insignificant that it is Thompson, himself a religious figure, who inspired Said most to call for a moral response to the wrongs of colonial occupation. Briefly alluding to Thompson in *Culture and Imperialism*,[19] Said increasingly acknowledged his indebtedness to him for insisting on a moral direction to amend colonialism's ills. "Atonement" is Said's term for the recognition of psychological hurt by those perpetrating such damage. Transferring Thompson's words, originally uttered in the context of Britain's relation to colonial India, to the Israeli–Palestinian situation, Said states in an interview, "I don't believe that there can ever be a reconciliation until there's a recognition by Israelis of what they have done and what their society has cost another people . . . We want recognition that something happened here." It is only from such moral recognition of wrongs committed that Said believes it is possible to develop "real dialogue, a real framework of understanding, a real reconciliation, of two cultures," but as long as Israel "absolves itself of any responsibility for what happened before September of 1993," he sees no possibility of equity or justice.[20]

Notes

1 Tariq Ali, *Conversations with Edward Said*, London: Seagull Books, 2006, p. 91.
2 Ibid., p. 90.
3 William Hart, *Edward Said and the Religious Effects of Culture*, Cambridge: Cambridge University Press, 2000, p. 76.
4 Edward Said, *Orientalism*, New York: Pantheon Books, 1978, p. 268.
5 Karen King, *What Is Gnosticism?*, Cambridge, MA: Harvard University Press, 2003, p. 7.
6 Ibid., p. 11.
7 Marcel Gauchet, *The Disenchantment of the World: A Political History of Religion*, trans. Oscar Burge, Princeton: Princeton University Press, 1997, p. 48.
8 Ibid., p. 48.
9 Max Weber, "Religious Rejections of the World and Their Directions," in Gerth and Mills, eds, *From Max Weber*, London: Routledge, 1970, p. 353.
10 Ibid., p. 351.
11 Ibid., p. 352.
12 Ibid., p. 353 (my emphasis).
13 Vincent Pecora, *Secularization and Cultural Criticism*, Chicago: University of Chicago Press, 2006, p. 53 (my emphasis).
14 Charles Taylor, "Closed World Structures," in *Religion after Metaphysics*, Mark A. Wrathall, ed., Cambridge: Cambridge University Press, 2003, p. 58.
15 Pecora, *Secularization and Cultural Criticism*, p. 20.
16 Ibid.

17 Ibid.

18 Gauri Viswanathan, "Beginnings," in Vinaswathan, ed., *Power, Politics and Culture: Interviews with Edward W. Said*, New York: Pantheon Books, 2001.

19 Edward Said, *Culture and Imperialism*, London: Chatto & Windus, 1993, p. 177.

20 Viswanathan, ed., *Power, Politics, and Culture*, p. 272.

14

On Blasphemy, Bigotry
and the Politics of Culture Talk

Mahmood Mamdani

This reflection focuses on the controversy around the Danish cartoons. Those who followed the controversy over the cartoons must have been struck by how fast issues moved from the question of free speech to that of the defense of civilization. Both sides lined up, one in defense of a secular civilization, another in defense of a religious heritage. There were two curious effects of this particular contest. The first was a tendency for the government and the people, on the right and the left, to stand together, on both sides, most unlike the tussle between government and people that we have come to expect of free speech contests.

The saga of the Danish cartoons resembled less a free speech festival than an opening salvo in a highly ideological and rapidly polarizing political contest with lines firmly drawn, pitting, depending on your point of view, secular against religious, non-Muslim against Muslim, or simply the majority against a minority. The polarizing dynamic was testimony to an eroding middle ground. My interest in the Danish cartoons stems from the fact that it brings out most clearly the political challenge that is worth facing: how to reconstitute the middle ground, for no contest can be won without winning the middle ground. My argument will be that the middle ground needs to be reconstituted conceptually, before it can be fought for politically. To explore that conceptual ground, I would like to begin by making a distinction between blasphemy and bigotry.

Blasphemy and Bigotry

When the Danish cartoon debate broke out I was in Nigeria. If you stroll the streets of Kano, a Muslim-majority city in northern Nigeria, you will have no problem finding material caricaturing Christianity sold by street vendors. And if you go to the east of Nigeria, to Enugu for example, you will find a similar supply of materials caricaturing Islam. None of this is blasphemy; most of it is bigotry. That is the distinction I want to bring out. It is well known that the Danish paper which published the offending cartoons was earlier offered cartoons of Jesus Christ. But the paper declined to print these on grounds that it would offend its Christian readers. Had the Danish paper published cartoons of Jesus Christ, that would have been blasphemy; the cartoons it did publish were evidence of bigotry, not blasphemy. Both blasphemy and bigotry belong to the larger tradition of free speech, but after a century of ethnic cleansing and genocide, we surely need to distinguish between the two strands of the same tradition. The language of contemporary politics makes that distinction by referring to bigotry as hate speech.

Just a few weeks after the Danish cartoons were published, the German writer Günter Grass was interviewed in a Portuguese weekly news magazine, *Visão*. In that interview, Grass said the Danish cartoons reminded him of anti-Semitic cartoons in a German magazine, *Der Stürmer*. The story was carried in a *New York Times* piece, which added that the publisher of *Der Stürmer* was tried at Nuremberg and executed.[1] I am not really interested in how close the similarity was between the Danish and the German cartoons, but more so in why a magazine publisher would be executed for publishing cartoons. One of the subjects I work on is the Rwanda genocide. The International Tribunal in Arusha has pinned criminal responsibility for the genocide not just on those who executed it but also on those who imagined it, including intellectuals, artists, and journalists on the radio station RTMC. The Rwandan trials are the latest to bring out the dark side, the underbelly, of free speech: its instrumentalization to frame a minority and present it for target practice.

We need to make a distinction between two kinds of bigotry, petty and grand. I characterize ethnocentrism, including discrimination against individuals, as petty bigotry. Grand bigotry, in contrast, is the stuff of demonization and the fuel of hate movements. It provides bricks and mortar for a hate ideology, which holds up, caricatures, frames and targets a minority as responsible for what is wrong with the world. Contrast, for example, individual racial discrimination with the organized racism of the Ku Klux Klan, or petty and grand apartheid in South Africa. Even when it comes to discrimination against entire groups, it is instructive to contrast anti-Semitism prior to the Nazis with Nazi anti-Semitism, which pointed to Jews as the explanation for what was wrong with the world.

Bigotry can be expressed in any language, religious or secular. The tendency to demonize one's enemies and to try to purify the world in one fell swoop has gone through a long historical development. The secular version forms a part of the history of ideology, where the language of demonization has been secularized as the language of race and of culture. The language of race has often – but not always – been distinguished from that of culture in the Western heartland, but the two languages have tended to be intermeshed in the colonies. This is the language of civilization, which originated with the Voyages of Discovery in the fifteenth century and led to the claim that colonialism itself was a civilizing mission.

Blasphemy and the Criticism of Religion

Bigotry, however, is not blasphemy. Blasphemy is the practice of questioning a tradition from the inside. In contrast, bigotry is an assault on that tradition from the outside. If blasphemy is an attempt to speak truth to power, bigotry is the reverse: an attempt by power to instrumentalize truth. A defining feature of the cartoon debate is that bigotry is being mistaken for blasphemy.

To understand why blasphemy was experienced as a liberating force, we need to historicize and particularize it. Blasphemy was aimed at the Church as an institutional power, which is why it is more of a European than an American tradition. Institutionalized religion in medieval Europe was organized as a form of hierarchical power, with an authority from the floor to the ceiling. Institutional Roman Catholicism has tended to mimic the institutional organization of the Roman Empire, just as the institutional organization of Protestant churches in Europe tend to resonate with the organization of power in the nation-states of Europe. But this tendency does not obtain in the United States of America. The puritan quest shifted the locus of individual morality from external constraint to internal discipline. This history displaced both the Pope and the Scriptures with inner conscience. The Christ of scriptures was to become the "Christ within," a doctrine pioneered by the Quakers.[2] Though blasphemy marked the moment of birth of the New World, the New World was not particularly receptive to blasphemy. The big change was political: Puritans and other Protestant denominations were organized more as congregations and sects, more like voluntary associations, than as hierarchical churches. Unlike in Europe, religion in the rapidly developing settler democracy in the United States was very much a part of the language of the American Revolution and of the public sphere. My point is that the European experience has to be seen as more the exception than the rule.

The European experience holds another lesson, one with perhaps greater relevance for the rest of us outside Europe. It is precisely in places like

Europe, where the Church has a history of institutionalized power, that compromises have been worked out both to protect the practice of free speech and to circumscribe it through laws that criminalize blasphemy. When internalized as civility, rather than imposed by public power, these compromises have been key to keeping social peace in divided societies. Let me give two examples to illustrate the point.

My first example dates back to 1967 when Britain's leading publishing house, Penguin, published an English edition of a book of cartoons by France's most acclaimed cartoonist, Siné. The Penguin edition was introduced by Malcolm Muggeridge. Siné's *Massacre* contained a number of anticlerical and blasphemous cartoons, some of them with a sexual theme. Many booksellers, who found the content offensive, conveyed their feelings to Allen Lane, who had by that time almost retired from Penguin. Though he was not a practicing Christian, Lane took seriously the offense that the book seemed to cause to a number of his practicing Christian friends. Here is Richard Webster's account of what followed: "One night, soon after the book had been published, he went into Penguin's Harmondsworth warehouse with four accomplices, filled a trailer with all the remaining copies of the book, drove away and burnt them. The next day the Penguin trade department reported the book 'out of print.'"[3] Now, Britain has laws against blasphemy, but neither Allen Lane nor Penguin was taken to court. Britain's laws on blasphemy were not called into action. Two issues, in particular, interest me here. One, Lane had internalized as civility what the law prescribed as externally enforced restraint. Second, since Lane was not a practicing Christian, the best explanation I can give for his action is that he had actually internalized legal restraint as civility, that is, as conduct necessary to upholding peaceful coexistence in a society with a history of religious conflict. To put it differently, the existence of political society requires the forging of a political pact, a compromise. It is not as much the restraint imposed by laws that reflect the terms of this compromise, but their internalization as civility that is key to peaceful day-to-day social existence.

My second example is from the United States. It concerns a radio show called *Amos 'n' Andy* that began on WMAQ in Chicago on 19 March 1928, and eventually became the longest running radio program in broadcast history. From one point of view, *Amos 'n' Andy* could be said to be a white show for black people, a show conceived by two white actors who mimicked the so-called Negro dialect to portray two black characters, Amos Jones and Andy Brown. *Amos 'n' Andy* was also the first major all-black show in mainstream US entertainment. The show moved from radio to TV, graduating to prime-time network television in 1951, and becoming a syndicated show after 1953.

Every year, the National Association for the Advancement of Colored People (NAACP) protested against the racist character of the portrayal that was the show. Giving seven reasons "why the *Amos 'n' Andy* show should be taken off the air," the NAACP said the show reinforced the prejudice that "Negroes are inferior, lazy, dumb, and dishonest," that every character in the all-black show "is either a clown or a crook." "Negro doctors are shown as quacks and thieves," Negro lawyers "as slippery cowards, ignorant of their profession and without ethics," and Negro women "as cackling, screaming shrews . . . just short of vulgarity." In sum, "all Negroes are shown as dodging work of any kind." But CBS disagreed. You can still read the CBS point of view on the official *Amos 'n' Andy* website, which still hopes that black people will learn to laugh at themselves: "Perhaps we will collectively learn to lighten up, not get so bent out of shape, and learn to laugh at ourselves a little more."[4]

The TV show ran for nearly 15 years, from 1951 to 1965. Every year the NAACP protested, but every year the show continued. Then, without explanation, CBS withdrew the show in 1965. What happened? In 1965 the Watts riots happened, and sparked the onset of a long, hot summer. The riots were triggered by a petty incident, an encounter between a racist cop and a black motorist. That everyday incident triggered a riot that left 34 persons dead. Many asked: What is wrong with these people? How can the response be so disproportionate to the injury? After the riots the Johnson administration appointed a commission, called the Kerner Commission, to answer this and other questions. The Kerner Commission Report made a distinction between what it called the trigger and the fuel: the trigger was an incident of petty racism, but the fuel was provided by centuries of racism. The lesson was clear: the country needed to address the consequences of a history of racism, not just its latest manifestation. Bob Gibson, the St Louis Cardinals pitcher, wrote about the Watts riots in his book *From Ghetto to Glory*. He compared the riots to a "brushback pitch" – a pitch thrown over the batter's head to keep him from crowding the plate, a way of sending a message that the pitcher needs more space.[5] CBS withdrew *Amos 'n' Andy* after the long, hot summer of 1965. The compelling argument the NAACP and other civil rights groups could not make, was made by the inarticulate rioters of Watts.

Why is this bit of history significant for us? CBS did not withdraw the show because the law had changed, for no such change happened. The reason for the change was political, not legal. For sure, there was a change of consciousness, but that change was triggered by political developments. CBS had learnt civility; more likely, it was taught civility. CBS had learnt that there was a difference between black people laughing at themselves, and white people laughing at black people! It was like the difference between blasphemy and bigotry. That learning was part of a larger shift in American society, one that began with the Civil War and continued with the civil rights movement that followed World War II. This larger shift was the inclusion of African-Americans in a restructured civil and political society. The saga of *Amos 'n' Andy* turned out to be a milestone, not in the history of free speech, but in a larger history, that of black people's struggle to defend their human rights and their rights of citizenship in the US.

The Challenge is Political, not Legal

In the public discussion on the Danish cartoons, two options have been on offer: greater censorship, and its opposite, total license. Both have problems. Some point to censorship – to the example of Europe in particular, where laws on blasphemy define the boundaries of free speech. The problem, according to this point of view, is that the laws reflect the cultural sensibility of particular countries in a particular historical period, so that blasphemy laws tend to protect the state religion only, such as Anglicanism in England and Lutheranism in Denmark. Europe also has laws against certain forms of bigotry, particularly anti-Semitism.

The laws in force in each of these countries express a political compromise, which in turn is no doubt a consequence of the process that constructed a political community. In each case, the restraint is more moral and political than legal. The law crystallizes both changing consciousness and an altered balance of forces that underlies a new compromise on the terms of constituting a political society.

An alternative solution was suggested by Ronald Dworkin in the *New York Review of Books*. Dworkin offers a consistent liberal position, that of no censorship, and calls for doing away with any laws that may impinge on free speech, including blasphemy laws or laws that criminalize Holocaust denial. What is striking about the Dworkin piece is its silence about hate speech and bigotry and how to confront it. Ask yourself: what, after all, is the rationale for criminalizing Holocaust denial? Clearly, not free speech. Rather, it is the more urgent imperative for peaceful coexistence between Christians and Jews in post-Holocaust Europe. Let us remember that the very notion of a Judeo-Christian civilization is mainly a post-Holocaust political project. Prior to the Holocaust, mainstream politics did not hyphenate Judaism with Christianity, but opposed one to the other.

The fact is that whereas the law can be a corrective to individual discrimination, it has seldom been an effective restraint on hate movements that target vulnerable minorities. If the episode of the Danish cartoons demonstrated one thing, it was that Islamophobia is a growing presence in Europe. One is struck by the ideological diversity of this phenomenon. Just as there was a left-wing anti-Semitism in Europe before fascism, contemporary Islamophobia too is articulated not only in the familiar language of the right, but also the less familiar language of the left. The latter language is secular, even feminist. The Danish cartoons and their enthusiastic republication throughout Europe, in both right and left-wing papers, was our first public glimpse of left and right Islamophobia marching in step formation. Its political effect has been to explode the middle ground, reminiscent of the blowing up of the shrine which triggered the civil war between Shia and Sunni in Iraq.

My sense is that we are now entering a period where Islamophobia in Europe is maturing into an ideology of hate, a grand ideology driven by a core explanation of what is wrong with the world: hence the growing claim that there is a clash of civilizations.

I want to close by suggesting a scale of responses, with an accent on more rather than less debate, and a focus more on the political than the legal. The real challenge is intellectual and political. The intellectual challenge lies in distinguishing between two strands in the history of free speech – blasphemy and bigotry.[6] The political challenge lies in building a local and global coalition against all forms of bigotry. If the local context is the dramatic growth of Muslim minorities in Europe and their struggle for human and citizenship rights, the global context is an equally dramatic turning point in world history. The history of the past five centuries has been one of Western domination. Beginning in 1491, Western colonialism understood and presented itself to the world at large as a civilizing and rescue mission. The colonizing discourse historically focused on barbarities among the colonized – sati, child marriage, and polygamy in India, female genital mutilation and slavery in Africa – and presented colonialism as a rescue mission for women, children, and minorities, at the same time claiming to be a larger project to civilize majorities. Meanwhile, Western minorities lived in the colonies with privilege and impunity. Taken together, it constitutes five centuries marked by an inability to live with difference in the world. The irony is that a growing number of mainstream European politicians, perhaps nostalgic about empire, are experimenting with importing these same time-tested rhetorical techniques into domestic politics: the idea is to compile a list of barbaric cultural practices among immigrant minorities, as a way first to isolate, then to stigmatize, and then to frame them.

But the world is changing. New powers are on the horizon: most obviously, China and India. Neither has a Muslim majority, but both have significant Muslim minorities. The Danish case teaches us by negative example how not to respond to a changing world with fear and anxiety, masked with arrogance, but rather to try a little humility so as to understand the ways in which the world is indeed changing.

There is also a lesson here for Muslim peoples. The Middle East and Islam are part of the middle ground in this contest on the horizon. Rather than be tempted to think that the struggle against Islamophobia is the main struggle – for it is not – let us put it in this larger context. For that larger context will both help us identify allies and highlight the importance of building alliances. This is not the time to close ranks, but to open them, so as to identify issues of common concern to all who wish to live together in this rapidly shrinking world.

Notes

1 *New York Times*, 17 February 2006, p. E7.
2 See Christopher Hill, *The World Turned Upside Down*, Harmondsworth: Penguin, 1975.
3 Richard Webster, *A Brief History of Blasphemy*, Southwold: Orwell Press, 1990, p. 26.
4 http://www.amosandy.com.
5 Cited in Robert Wright, "The Silent Treatment," *New York Times*, 17 February 2006, p. A23.
6 Even though there are important instances where the boundary is blurred, as in the case of responses to Salman Rushdie's *Satanic Verses*.

Notes on Editors and Contributors

Meltem Ahıska is associate professor of sociology at Boğaziçi University. She is the author of *Occidentalism in Turkey: Questions of Modernity and National Identity in Turkish Radio Broadcasting* (forthcoming; published in Turkish as *Radyonun Sihirli Kapısı: Garbiyatılık ve Politik Öznellik*, 2005). Her articles, essays and poems have appeared in various publications including *Defter*, *Toplum ve Bilim*, *New Perspectives on Turkey*, and *South Atlantic Quarterly*, and she was a member of the editorial board of several journals, including *Akıntıya Karşı*, *Zemin*, *Pazartesi* and *Defter*, a journal of cultural criticism published in Turkey from 1987 to 2002. She has published a book of poems, *Havalandırma* (2002), and co-curated several exhibitions, the most recent being "The Person You Are Calling Cannot Be Reached at the Moment: Representations of Lifestyle in Turkey, 1980–2005."

Tuncay Birkan graduated from Boğaziçi University English Language and Literature Department in 1991. He worked as an editor at Ayrıntı Publications until 1996, and later as a freelance translator. He translated thirty-five titles into Turkish. He has been working as an editor at Metis Publications since 2004. He has written articles on political and cultural topics, and is currently the president of the Turkish Literary Translators' Society.

Timothy Brennan is Professor of English and Comparative Literature at the University of Minnesota. A recipient of fellowships from the Fulbright Foundation, the National Endowment for the Humanities, and the American Council of Learned Societies, Prof. Brennan has taught at Cornell University, the Humboldt University (Berlin), the University of California at Irvine, and Rutgers University. He received an award from the Council of Editors of Learned Journals for his special issue of "Narratives of Colonial Resistance." He is the author, most recently, of *Wars of Position: The Cultural*

Politics of Left and Right (2006). A former journalist in Central America, and consultant for American Public Television, his recent books include *At Home in the World: Cosmopolitanism Now* (1997) and the forthcoming *Secular Devotion: Afro-Latin Music and Imperial Jazz* (2007). His essays on literature, cultural politics, and intellectuals have appeared in a variety of publications, including the *Nation*, the *Times Literary Supplement*, *Critical Inquiry*, and *New Left Review*.

Başak Ertür completed her MA in Liberal Studies at the New School for Social Research in New York. She has worked as an editor for Metis Publications in Istanbul, and translated several works of philosophy into Turkish, including Judith Butler's *Gender Trouble*. She is the co-producer and director of a documentary entitled *For the Record: The World Tribunal on Iraq* (2007). She currently lives and works in London.

Harry Harootunian is one of the foremost historians of Japan in the Anglo-Saxon world. He is currently Professor of East Asian Studies and History at New York University. He is former editor of the *Journal of Asian Studies*, and has served on the editorial board of *Critical Inquiry*, *Hihyo Kukan* and the *Journal of Japanese Studies*, and is a member of the American Academy of Arts and Sciences. He is the author of *Things Seen and Unseen: Discourse and Ideology in Tokugawa Nativism* (1988), *Toward Restoration* (1991), *Overcome by Modernity: History, Culture, and Community in Interwar Japan* (2000), *History Disquiet: Modernity, Cultural Practice and the Question of the Everyday Life* (2000), and *Empire's New Clothes: Paradigm Lost, and Regained* (2004). He recently published, with Tomiko Yoda, *Japan After Japan* (2006).

Rashid Khalidi is Edward Said Professor of Arab Studies and Director of the Middle East Institute at Columbia University. Previously he taught at the University of Chicago, the Lebanese University, the American University of Beirut, and Georgetown University. Khalidi is editor of the *Journal of Palestine Studies,* and he was President of the Middle East Studies Association, and an advisor to the Palestinian delegation to the Madrid and Washington Arab–Israeli peace negotiations from October 1991 until June 1993. His most recent book is *Resurrecting Empire: Western Footprints and America's Perilous Path in the Middle East* (2004), which has been translated into French, Italian, Spanish and Arabic. His *Palestinian Identity: The Construction of Modern National Consciousness*, published by Columbia University Press, was a co-winner of the Middle East Studies Association's Albert Hourani Prize as the best book of 1997. He is also the author of *British Policy Towards Syria and Palestine, 1906–1914* (1980) and *Under Siege: PLO*

Decision-Making During the 1982 War (1986), and was the co-editor of *Palestine and the Gulf* (1982) and *The Origins of Arab Nationalism* (1991). He has written over eighty scholarly articles on aspects of Middle East history and politics, as well as op-ed pieces in *New York Times*, *Financial Times*, *Boston Globe*, *Los Angeles Times*, *Chicago Tribune* and the *Nation*.

Born in Beirut in 1948, **Elias Khoury** is the author of eleven novels, four volumes of literary criticism, and three plays. The publication of his first novel, *On the Relations of the Circle* (1975), landed him in the vanguard of modern Arabic literature. Khoury's commitment to the question of Palestine began when he visited a refugee camp in Jordan at the age of nineteen. He has been an advocate of Palestinians' right to sovereignty and justice ever since, working at the Palestine Research Center in Beirut and speaking out in articles and essays, as well as through his fiction. Khoury is currently the editor in chief of the cultural supplement of Beirut's daily newspaper, *An-Nahar*, and is a Global Distinguished Professor of Middle Eastern and Islamic Studies at New York University. In 1998 he was awarded the Palestine Prize for *Gate of the Sun*, and in 2000 the novel was named *Le Monde Diplomatique*'s Book of the Year. Elias Khoury is a public intellectual and cultural activist who plays a major role in contemporary Arabic culture, and in the defense of freedom of expression and democracy.

Saree Makdisi is Professor of English and Comparative Literature at the University of California, Los Angeles. He has published widely on eighteenth- and nineteenth-century British literature and culture, including two books – *Romantic Imperialism: Universal Empire and the Culture of Modernity* (1998), and *William Blake and the Impossible History of the 1790s* (2003). He has also published scholarly articles on the cultural politics of the contemporary Arab world. In addition to his academic work, he has written about the Israeli–Palestinian conflict for a number of publications, including *Chicago Tribune*, the *Nation*, the *London Review of Books*, and the *Los Angeles Times*, to which he is a frequent contributor. His next book, on Palestine, will be published in 2008.

Mahmood Mamdani is from Kampala, Uganda. He is currently Herbert Lehman Professor of Government in the Department of Anthropology and Political Science and the School of International and Public Affairs at Columbia University, where he was also director of the Institute of African Studies from 1999 to 2004. He has taught at the University of Dar-es-Salaam (1973–79), Makerere University (1980–93), and the University of Cape Town (1996–99), and was the founding director of the Centre for

Basic Research in Kampala, Uganda (1987–96). He is the author of *Good Muslim, Bad Muslim: America, the Cold War and the Origins of Terror* (2004), *When Victims Become Killers: Colonialism, Nativism and Genocide in Rwanda* (2001) and *Citizen and Subject: Contemporary Africa and the Legacy of Late Colonialism* (1996) and ten other books. *Citizen and Subject* was recognized as "one of Africa's 100 best books of the twentieth century" in Cape Town in 2003, and was also awarded the Herskovitz Prize of the African Studies Association of the USA as "the best book on Africa published in the English language in 1996." Mamdani was President of the Council for the Development of Social Research in Africa from 1999 to 2002. In 2001, he was invited to present one of nine papers at the Nobel Peace Prize Centennial Symposium in Oslo. In 2004, he presented one of nine papers at the African Union–organized Global Meeting of Intellectuals from Africa and the African Diaspora, in Dakar.

Joseph Massad is Associate Professor of Modern Arab Politics and Intellectual History at Columbia University. He is author of *Colonial Effects: The Making of National Identity in Jordan* (2001), *The Persistence of the Palestinian Question: Essays on Zionism and the Palestinians* (2006), and *Desiring Arabs* (2007). Professor Massad has published numerous academic articles and has a regular newspaper column in the Egyptian *Al-Ahram Weekly*.

Karma Nabulsi is the Fellow in politics at St Edmund Hall, Oxford, and University Lecturer at the Department of Politics and International Relations, Oxford University. She was a PLO representative from 1977–90, working at the United Nations, Beirut, Tunis, and the UK. She was an advisory member of the Palestinian delegation to the peace talks in Washington from 1991–93. She served as the specialist adviser to the UK all-party parliamentary commission of inquiry on Palestinian refugees (and its report, *Right of Return*, 2000) and specialist adviser to the House of Commons select committee's inquiry on assistance and the occupied Palestinian territories, and its report. She directed *Foundations for Participation: Civic Structures in Palestinian Refugee Camps and Exile Communities*, a collective participatory research project which took place in over 25 countries, the findings of which were recently published as *Palestinians Register* (2006). She is the author of *Traditions of War: Occupation, Resistance and the Law* (1999) and writes on the philosophy and ethics of war, the laws of war, European political history and theory, and Palestinian history and politics. Karma Nabulsi is currently writing *Conspirators for Liberty: The Underground Struggle for Democracy in 19th Century Europe* for W.W. Norton. She is a columnist for the *Guardian*.

Ilan Pappé is a professor in the History Department at University of Exeter. He was a senior lecturer in the department of Political Science at Haifa University and is the Chair of the Emil Touma Institute for Palestinian Studies in Haifa. He was also the Academic Director of the Research Institute for Peace at Givat Haviva. Ilan Pappé is well-known as a revisionist or "post-Zionist" Israeli historian. He is the author of many books relating to the Israeli-Palestinian conflict. His most recent books are *The Ethnic Cleansing of Palestine* (2006), *The Modern Middle East* (2005), and *A History of Modern Palestine: One Land, Two Peoples* (2004). His previous books include *The Making of the Arab-Israeli Conflict, 1948–1951* (1992) and *The Israel/Palestine Question* (1999).

Jacqueline Rose is Professor of English at Queen Mary, University of London, and one of the steering committee of Independent Jewish Voices. She writes and lectures on literature, psychoanalysis and politics. Her publications include *Sexuality in the Field of Vision* (1986, 2006), *The Haunting of Sylvia Plath* (1991), the 1994 Oxford Clarendon Lectures *States of Fantasy* (1996), the novel, *Albertine* (2001), *On Not Being Able to Sleep: Psychoanalysis and the Modern World* (2003), the 2003 Christian Gauss seminars, *The Question of Zion* (2005) and *The Last Resistance* (forthcoming in June). She was the writer and presenter of the television documentary, *Dangerous Liaison: Israel and America* for Channel 4 in 2002, and wrote the response to Edward W. Said, *Freud and the Non-European* (2003).

Mariam Said was born and raised in Beirut, Lebanon. She received an undergraduate degree from the American University of Beirut (AUB), Lebanon, and two graduate degrees from Columbia University, New York. She has worked in the financial world in New York for twenty years. Currently retired, she is involved in the Barenboim-Said Foundation, a project that her late husband, Edward W. Said, and Daniel Barenboim established together. It runs several musical education programs in Palestine and Israel, a musical kindergarten in Ramallah, the West-Eastern Divan Orchestra – an orchestra comprising Arabs and Israelis. The Foundation is sponsored by the Regional Government of Andalusia, and its workshop takes place every summer in Pilas, near Seville.

Raja Shehadeh graduated in 1973 with a degree in English Literature and Philosophy from the American University of Beirut. He studied law in London, was called to the English Bar at Lincoln's Inn in 1976 and has been in private practice in Ramallah since 1978. In 1979 he co-founded the pioneering human rights organization Al Haq, the Palestinian affiliate of the

International Commission of Jurists which he co-directed until 1991. In the course of his practice of law he handled and participated in a number of precedent-setting cases including the recent request to the International Court of Justice at the Hague regarding the Legal Consequences of the Construction of a wall in the Occupied Palestinian Territories. He wrote several books on the legal aspects of the Israeli occupation of Palestinian Territories including *Occupiers Law* (1985 revised 1988) The *Law of the Land* (1993) and *From Occupation to Interim Accords* (1997). His latest published books are his memoir, *Strangers in the House* (2002) and *When the Bulbul Stopped Singing* (2004) which was adapted to the theater and performed in Edinburgh, Tehran, New York and Amman. Shehadeh won the 2008 Orwell Book Prize for his most recent book *Palestinian Walks, Notes on a Vanishing Landscape* (2007).

Müge Gürsoy Sökmen is an editor, translator, and co-founder of Metis Publications. She has been a member of the editorial board of the translation journal *Metis Çeviri*, and of *Defter*, a critical thought quarterly. She edited *World Tribunal on Iraq: Making the Case Against War* (2008). She has translated works of authors such as John Berger, Ursula K. LeGuin, F.G. Lorca and Susan Sontag and has contributed to the organisation of many seminars, conferences and symposiums. Müge Gürsoy Sökmen has chaired the Writers in Prison Committee of Turkish PEN for many years and is a member of the Alliance of Independent Publishers for an Alternative Globalization.

Fawwaz Traboulsi is Associate Professor of History and Politics at the Lebanese American University, Beirut and Visiting Professor in Modern Arab Studies at Columbia University, New York. He has written on history, Arab politics, social movements and popular culture. He has translated Edward Said's *Out of Place* and his posthumous *Humanism and Democratic Critique* into Arabic. He has also translated works by Karl Marx, John Reed, Antonio Gramsci, Isaac Deutscher, John Berger, Etel Adnan and Sa'di Yusuf. Fawwaz Traboulsi's most recent book is *A History of Modern Lebanon* (2007).

Gauri Viswanathan is Class of 1933 Professor in the Humanities at Columbia University. She has held numerous distinguished visiting pro-fessorships, most recently at Berkeley as Beckman Professor. Her fields of interest are education, religion, and culture; nineteenth-century British and colonial cultural studies; and the history of modern disciplines. She is the author of *Masks of Conquest: Literary Study and British Rule in India* (1989) and *Outside the Fold: Conversion, Modernity, and Belief* (1998), which won the

Harry Levin Prize awarded by the American Comparative Literature Association, the James Russell Prize awarded by the Modern Language Association of America, and the Ananda K. Coomaraswamy Prize awarded by the Association for Asian Studies. She has also edited *Power, Politics, and Culture: Interviews with Edward W. Said* (2001), as well as a special issue of *ARIEL: A Review of English Literature* (2000) on "Institutionalizing English Studies: The Postcolonial/Postindependence Challenge." Her numerous articles have appeared in many leading journals and edited volumes. Professor Viswanathan's current work is on memory, history, and modern occultism.

Index

abjects 148
Abu Ghraib 23
academy 70–1
Academy of Hebrew Language 19
Achebe, Chinua 16
Adorno, Theodor 6, 59, 173
affiliation 130
Africa 160, 161, 182
African National Congress (ANC) 111
After the Last Sky (Said) 44, 111, 123, 126–8, 129
Ahmad, Aijaz 35
Ahmadinejad, President Mahmoud 41
Alaa, Abu 94, 101
Alexandria Platform 42–3
Algeria xix, 110, 158, 160
Algiers meeting (1988), declaration of Palestinian state 99
Ali, Sabahattin 69
Ali, Tariq 164
amateurism 55
Amel, Mahdi xix
American University of Beirut 34
Amos 'n' Andy (radio/TV show) 179–81
An-Nahar 41, 43
Anatolia 160, 161
Anderson, Benedict 147
anti-colonial struggle 157
anti-Semitism
  before and after Nazis 177
  cartoons in *Der Sturmer* 177
  European Jewish struggle against 132
  European laws against 181
  left-wing 182
  link with Orientalism 125–6, 128
  and Occidentalism 35
anti-Westernism
  as distorted Westernism in Turkey 139, 145

popular meaning of Occidentalism today 138, 147
Antonius, George xv, 58
apartheid 51, 177
Arab culture, Said's role in xiv–xv
Arab intellectuals
  crisis xvi–xx
  Hanafi's project for creating tradition of 138
  Said's criticism of 34
  Said's place in tradition of 36
Arab liberation movements 110
Arab nationalism 88, 90
Arab regimes
  impotence in face of Israeli occupation of West Bank xviii–xix
  Said's criticisms of 34, 88, 132
Arab writer, predicament 17, 18
'Arabic Prose and Prose Fiction After 1948' (Said) 17
Arabs
  Alexandria Document 42–3
  hijacking of Said's critique of Orientalism 33
  negative representations in West 125–6, 148
  Said's communications with 49
  Said's plea for better understanding of 85
  see also Mizrachim
Arafat, Yasser 34, 90, 94, 102–3, 103
archaeology, in Israeli project of Jewish identity 157–8
Arendt, Hannah 10
Armenians, genocide 159, 162, 163
art
  religious objects placed in museums 170
  and resistance 173
Asia, colonial expulsion of populations 160, 161